PRAISE FOR AFTERLIFE OF A KEPT BOY

"Dale Corvino's vivid memoir of hustling is an unflinching look at the thrill and pain of transactional relationships. His singular, amoral voice describes an unexamined life of privilege that descends into a dark complicity and back through the other side."
-Daniel Minahan, Director of *HALSTON* and *ON SWIFT HORSES*

"What does it mean to be a kept boy and what does it mean to break free? In acute prose, Corvino takes the reader on a journey of survival and liberation, of the roles we choose and the roles that choose us, and, ultimately, of what it means to transcend. Many books trace the activities of sex workers, but so few do as this does—to trace the fragile outline of the sex worker heart. Treasure this."
-Lily Burana, author of *Grace for Amateurs* and *Strip City*

"In *Afterlife of a Kept Boy*, Dale Corvino has written nothing short of a masterpiece. I swear this book activated something ancient and homosexual in me. You do not simply read *Afterlife of a Kept Boy*, you nod your head, snap your fingers, call your best friend and say, 'Girl...' And Corvino is not just funny—though I kept scream-laughing throughout—his stories about navigating the sex work industry are also smart, tender-hearted, and absolutely fearless. Rich in atmosphere, full of lyrical prose and hard-earned wisdom, I was swept away from the first page and sighing with deep satisfaction by the last. I really love this book."
-Edgar Gomez, author of *Alligator Tears: A Memoir-in-Essays*

"You're unlikely to find anything resembling this story in the archives of gay literature, or maybe any kind of literature at all. Those who spend a significant portion of their lives as 'Kept' usually don't get the chance to acquire either the literary skills or the understanding to recount what happened. *Afterlife of a Kept Boy* is one fantastic exception, an invigorating tale of survival that led to the flourishing of a glorious new identity."
-Bruce Benderson, Prix de Flore winner for *The Romanian*

"Sex work, passion, disillusionment, wisdom and coke all overflow in this delicious diary of an unstoppable dreamer. Condoms not included."
-Michael Musto, columnist and author

"An unapologetically raunchy queer odyssey that challenges the art of memoir writ large, demanding the truths we expose of ourselves be deeper and more colorful. Dale Corvino's self-awareness is immediately inviting, putting the reader at ease while feeding them a buffet of debauchery that seamlessly transmutes into profound wisdom. This is the kind of story where you cry and cackle in the same gesture. If this prose is what Corvino does with his personal history, I can only imagine the force he'll become in the queer lit sphere. And yet as much as I loved the ending, I wanted more and more!"
-Jason Yamas, Lambda Literary Award winner for *Tweakerworld*

"A complex story of gaining access to wealth and forming bonds of care, while also simmering with resentments for both. This is a diary of raunch and excess, a travelogue of one man's experiences of being kept and unkept, and a reflection on important and under-considered aspects of gay male culture.
-Audacia Ray, activist and author of *Naked on the Internet*

"Dale Corvino's beautiful writing is a roller-coaster ride of emotion through modern gay and queer history that runs on a hard core track. Corvino challenges us to a world view of exploitation and social justice with sex work as a path to liberation."
-Veronica Vera, author, dean of *Miss Vera's Academy*, sex worker

"A sensational read, immediate, engrossing, frank and at times way out there. Corvino's detailing in at least the first part is so intricate and accurate one could reproduce the upper-upper's lunch and dining down to the wallpaper. His portrait of the 1990's East Side Bohemian life that seems so far away now is fresh and his character sketches often affectionately rounded."
-Felice Picano

AFTERLIFE OF A KEPT BOY

DALE CORVINO

C&R Press
Conscious & Responsible

All Rights Reserved

Printed in the United States of America

First Edition
1 2 3 4 5 6 7 8 9

Selections of up to two pages may be reproduced without permission. To reproduce more than two pages of any one portion of this book, write to C&R Press publishers John Gosslee and Andrew Sullivan.

Copyright ©2025 Dale Corvino
Cover by Dale Corvino

ISBN 978-1-949540-52-9
LCCN 2024931532

C&R Press
Conscious & Responsible
crpress.org

For special discounted bulk purchases, please contact:
C&R Press sales@crpress.org

While this is a work of nonfiction, some names and identifying features have been changed or withheld in order to protect privacy. This memoir draws upon diary entries, photos, artifacts, research, and least reliably, my memory—all bolstered by the recollections and record-keeping of Andrés.

AFTERLIFE OF A KEPT BOY

TABLE OF CONTENTS

1. Sugar Daddy   5
2. Nature to his Ruin   21
3. Garden Poses   42
4. Sunken Cargo   58
5. Merely Decorative Value   75
6. Voluntary Departures   96
7. Guido Stud for Hire   110
8. R U Available?   145
9. Andrés   167
10. Color Chart   180

1. SUGAR DADDY

Our drunk bodies landed on his bed. We'd been at it all night, though at crossed purposes: I drank along with him so he'd pass out and he wanted the alcohol to erode my boundaries. Most nights were a draw. His bed is enormous and more like its own room, the frame of solid mahogany, in the Jacobean style, with twisting hand-carved posts, a canopy overhead, and curtains along the sides. The sheets are Pratesi, in crisp white, outlined in royal blue embroidery, and ironed perfectly flat... As their soft sheen brushed across my cheek, I inhaled notes of detergent and singed cotton.

"Dale, Dale! Over here...*Hurry!*"

A voice I didn't recognize over the din of traffic jolted me out of my solitude as I walked up Fifth Avenue. *Why would anyone yell* my *name?* It seemed to be coming from a stopped car. The taxi drivers stuck behind it jabbed at their horns. *No one I know would do this-?* I'd adhered to my own made-up rules of city life since moving out of the Long Island town of my upbringing at eighteen: 1. Don't attract attention. 2. Don't block traffic. This yelling person was breaking both. I turned away from the Central Park entrance and scrambled between cars to come upon a navy blue Jaguar with a hand waving frantically out of the open rear window. *What am I even doing on the East Side?*

That day I'd gotten diverted. I was in the habit of walking home after my architecture studio classes at the Cooper Union. These solitary hikes helped to soothe my inner turmoil; the school's high-concept pedagogy was way over my head, and my body ached for a sensual life beyond my imaginings. It was four miles from the punk Bohemia of the East Village to the rougher edges of the wealthier Upper West Side. On Broadway, a gruff man had jostled me as he maneuvered a hand-truck stacked high with boxes. Fixated on his sturdy build, his sweaty brow, I could barely made out his barked insults. *Is that longing in his eyes?* I followed him for a couple of blocks, losing him near needle-strewn Union Square Park. There, a rangy, black-clad dope dealer who didn't like my look chased me out, hurling threats. That was the street scene downtown, but I could usually skulk through uptown unnoticed.

I approached the Jaguar. Behind the steering wheel sat a man with a brushy mustache, in a chauffeur's cap, wearily gesturing to the hacks to go around. In the back seat sat Andrés, my recently moved-in roommate, and an older man. Andrés was new at Cooper Union; he'd responded to a notice I'd posted in the school's housing office. My walk-up was cheap enough, but I'd reasoned that cutting my rent in half would leave me with some spending money.

Andrés had arrived to meet me and see the apartment wearing a striped jacket and a flowy scarf, with cash in hand. From Chile, he'd grown up in the Detroit suburbs. His bright eyes darted, consuming the entire space; his tawny skin was as smooth and even as one of his earth-toned paints from the tube. He was stylish, outgoing, and obviously gay, whereas I was a sexually confused loner. I wanted this handsome dandy in my life, to counteract my moody self-absorption and a provincial cast I couldn't seem to shuck. It hadn't been clear to me then, but I was inviting change into the narrow life I'd carved out for myself in that narrow apartment, more than trying to save money.

Andrés had a boyfriend, Joseph, a closeted grad student at Columbia from a wealthy Baltimore family. I imagined it would be hard to stay closeted around Andrés. After a fight, Joseph had demanded that Andrés move out and dropped him off at my place. Joseph, who was running a fever, broke it off with finality right there on the doorstep while I tried not to watch. His tall, lanky frame was nearly buckled by his aggrieved posturing, his reddish hair set aflame. Andrés, subdued, blinked. As his now-ex stomped off, he closed the door behind him and rolled his eyes. *These gays are dramatic...*

"Are you okay?"

"Oh yea...Wait, I feel a fever coming on, too. Check..." He put my hand on his forehead.

"You do feel warm."

Is this guy a hypochondriac, or just dramatic? A little of both? I wondered as he held my hand in place.

Right after moving in, Andrés took off to Spain. He owned a portable easel and painted wherever he traveled. Andrés was enrolled in the architecture program like me, but treated it like art school. I'd wanted to apply to the art school, but fearful that it was too gay a choice, opted for what seemed the more masculine, professional architecture track. Andrés painted on handmade papers with gouache paints. His subjects were abstractions—haunted carousels, biomorphic mechanisms, debris fields—all rendered in mineral colors. His professors loved his work, whereas mine were less impressed with my tentative, plodding efforts. He'd developed these sophisticated techniques and themes before even starting Cooper Union; I'd gotten in with studious but unremarkable samples from my high school art classes.

When he was home he made a lot of international phone calls. He'd yammer on ostentatiously in Spanish, French, and Italian with equal fluidity. I'd taken French in high school and had only picked up a few broken phrases of Italian listening to my grandparents talk about us. My parents' generation had been pitched towards assimilating into the American mainstream. I was bowled over by Andrés' language skills and still nursing a resentment over never having been taught Italian at home.

The more I got to know about Andrés—artist, polyglot, dandy—the more starstruck I became, and the more I felt like a bystander to his extraordinary life from the perch of my own apartment. Upon his return from Spain, he'd detonated his giant suitcase, filled to bursting with books, clothes, medications, toiletries, liquor—and underneath, flattened auto parts he'd found on roadbeds. He'd ink these and pull prints from them, acing his printmaking class. As he sorted through all these acquisitions I wondered where he'd gotten the money to travel like this. *He told me he was living on a student loan*...I couldn't find a moment to ask him about it—he spent very few nights at home even when he was in town. Some days he'd just run in, change into some new outfit, and run right back out.

I was still in starstruck mode and hadn't really gotten to know him the day he stopped traffic. He was mildly annoyed at me for having taken so long to find him as I approached the open window:

"Yasss, finally. I thought you two should meet. Mr. Greet, this is Dale."

Seated next to Andrés was an exasperated older man, large and pink, with wisps of thin blond hair. He was dressed in a suit and tie, and I noticed the garters holding up his socks. He had that uptown poise and the rosy front of a seasoned drinker. As we shook hands through the open window, this gentleman in his finery and his chauffeured sedan straightened slightly and pitched towards me, tugging on my arm a bit. His sour expression lifted and his blue eyes sparkled in the dappled light. "We're having dinner at El Internacional, you know, in TriBeCa." said Andrés. I didn't know. Mr. Greet muttered something about their reservation and ordered the driver on, finally putting an end to the commotion. The hacks stomped on their gas pedals, and a lurching yellow blur accompanied the Jaguar downtown.

I caught up with Andrés days later: "Child, that dinner was a complete disaster…" Greet had turned up his nose at the Latin fusion menu. From an air duct overhead, condensation bounced off the retro vinyl banquette seating, splattering his custom suit. The final blow came when Andrés left to use a pay phone. Abandoned at a leaky table in a noisy, trendy venue, Greet summoned the chauffeur and retreated uptown.

"I had to borrow money for the bill," lamented Andrés.

"Oh, no. But how do you…" my question was interrupted.

"The single bright spot in his terrible evening was meeting you," gushed Andrés. "He finds you *delightful* and wants to have drinks."

"But all I said was, 'Nice to meet you.'"

"He's got a thing for Italians."

A thing for Italians…I've heard that before. My high school girlfriend, a Jewish girl named Joy, had told me that once as she fawned over my black curls. Andrés explained that Greet was a renowned society decorator who lived in this East Side townhouse filled with beautiful antiques, and counted among his clients old-money matrons, nouveau riche, and even celebrities. Andrés was his paid companion; they'd meet for drinks, then go to a restaurant for dinner. Sometimes they'd hit a few bars afterwards, too. He'd keep him company, and get some money. If I came along I could expect the same.

"His apartment is in a townhouse?"

"It's his whole house, on East Seventy-Second Street." Andrés replied, sketching the façade in the air. "Is this sinking in?"

I was all for a fancy dinner after a semester of falafels. Andrés confessed that he'd been the one who had pushed Greet into trying El Internacional, and after their night had ended in disaster, they'd be sticking to his familiar haunts: uptown, upscale, traditional French and Italian restaurants.

"He drinks a lot, and expects you to keep up. Eat, drink, make small talk, laugh at his jokes."

"And he pays you?"

"Yasss, child." Andrés seemed to call all of his friends 'child.' He later told me about his first roommate in downtown Detroit, Delia, a Southern Black woman. They shared an entire floor of a vacant department store, and would yell out "Yasss, child" to find each other. (I fully believed this explanation at the time but now I'm not sure it would hold up to scrutiny—Delia may have lived in his head, not in a department store.) Andrés called me *child* but he wasn't exactly motherly. He was more like a bossy schoolmarm.

"Do you have to do it with him?"

"Well, he can't really..." Andrés made a raising motion with his index finger, "...any more, but he still has interest. He tucks a couple of bills in my pocket afterwards," he added with a manic grin.

"So you don't do anything?"

"Child..." Andrés sorted through his bounty. "Sometimes I just put on a show for him. Last time, he called in the houseboy. We got busy, and the old man watched..."

"Well don't expect me to do anything..."

"Please come, it'll be fun. We'll tell him you're bi, okay?"

I remained unconvinced.

"And that you have a girlfriend." This was technically true; I was dating the sister of a classmate, although Andrés hadn't met her. I'd had a few isolated gay encounters since coming to the city, usually drunken, often fumbling, all with men who'd made the first move. The first happened when I was seventeen. I'd cut high school and taken the train into the city. I was loitering around Penn Station late that afternoon when a dark-skinned delivery man with a penetrating stare nodded at me. He guided me into an empty loading dock and dry-humped me behind a dumpster. I hadn't ever initiated sex with a man. I'd just let things like that happen—that way I could count them as "experiences" rather than look any deeper into my own desire.

 The date with Greet was set. I put on my only suit, the one I'd worn to weddings and college interviews. Andrés sprung for a taxi; he fixed my tie as we crossed town along the Central Park traverse. The address was an unimposing brownstone with a garage door, a holdout on a main cross-street with mostly high-rise apartment buildings. The decorator indeed owned a four-story house with a small, shady backyard. His staff included a driver—Alvaro, the man with the brushy mustache—and Juan, a handsome, solidly built, stoic man who Greet called "John" or "the Colombian" or "the houseboy." Each antiques-furnished room was painted or papered a different color; every surface had been considered. There were fresh flowers, art works, plush carpets underfoot, and marble-and-gilt furniture. From one corner, a porphyry bust of a Moor on a carved pedestal glared for eternity. All over, objects were arranged in tidy symmetries. Some of those antiques were real treasures, while others had "merely decorative value," as the appraisers would later put it.
 Gliding from room to room, I was in awe of the interiors' detailed perfection. It signaled a level of personal wealth I'd never encountered. I'd studied this style in design history class and on trips to the Met, where such rooms had stanchions to keep people out. It was a version of Classicism; the British aristocracy cosseted themselves in colors and patterns that evoked the glories of nature, Mother England herself. Precious objects were juxtaposed in carefully composed interiors, projecting a veneer of serene order. (I would later note an Imperialist edge to his style, recognizing many of his objects as plunder from the farthest reaches of the British Empire.)
 In the living room, Andrés and I sat on matching chairs, gilt Gothic Revival, with pointed arched backs, upholstered in peacock blue. Sinking in to the crush of velvet, everyone's eyes were on me—Greet's, Juan's, Andrés', even the figure in the painting over the mantle. I felt like the center of attention in a way I hadn't since I was a boy; as the first-born son of a traditional Italian family, I'd been the pampered little

prince at the table. A feeling of power surged through me, its contours vaguely familiar. Juan stopped staring, resetting his expression to stone-faced deference as he replaced our drinks. Andrés raised an eyebrow as he passed.

"That's quite a painting," said Andrés, pointing over the mantle. "The oil is somewhat muddy, the proportions are a bit off, and this hatching…it's incomplete."

"Academic Study of a Youth," I read off the plaque affixed to the frame.

"An amateur work, but it has a certain charm," replied Greet.

The painting depicted a young man in blue shorts—open at the fly— with black hair and muscular thighs. He wore a crooked smile as he posed provocatively in a studio scattered with empty stools and easels.

"You remind me of the model," Greet said to me, adding, "something in his smirk."

"Yasss, in the package, too," Andrés replied, and Greet snorted.

"Package?" I didn't know enough camp code to understand the joke. My naïveté prompted more laughter. I noticed Greet sneaking glances at my body, sometimes shyly, sometimes boldly, his glare burning through my suit.

Greet told us wild stories of his London days: hazy nights in rough bars with Francis Bacon, partying with the ruling class at Annabel's, the legendary private club in Mayfair, and mingling with Eartha Kitt and her band at the Café de Paris. He'd launch into these stories, delivered in his British accent with touches of mangled French, and he seemed to know how they played against his formal, uptight appearance and aristocratic bearing. He'd made allusions to his own peerage, according to Andrés. With me there, Andrés was emboldened enough to come out and ask: "So, what are you anyway? A lord, a duke, a baron?"

"You know darling, I was always taught that when in America, we leave our titles at Jay-Eff-Kay." Andrés laughed, and I filed this reply away.

After drinks, we headed to Felidia, an understated bastion of Istrian cuisine. Greet lauded my Italian background, praising the people, the land, the art. He quoted Verdi: "You may have the world if I may have Italy." When I told him my grandmother was born in Amalfi, he raved about the Amalfi Coast, insisted I visit, and thereafter bestowed upon me all the virtues he associated with our people.

I ordered osso buco, which my grandmother used to make on special occasions, to Greet's gushing approval. I'd never eaten it anywhere else but at her house at one of our raucous Sunday dinners. I'd sit with the adults in her Venetian-inspired dining room, witness to unfolding family melodramas. The waiter discreetly instructed me in extracting the marrow out of the bone with the tiny fork he'd brought. I slurped the warm jelly, its creamy body having absorbed the roasted bone flavor. Even with that dainty fork, it felt primitive in such a posh setting. Dessert was a cloud of zabaglione served with wild strawberries fresh from the chef's own property. If I didn't already feel like a prince from sitting in that blue chair, this feast sealed it.

We returned to the townhouse, sated and drunk on Barolo and Grappa, and formed a clumsy parade stumbling into the bedroom, with its pale yellow walls and crisp white crown molding outlining a sky blue ceiling. Hand-colored lithographs of Roman monuments (which now hang in my apartment) adorned the walls. Andrés and I climbed up on that enormous Jacobean bed, which would soon become the site of a twelve-year battle over my body. With the canopy overhead and the curtains along the sides drawn, it became a swirling room-within a room, a capsule of space where my judgment would be atomized, as if by the floral chintz. As I hit the ironed sheets, Andrés turned his head to mine, kissed me, and felt my body. The vectors of their desire pierced the fog of drink.

Greet hovered over us in a striped robe, a cut crystal tumbler in hand, sloshing around the last of his drink, now and then timidly copping a feel. Andrés went down on me. Despite the numbing effects of alcohol, I got a hard-on; Greet's glassy eyes widened as he took it all in. Andrés' blow job became more performative, with exaggerated head movements, gulps, and leering. He stroked me until I shot off. It was the first time I'd really ever had an audience and it was pretty impressive. I caught on to Andrés' cues and moaned loudly while shooting a forceful arc through the air. "This one's a headboard hitter," Andrés pronounced with a manic leer. He'd already come up with a branding slogan for me. Greet fixed on the scene with his mouth hanging open.

We went into his marble-clad bathroom for a hasty and sobering clean-up. I looked expectantly at Andrés and asked if we were done; he raised a finger to his mouth. As we were saying our goodbyes, Greet put down his glass and tucked crisp hundred dollar bills into our jacket pockets.

"For art supplies..." he said as he kissed me goodbye, in the French manner, left cheek, right cheek. I caught an acidic whiff of metabolized alcohol from the sweat on his neck.

We took the cross-town bus home. *Was that it? I could handle that—as long as I don't have to do anything with him.* Andrés camped up and down the aisle, in view of the late-shift workers—maids, nannies, housekeepers—and sang out the chorus of Blondie's "Call Me."

He twirled and prompted me to sing along: *"Chiama me..."*

A few of the weary passengers cracked smiles. As we reached the West Side, he turned to me and patted my breast pocket, saying, "Yasss child, you just turned your first trick." I acknowledged his praise, still failing to grasp what it all meant.

The next day I was awoken by the late morning sun as it angled in from behind the buildings along Central Park West. As I adjusted to the brightness compounding my hangover, I regretted the decision to forgo window treatments. Over breakfast, Andrés explained his relationship with Greet in more sober terms.

"I met him at Rounds. It's a bar on the East Side."

"Oh, on that stretch?"

"Yasss, Fifty-third. So you've been there?"

"Oh—No, but it's hard not to notice the street action..."

"It's a place for uptown tricks to meet young trade. There's even a song about it..." He sang the chorus of "53rd & 3rd" by the Ramones. Reportedly, Dee Dee Ramone had hustled on the strip to support his dope habit.

"So you mean you're..."

"Working my way through college, yasss..."

He looked at me expectantly as this information landed.

"Isn't it dangerous?"

"Not really...On the street, maybe, but that's why I dress up. I'm looking for sugar daddy potential..." Andrés explained how he'd hit Rounds in a jacket and tie, looking to attract rich johns–Upper East Siders, business travelers, European tourists. *So that's how he could afford all those clothes and all the travel.* My roommate was a jet-setting escort and I'd been too naïve to piece it together.

"What do you mean, sugar daddy?"

"That's an older man who's looking for a regular, for dates and travel…"

"Are there a lot of guys like that?"

"Child, I only need one…" I laughed. He'd made his case. "I've been working on Greet for a while. Help me out with him, please? It'll be good for both of us."

For years after its end, as I inventoried the effects of the twelve-year relationship in which I would soon be embroiled, I'd refer to him using this handed-down term: *He was my sugar daddy*. Not long after, I'd learn its complement: I was his *kept boy*.

I was invited for another dinner, this time French, La Côte Basque, described in the press as a "high-society temple," the site of Truman Capote's 1975 exposé. Greet was friendly with the owner/chef, Jean-Jacques Rachou. Andrés again begged me to go, to keep in Greet's good graces. Things hadn't been the same between them since the debacle downtown. We met up at the townhouse again, and after a hurried round of cocktails, the decorator yelled for Alvaro. As he careened towards the idling car, he stumbled a bit, his dainty, half-drunk steps in tasseled leather shoes no match for the New York City curb. He managed to lower himself into the car, and Alvaro whisked us down to Fifty-Fifth Street.

A giant floral display honeyed the air and dwarfed the young woman at the front desk. The Italian place, though fancy, had been familiar enough ground for me to feel comfortable, but picking up on the sophisticated Francophile vibe of this place wrested me out of my tipsy state. *This crowd will see right through my department-store suit and borrowed tie… my shoes are scuffed…they'll clock me as an imposter.* To ease my uptown anxiety, I calculated the distance to Saint Mark's Place, epicenter of my student/punk downtown reality: *Forty-seven blocks down, twenty blocks to a mile, two avenues over…* It helped just thinking that I could run out and find my way back to a familiar city.

Rachou jumped up and embraced Greet affectionately.

"*Monsieur Greet, bienvenue, mon beau…*"

"Monsieur Rachou, always an honor…"

He welcomed Andrés and I warmly, his gravelly voice belying a soft, affectionate demeanor. He beamed with pride over the lively room, a mix of rich older patrons and a younger, well-dressed business crowd.

Andrés and I were definitely the youngest people there other than the coat-check attendant. M. Rachou seemed oblivious to any potential scandal in the sight of two college students accompanying a rich old man, although we turned heads as he escorted us to a choice table. The crowd's attention raised the heat behind my ears.

When it came time to order, Rachou took over from the waiter. I impressed him with my high-school French and my selection: *"Je prendrai le caneton aux cérises."* He beamed, evidently relieved that he did not have to deal with another dieter. I came to learn that it was Rachou's existential struggle to make classic French cuisine, often maligned as heavy and sauced, appeal to capricious Americans. Andrés also ordered in French, but asked endless questions, each an apparent slight to the chef. As he left, Greet turned to me and whispered, "That's Monsieur Rachou's signature dish." At least I'd gotten ordering right.

Greet's focus seemed to have shifted, away from Andrés and towards me. I grew a bit more confident: *Maybe I'm better suited to this scenario than Andrés…He's such a picky eater.* I was relieved when the waiter slid my plate before me. I wasn't entirely sure of what I'd ordered, but it smelled fatty and sweet, was cooked to a crisp, and bathed in sauce. I savored the generous portion of what turned out to be duckling—its rich meat offset by a tart cherry sauce—while gauging Greet's growing admiration. Though there were moments when I over-identified with that sauced and seared duckling, one thing I could rely upon was my appetite. We capped off dinner with Grand Marnier soufflés.

Over a few more nights out as a trio, alternating between Italian and French restaurants, I adapted to both the leering gay scrutiny from the table and the uptown social scene beyond it. There were more signals that Greet was more interested in me than Andrés. He'd bristle whenever Andrés acted in too "flamboyant" a manner out in public, although he'd play right along in private settings. He wanted a staid, civilized companion, not an attention-seeker. My reticence seemed to play better than Andrés' acting out. The Upper East Side elites whom Greet sought to impress might clock Andrés as gay; I was less obvious. I just needed to polish off the suburban affect.

Andrés had mentioned that Greet had "a thing for Italians." I didn't think of myself as especially Italian-looking; what stood out in my mind about my appearance was a lanky awkwardness, and that was not part of the archetype of the Italian male as I understood it. Andrés set me straight: "Child, you heard how he carries on about Italians…With those eyes, your black curls, your Mediterranean complexion? You are trade, right out of a Caravaggio…" I didn't really get the reference.

I could drink, too, better than Andrés, who was a lightweight; drinking was a major part of the job. Greet would have Juan serve us pre-dinner cocktails at home, then have one or two upon arrival at the restaurant. We were expected to drink along with him. My cocktail of choice for many years out with Greet was the Negroni: Bitter, red, and Italian, it played well into my performance. Greet favored vodka with a mixer. Once at the table, we'd drink wine all through dinner, and after-dinner, he'd order up an amaro or a cognac. My body would not know the ravages of this routine for a few years.

Back at the railroad flat after a dozen or so dates, Andrés was packing up his paints, canvasses, and travel easel for a trip to Turkey.

"I'm flying to Istanbul, so much to see…Hagia Sophia, the Bosphorus, and child, the *men*…"

"How long are you going to be away?"

"Five days in Istanbul and a side trip to Cappadocia."

Cappadocia's volcanic landscape sculpted by erosion, its hoodoos and carved-rock dwellings, would influence his paintings for years thereafter. With the way his travels informed his subjects, I came to think of his work as a kind of nomadic modernism.

"You should go out with Mister Greet one night…keep those fires burning."

"You think so? What would we do?"

"Keep him company 'til we can all go out again. Just don't get any ideas about stealing my sugar daddy away…"

I sensed that there was some genuine anxiety beneath his joking. I had no such plot in mind but was working on a way to benefit from the decorator's favor. Though I didn't want to ruin anything for Andrés, it was hard to account for what I owed him. He'd moved into my apartment, and soon after, he and Greet had taken over my life. I'd sometimes recall the narrow confines of my former quiet student routine fondly and a resentment would burrow: *Andrés tricked me*. I'd invited change, at least subconsciously, but didn't remember signing on to all of this.

Greet took me to Le Cirque, which had been chronicled as "one of the city's most socially prestigious dining rooms." This was the original location on East Sixty-Fifth Street, inside the Mayfair House. The proprietor was Sirio Maccioni, a Tuscan-born self-made restauranteur who'd gotten his start as a waiter on a cruise ship. Maccioni later moved the restaurant into a garish theme-park design at Villard House. He closed that location rather than honor union workers' contracts, relocating for a second time to an even more garish build-out in the Bloomberg Building. Neither had the same clubby intimacy or clout as the original; the last eventually shuttered.

Greet introduced me to Maccioni, who, upon hearing my last name, welcomed me in Italian; I stammered through some phrases I'd picked up from Andrés. I thought I detected a hint of suspicion from him—a raised eyebrow directed my way—but he seemed to have put it behind him and accepted me as *famigliare* by the time we got to the table.

The room was a peach soufflé of Old World elegance. As I scanned the tables, sometimes locking eyes with the other guests, mostly well-dressed society matrons, my gaze repeatedly reset to the painted panel above our table; it depicted monkeys dressed as French courtesans. I soon realized that the whole room was adorned with panels of the same theme: snobby rococo monkeys playing the piano, strolling in a garden, having afternoon tea. I couldn't help but feel that the pretension-skewering monkeys were on my side as I took in the social scene. None of the other diners seemed to give them a thought.

Greet ordered a bottle of champagne and filled me in on the allure of Le Cirque. The social hierarchy was reflected in the intimate room's seating chart: "The regulars each have their favorite table, and Sirio has to juggle them every night…" As a well-dressed, well-connected decorator with Park Avenue clients, he'd been showered with ingratiating charm. "Sirio adores me. Nevertheless, I stopped by this afternoon to make sure we'd get this corner. It's a special night…"

I puzzled over his last remark as we settled in; the waiter popped the champagne. Greet fixed his gaze upon me and began a rambling pronouncement. He told me how "charming" he found me, how "wonderful" it was to spend time with me. He had a tic of tagging each thought with "involved" as a kind of verbal ellipsis: "I've developed feelings for you, quite strong feelings, involved…" I tried to listen to what he was saying, but it was both jumbled and beyond my belief. When he used the word "love" in some context, I fixated on the bubbles wriggling up through the champagne.

He waited expectantly. It all sounded nonsensical, praise that

I did not deserve, emotions that were unearned. I had to stop myself from looking around: *Who is he talking about? He doesn't even know me.* I felt trapped in a absurdist stage play, not knowing whether to laugh or bolt. I managed a half-smile and an impassive shrug.

"Perhaps you will develop feelings for me over time… I would like you to be my full-time companion…"

"What does that mean?"

"Well, we'll have our dates…we don't always have to go to restaurants, we could visit museums, gardens, involved…and travel. I go on buying trips—and for inspiration—London, Paris…One of my major clients, Anne Cox Chambers, she was Jimmy Carter's ambassador to Belgium, has a beautiful house in Provence…and of course Italy, you must see Capri…there would be a stipend involved…of course, we'll have to have some suits made…"

Andrés' fears had proven correct. I gulped. I tried to comprehend what was being asked of me. In the moment, it was to accept this declaration of love and this proposal and seal it with a clink of champagne flutes. Going forward, I'd be agreeing to date this old man, be dressed up by him, even get on planes to Europe with him. The monkeys seemed to turn on me. In the jumble of benefits offered, the prospect of travel stuck out. I'd flown to Paris the prior summer after scoring cheap airfare but had run out of money before my return flight. I also remembered hearing the word "stipend." What was that, exactly? I was too shy to ask the dollar amount. After a too-long pause, I came back to my senses and managed to formulate a counter offer.

"Mr. Greet, you know that I'm studying design, right? I can help you with your projects."

He was stung. His mouth dropped and he shooed the waiter off. He recovered enough to propose a compromise: He'd hire me to organize his office and accompany him on buying trips, but we'd have dates, too.

"But what about school?"

He assured me that he'd work around my class schedule. I realized that during all of our nights out, he hadn't ever once asked me about school, what I was studying, how I liked it. I voiced concerns about keeping on top of my classes but hardly believed them myself. I had the feeling that this was another golden ticket moment before me, like with Cooper Union. Acceptance to a tuition-free college had preempted any worries my parents had about me moving into the city on my own.

I envisioned our relationship maturing beyond his initial, unrequited sexual desire for me into one of professionalism and respect.

"And Andrés?" I asked.

"He's a bit too camp…" The complaint struck me as odd, because I'd seen him camp it up, too. "Please understand, I admire him greatly, but I feel that we are temperamentally unsuited to each other, involved…"

I came to read between the lines; Whenever he called Andrés "flamboyant," he was signaling that he was too overtly gay to be seen with him. It reminded me of Andrés' failed relationship with the closeted grad student, and Joseph's aggrieved posturing at my doorstep, how it all seemed colored with gay shame.

I didn't think of myself as masculine, but was definitely more masculine-presenting than Andrés. The decorator lived in a glass closet, the kind sanctioned in wealthy circles, whereby a gay man could be accepted on the scene as long as he was discreet. Andrés cracked the glass. He'd also proven unreliable, having abandoned him downtown. Greet further complained that Andrés had "too much of an artistic temperament." Andrés did look upon the world with an artist's all-consuming eye. On the other hand, I could be like the sullen boy in the painting, a subject among objects. I could sit there under his gaze, like an artist's model, upon whom he projects his desires: an academic study of a youth.

Up until this rococo monkey night—as with my furtive encounters with men—I'd let everything that had happened between us just happen. His proposal was uncharacteristically frank, coming from a man who seemed to live by unspoken terms. I'd given him an uncharacteristic reply, laying out terms of my own instead of just letting this relationship happen to me. I glanced over at some businessmen at the bar; they appeared to be negotiating something, too. If I were to accept, I could no longer claim I'd been tricked or was just along for the ride. At the same time, I worried about how Andrés would take the news.

"All right, Mr. Greet," I said with a smirk. I touched my flute to his as it trembled in his hand. Though we hadn't fully settled on terms, the rites of alcohol would not be stopped. The champagne went down and the burst of bubbles pricked at my conscience.

2. NATURE TO HIS RUIN

Spring 1982, the Lebowitz' driveway

I went and picked up my tux and put it on with the red bow tie Joy insisted I buy for the occasion. Then I picked up her wrist corsage—it looked so big, at least through the cellophane window in the florist's box. As I drove up, Joy ran out, her mother behind her with scissors, cutting stray threads off of her dress. She'd made it herself (with help from her mom)...vivid red, with a fitted bodice, ruffled sleeves, a full skirt, like a flamenco dancer...

"Wow, you look amazing..."

She deferred the compliment, instead swooning over the corsage. I couldn't tell if she was being sincere or ironic.

"Let's get some pictures..Dad? Dale, straighten your bow tie..."

Clutch. Smile. Click.

My high school prom date and I grew up in houses not too far from each other. She was a tall girl with a deep voice, very outspoken and wild, but managed to present as a good kid. She went to a specialized public school in the city: the High School of Art & Design. In the photos her dad took that day, she doesn't look like a high schooler: her mature body is on full display, her makeup professional-looking, her hair a feathered mantle. I fully look like a high school kid swimming in a rented tux, awkward in my body, my face round with adolescent fat under a tangle of curls. I was really impressed with that dress. It was a bold choice, a departure from the prom dress code of the day, which demanded pretty, soft pastels and flowy silhouettes.

By my last semester at Oceanside High I'd already completed enough credits to graduate. I had a schedule of mostly art and theater classes and my teachers were fairly lenient. What a relief it was to flee the school's repressive social order, though by senior year I'd reached a kind of detente with the bullies; they'd moved on to easier targets. There was a useful rumor going around that my dad was in the Mafia. He'd done well enough in his own business to buy a big waterfront house, a couple of blocks over from where he and my mom had grown up. In a town where Italian-Americans were largely blue collar (plumbers, butchers, cops) and the Jewish families skewed white collar (doctors, lawyers, teachers), our family stood out. Someone must have concluded that my dad was mafioso and the rumor took hold. We'd laugh about it when it would circle back to us. Still, the halls of Oceanside High were the site of years of humiliations: clocked for a sissyish strut, called out for crossing my legs, an uncoordinated wreck on the ball field, mocked for gay voice.

During that final semester, Joy would call me on school nights and command: "Come with me to the city tomorrow." Any chance I got, I'd skip, and we'd take the Long Island Rail Road together. She would sweet talk the security guard into letting me into her school, and I'd hang out in the stairwell that was her clique's meeting point, while they came and went, spending their free periods with me. They were artistic kids from all boroughs, Black, Latino, Asian; most were queer. I was accustomed to the predominantly Jewish/Italian makeup of our hometown; there was exactly one Black family with sons enrolled in my high school, who seemed to manage because they were jocks, and one Chinese family, whose son was a friend for a while. In addition to the jocks, there were academic and theatre cliques inside the walls, while outside, suburban toughs in leather jackets, self-appointed enforcers of the social order, ruled with menace. The queer kids concentrated in the theatre cliques but were mostly too scared to be out. Hanging out at Art & Design felt like slipping into an inverted reality; the would-be targets of bullies ran the place and the sensitivity we'd been bullied for was cultivated.

Winding out of her graphic design class, Joy slapped a card in my hand.

"Welcome to Art & Design." It was a school ID with my name and photo.

"How did you do that?"

"Just a little ink, an X-Acto knife, and the laminating machine. Plus a photo I got from your mom…"

I examined her work with admiration. In the day, city school kids rode for free on the subway (let's bring that back). All I had to do now was flash it at the token clerk. That fake ID was a ticket to ride.

Many of Joy's friends were banjee boys, fronting butch in the streets, cutting up as queens when there was strength in numbers. We'd smoke joints and hang out in the atrium of the Citicorp building and they would read the office workers as they walked by, picking apart their clothes, their styling, judging books by covers: "Miss Lady is giving me juniors department at the workplace…" "Is that her *daughter's* dress?" It was savage. Sometimes I saw Joy as their ringleader; on other days she seemed like a pushy white girl hanger-on. I was just happy to be included, even if my presence raised some eyebrows.

At night, we'd go to discos. These were the days of the reopened Studio 54, after it had been famously shut down, the owners jailed for tax evasion. It was still a scene at the door even if it wasn't as exclusive as before. We were underage and that actually helped; clubs were lax about carding and seemed to want hip city kids in the mix. We went to other uptown clubs too, like Magique on First Avenue, which had a laser system, and the Red Parrot on West Fifty-Seventh Street. We'd get in on comp cards Joy and her friends always managed to score. If Art & Design felt like slipping into an inverted reality, nightclubbing on comp cards with these kids felt like sliding through a loophole only they knew about. Once through, our adolescent bodies were immersed in the thump and the heat, in sync with and up against the adults. "Wear your Jordaches, we're going out," she would command the morning of our trips, referring to the one pair of designer jeans I owned. I bore my entrée into the grown-up world of city clubs as a shield against the petty provincialism of my home town.

Dating Joy was a version of heterosexuality I could muster at that stage in my confusion. Her body was familiar in some ways—we were close in height, she had thick black hair and a Mediterranean complexion from her Sephardic forebears. She had womanly curves, but also grew hair in places on her body I'd grown hair, too, some sprouting around her nipples. She didn't seem to mind. She'd been effectively socialized as a gay man and was an instigator. We'd made a couple of amateurish attempts at sex in my car before she said, "Let's just stick to second base," so *that* pressure was off. Being her boyfriend gave me access to her circle of gay friends, though technically I was off limits to them, on strict orders from Joy. (I would later visit one of her friends, Edwin, a slim Latino, at his place in Corona; he smoked me up and we burned that order.) Being my girlfriend gave Joy a date taller than she was and access to the Oceanside High School prom, at which she thoroughly enjoyed making a special appearance, catching up with friends from middle school and dancing all night until she burst out of the bodice of that dress.

My time trailing a queer city clique was a remote flash by the time Andrés had come along: wild Joy, self-described fag hag, had become immersed in Scientology, a controlling and homophobic cult. Without an instigator at my side, I'd retreated into loner habits. I was fairly lost in my new context; Architecture as taught at Cooper Union was an open-ended exploration of poetics and myth—not exactly grounded in the profession's realities. I couldn't follow the assignments the way I had in the applied arts classes taught at my school. Despite its founder's mission— to provide a free arts education to talented working-class people of all races—the students were nothing like the kids from Art & Design. Most of my classmates were from privileged backgrounds, and relatively few were straight out of high school, like me. I was thrown in with an older group, some of whom had degrees in other disciplines, others who were working artists.

My stomach sank upon realizing how much I was in over my head; my golden ticket began to feel like a mistake. I scrambled to catch up on an extensive reading list, up to and including French theorists like Gaston Bachelard, whose influential work *The Poetics of Space* proposed a phenomenology of architecture. I found myself parroting the artspeak and the theoretical jargon. The school's Foundation Building was a sanctum in the clouds, an esoteric fortress at the threshold of the gritty East Village. I was still finding my footing on this track when Andrés came along, upended my plodding, and pulled me back into the city outside the sanctum. He'd been on the scene for a whole year by the time he moved in with me. Like Joy, he was a street savvy instigator who knew all the clubs. He'd scoped out all the gay spots, from Boybar to the Christopher Street Piers to the hustlers on Fifty-Third.

Under the guise of roommate-seeking, I'd invited change, and change had come at me full force. Once he started actually spending time at home, living with Andrés was a whirlwind. One night, he was on yet another international call, yammering ostentatiously, switching between French and Italian. Upon hanging up, he turned to me.

"Yasss child, Franca, she's fabulous. I met her in Rome, she lives in Paris now..."

"Ok, that was a pretty long call..." I was nervous about the charges.

"What are you doing tonight?" he asked, changing the subject. "We're going to Danceteria. You should come."

"Don't you have to know someone to get in there?"

"Child, you know *me*," he said, flashing an invite. "We just have to do something about your clothes..." he added, circling my figure with a disapproving finger. The only trend I'd kept up with while buckling down at Cooper Union was black basics; that wasn't going to cut it with Andrés' nightlife crowd. He rifled through his clothing rack and pulled an outfit: a flowy Matsuda shirt, cropped pants, and a beaded necklace. He teased my hair into a mane of wild curls.

Some of his friends came over—Daisy, a passable drag queen who would later work at Lucky Cheng's, and two cute visiting German students. We were swept into Danceteria as promised. There was a scene in the coat check room, so Andrés gathered up our jackets and stuffed them behind a speaker. He dragged me upstairs to the dance floor and strutted through the crowd. I met his circle of friends who pronounced me *adorable!* In the taxi home, he kissed me, just once, hard but fast so the driver wouldn't notice.

We'd had sex in front of Greet but those were performances. Alone in the quiet of a New York night, no eyes upon us except our own, we made out and felt each others' bodies. When Andrés went down on me in the dark, I surprised him by taking his uncut cock in my mouth, making us a swirl on the futon. For the first time, I didn't just let gay sex passively happen to me, I let myself desire his male body, taste his salt, caress his torso in long, tentative sweeps. By the incidental light of rear windows, I watched him drop his mask of mischief and show me almost maternal tenderness. *Yasss, child.*

In the days that followed, we presented as a couple, at least to our circle. I still saw my girlfriend on some nights, but not for much longer. B—— was Serbian, with soft curves and black curls like mine. After joining me on one of my long walks home we'd fallen into an easy intimacy. Our relationship had ended not just because my life had taken a turn, it was something else, something between us. Soon after introducing a recently-released contraceptive sponge to our sex lives, she let me know that she was pregnant. Though we both put on brave faces and said the right things, we seemed unable to move past the heavy fact of our abortion. As easily as we'd come together we just fell apart. This was concurrent with my getting caught up in the whirlwind of Andrés.

For me if not him, my new relationship with Andrés marked an end as much as a beginning. I no longer took solitary walks; we'd jump on the subway together after classes and get ready for a night of clubbing. We occupied that railroad flat as a unit, at least when we were both around. There were nights he'd disappear, nights he'd underplay in retellings: "I'm still trying to catch a sugar daddy…" but I could smell the sex under the citrus notes of his favorite cologne, No. 4711, and could see that the cash was still rolling in. I had no hold over him.

Within a year of his moving in, we started on some renovations, prompted by Andrés. We removed the dropped plaster ceiling from the entire apartment; there were patches of prior water damage. I wound up doing most of the demolition, since Andrés was sensitive to mold and dust. I leaned into the butch construction worker role to offset what seemed like an obvious manipulation, removing the ceiling exposed the original wooden joists that held up the roof. We (I) took down all the door jambs, installed new plywood flooring, backlit the skylight, and trained vines to grow on its walls. There were no closets, so Andrés bought two industrial wheeled clothing racks. We transformed the space from ordinary railroad flat into lofty aerie. In less than a year, Andrés had turned me out and transformed my style of dress, my living space, and my habits.

He'd turned me out and he'd pimped me out, but with unintended consequences. Once it was clear that Greet wanted to see more of me and less of him, he fumed. He couldn't stay mad at me but he heaped insults on the decorator. He'd push himself on our dinner plans whenever possible; Greet would usually acquiesce, despite his misgivings: "Two's company, four's a party, three's an empty chair…" he'd intone. I wanted Andrés there as a safety but at the same time allied myself with the decorator's growing disapproval.

Some nights, Andrés would be invited back to the townhouse, which meant that we'd be putting on a show for him—that the headboard hitter would be called upon. Other nights, the decorator would tuck a bill in his pocket after dinner just to get rid of him, so that he could spend the rest of the night with me. So much was changing at once that I didn't even have time to acknowledge that my first gay relationship was knotted up in transactions.

After our negotiation at Le Cirque, our regular date nights were set. For a time, he was careful to accommodate my class schedule and my workload. He stalled off on getting me started in his studio for that reason, and I agreed it would be easier once the semester ended. Andrés was traveling a lot that summer but would appear at Greet's table whenever he was around, something between a third wheel and a pimp demanding his cut. I couldn't begrudge him.

When Harry Cipriani opened at the Sherry-Netherland hotel it became our regular spot for nights out. The restaurant had Venetian bona fides that put the decorator in a Von Aschenbach-chasing-Tadzio swoon, and gave me a sparkling new set on which to play up my exiled prince performance. I burnished my restaurant Italian for the full effect and we indulged in *vitello tonnato* or halibut and zucchini chips, washed down with Bellinis. Anthony Bourdain once said, "everyone at Cipriani is complicit," and that held true of me, too. I even sat politely while Greet greeted First Lady Nancy Reagan—then a laughingstock for her simplistic "Just Say No" anti-drug slogan—at a nearby table when I thought I should say *something*. He'd later take me to the original Harry's Bar and the Hotel Villa Cipriani on the island of Giudecca, a dislocation in time and space I was convinced my bedroom performances had manifested.

For all of his connections, his lavish habits, and his aristocratic affect, Greet saw himself as a down-to-earth fellow. On many nights when I sat across from him at a table, he'd launch into a mangled quote from Kipling: "If you can walk with kings, but never lose the common touch...you'll be a man, my son." I'm not sure what years of dining in posh restaurants was supposed to prepare me for, but he considered it central to my education as a young gentleman. I learned about cuisine, developed refined table manners, became adept at making small talk in hushed rooms, and learned to play to role of outré charmer without pushing limits. I got to know the social order as it was inscribed in the seating charts of a constellation of favored establishments dotted across the uptown firmament. Showing off wealth, prestige, pecking order, and social influence was the main event; dining was performative, proof that they were, after all, humans. I came back from one dinner and vented to Andrés. "I feel like an anthropologist doing field work...the tribal consumption rituals of Upper East Siders..."

Greet had started me out on a weekly stipend—seven crisp hundreds and one fifty—tucked into my jacket pocket, as usual. To put that sum in perspective, the monthly rent on the railroad flat was just under $400, which I was then splitting with Andrés. He could make his share of the rent in one good night at Rounds. Andrés would spend his cash as it came in: "Child, I just let the currency flow through me." The bills came at me so much faster than I could spend them that I started stashing them under the floor boards.

On the day Greet finally decided I'd start work, I was admitted through the basement door by a wordless Juan. I wore that one suit of mine—a gray Armani knock-off, which I'd bought off the rack at Century 21 for a wedding—with a shirt and tie that were gifts from the decorator. I never felt at ease in that suit; I didn't think its slouchy Italian cut did my lanky frame any favors. It was an important day for me, as I pictured working together a path to legitimizing our relationship.

His workroom, which occupied the basement of the townhouse, surprised me with its modern design: checkered flooring, sleek steel filing units. His desk, which I would never see him sit at, was strewn with samples: fabric swatches, wood finishes, blocks of stone, tiles in unruly stacks. The swatches were on loan from Clarence House, Scalamandré, Cowtan & Tout, many of the high-end fabric houses. Most were long overdue, according to the labels. Greet would affix an embossed note card to a sample to identify it by room and project. I could only think to bring some order into this annotated swirl of colors and textures.

Greg, an interior designer who freelanced as Greet's draftsman, arrived, eyeing me suspiciously. We'd met once or twice for drinks; I surmised that he'd come to look down upon me as yet another hustler (I wasn't entirely sure he was wrong). Andrés had since found out that the decorator had a history and a reputation among the working boys at Rounds. One of the regulars had assessed him as "generous, a heavy drinker…thinks he can turn you into his boyfriend." While Greg put together a set of drawings, I spent the morning organizing samples in binders by project and room and gathering up bags of swatches to be returned. Greg brushed off the drawing, seemingly finished, and I took the opening to start a conversation.

"So which project are you working on?"

"Actually, it's an old project, I'm just touching up this set for my own portfolio…"

"Isn't there anything new to work on?"

"Still waiting on my marching orders," he said as he flipped through the drawings. "These are from the Saul Steinberg residence. You know, the corporate raider?"

"Never heard of him…"

"Saul somehow managed to get into 740 Park, a real snobby building…" I studied the drawings. "He's on his third wife, Gayfryd. Gorgeous, a terror, but aren't they all? She hired Mr. Greet to redo these rooms." He circled an area on the floor plan. "Even though wife number two—I've already forgotten her name— had Sister Parrish redo them, not even that long ago…"

"I guess third wives are good for business…"

"Ha! His reputation really took off after this project, you know. Ever since them, it's been a steady stream of Jews pushing to get into good buildings…"

Greet came down at ten, dressed in a suit with a patterned shirt and contrasting tie. He reserved white cuffs and collars for evenings. He immediately set about pulling my work apart, selecting this sheer for those curtains and this marble for that bathroom.

"Greg, Mr. Corvino and I are going to hit the showrooms, involved…"

"Just leave something for the rest of us," he joked.

Greet laughed and put on his jacket.

"Alvaro, let's get this over with…"

As I gathered up the samples to be returned, Greet gave me a confused look. Greg spoke up: "We *should* return once in a while, make a good show of it…" Greet shrugged. Alvaro started the Jaguar and we were on our way. Greet ran in and out of the showrooms like a linebacker, fairly terrorizing the clerks, running through the racks with a focused eye as they chased behind him marking down his selections. Despite his protestations of dreading this part of the job it was the most alive I'd ever seen him. After knocking off all the showrooms on his mental list, he got back in the car and commanded Alvaro to take us to Gino.

"*Buon giorno, Signore* Greet," Gino Circiello enthused as we entered. It was a clubby Italian joint on Lexington Avenue, its narrow, nondescript dining room enlivened by wallpaper from Scalamandré, a repeating pattern of zebras escaping arrows on a Masai red background. Founded by Caprese Circiello in 1945, regular Gay Talese once called it a "time capsule." I was introduced to Cesare, the maitre d', as Greet's assistant. I could tell by the glances exchanged that inferences were being made, but the old-school Italian waiters welcomed me with sympathetic nods. Gino was essentially his cafeteria for all the years we were together, until near the end. Once a month, he'd go down there with a wad of cash to settle his tab. He loved holding court at the bar. Since we were supposed to be working, I tried ordering a soda, but was immediately scolded. He glared at me, then yelled to the bartender, "Mario, bring Mr. Corvino a Negroni…" Although I prided myself on being able to keep up with Greet by night, I found the day drinking ruinous. Greet seemed to be able to function, at least until the cumulative effect of his drinking would unleash his romantic melancholy. Before long I worked out a signal with Mario to make me up a virgin drink that looked enough like the cocktail.

There wasn't much left to the day by the time we got back to the townhouse. I'd done my best to sip the wine at lunch, but Greet drank like he always did and was ready for a nap. Greg and I gossiped for a bit; it became clear that he would be keeping the drafting work for himself.

Greet and I never coalesced around a consistent work schedule; I soon accepted that my role would be limited to accompanying him on buying trips, job site visits to watch him harass contractors, and lunch. After a few weeks, I noticed that Greet's hands would start shaking while zooming between showrooms; he couldn't make it too far past noon without alcohol.

I was increasingly pushed and pulled between uptown and downtown. I missed classes, but having a part-time job with a decorator was a valid cover story, even if my time was spent drinking and shopping. On days I went from work to school, I'd duck into the men's room at Bloomingdales to change into black jeans and Doc Martens. Going to the East Village in a suit and tie was not the look. I was commuting between two lives, downtown student and uptown companion. The distinctions between these split realms were sharper in the Eighties than they are now; uptown and downtown were two different economies, with distinct social orders and dress codes. There were no chic boutiques below 14th Street, where anarchy was in the air, and not just as a style. Downtown in those days was as subversive as uptown was materialistic.

Classes let out for the semester, and Greet took Andrés and I to Cipriani. We were already in a giddy mood over having gotten through the school year when Greet dangled the bait of a summer trip for the three of us:

"We'll fly in to Naples… from there we can visit Capri, Sorrento, the Amalfi Coast, all the excursions, involved… Andrés, your language skills will come in handy…"

We took his bait, and the show we put on for him later that night quaked the serene order of his bedroom.

I excitedly told my family that I was going to Italy—with my roommate. I couldn't explain to them how it was that this man who'd supposedly hired me as a part-time draftsman would be taking me on a month-long summer vacation (to our ancestral home no less) without raising suspicion.

My grandparents had come to this country as children, part of the great trans-Atlantic migration of the early twentieth century. My parents had married as high-school sweethearts with me on the way, and we all lived in my maternal grandparents' attic apartment. My mother's mother, Helen, was a fair, dark-haired beauty in her day who was born in Amalfi, and when I told Greet about her, he swooned. "Oh, you *must* see the Amalfi Drive, involved...." Helen had married my swarthy, Sicilian-born grandfather over her family's objections—her mother spat at her, "You're not marrying that *Africano*"—and they fled from their disapproval. They'd raised their children to speak English-only as good assimilationists.

In preparation for our trip, Greet scheduled an appointment with his New York tailor. Andrés' wardrobe was already presentable, if a bit dandyish, but that one suit of mine was looking tattered.

"One day, I'll have to take you to London to see my man at Turnbull & Asser, but for now, we'll have Victor make up a couple of suits and some jackets, involved..."

Victor, his New York tailor (who was actually from Hong Kong), put me on a platform and measured me in front of a three-way mirror, while Greet looked on, scrutinizing his work, or at least pretending. We clashed over the cut: I insisted upon form-fitting tailoring which he could not wear given his heft. "You'll look like an uptight British banker," he griped. Our disagreement represented a reversal, since I was leaning towards the English cut—tapered, snug, three-button—while Greet favored the looser American two-button style. It was really the first time I'd asserted my taste and it led to a battle of wills, its lines drawn along my body in tailor's chalk. Victor weighed in on my side, and after an uncomfortable silence, Greet relented. We also went to Louis Vuitton, where he purchased a set of hard suitcases in a plain finish—

old-money "Alzer" in pebbled brown leather, not the heavily branded patterns currently in style.

I swaggered victoriously when the suits were delivered.

After our battle at the tailor's we settled into a routine of days and evenings together, drinking and sexual tension both constants. Andrés was invited occasionally, as a special guest star; those were the nights I knew I'd been called upon to put on another show. Whatever successes I'd managed operating within Greet's social realm—despite my insecurities—I had a growing sense that my performances in his bed were a larger part of my value to him. Andrés, now valued by the decorator as a sexual instigator, had dropped his resentments as he looked forward to a month in Italy.

Over lunch at Gino, Greet outlined our itinerary: "The travel agent booked us on Alitalia, first class to Rome, with a connection to Naples, involved...We arrive in Naples late, so we'll have one night there and then take the aliscafo the next morning...The approach to Capri is *magnifico*..." He referred to the high-speed ferry that made the crossing in under an hour. I excitedly filled Andrés in on the details.

When I told my mom about the trip, she was excited, too: "That's wonderful, honey. I've always wanted to go..." I pitched it as a visit to important architectural sites and a chance to connect with our heritage. Although my parents had long expressed a desire to go (and had the means), they've never set foot in Italy, even to this day. My mom in particular has loved hearing about my travels; her vicarious pleasure started in earnest with this trip. To my surprise, she didn't have any probing questions, like how could the two of us afford a month-long trip. She'd been suspicious of Andrés since they'd met. He'd struck her as pretentious and worried that he was a "bad influence." I sensed that there was some coded fear about my sexuality in her dislike of him. On the other hand, I'd picked up some Italian living with him, which delighted her. She was enthusiastic about our travel plans and especially my intention to learn more of the language. She'd also felt the estrangement of the assimilationist program: "I only ever picked up a few curses in dialect. Your grandparents used to speak Italian to talk about us, too."

I'd also bragged about my new boss to my grandma Helen. She

always had a soft spot for me as her first grandchild. My fascination with her glamorous past—she'd enjoyed a brief friendship with Marilyn Monroe, while Monroe was dating Joe DiMaggio (another "swarthy" Sicilian), and she'd been a local beauty pageant contestant, evidenced by a newspaper clipping of her posing in a one-piece bathing suit and wedge heels, showing off her curves—also endeared me to her. I remember her lounging in a housecoat, her dyed black hair in a dated bouffant style that resolved into one sweeping curl. She had a beauty mark over her painted lips like punctuation, and as she pulled on a Parliament light, she'd told me, "You wouldn't know it to look at me now, but I worked for a respected lawyer in the city, before I got into running the lounge," of her life outside of marriage. I was fascinated with the gowns that hung in her hall closet, which she'd worn to hostess at that lounge, a jazz club in the neighboring town of Long Beach. I'd sneak into the closet and run my hand along the sequins. I'd happily embraced my favored status within her house and lorded it over the other kids. I too had mythologized Amalfi as the source of her fair-skinned beauty.

I told Grandma Helen about all the Italian dishes I'd been eating, the osso buco at Felidia, the *vitello tonnato* at Cipriani. She too accepted my relationship with the decorator as I represented it. The story I told tracked with the prevailing narrative of an earnest young man going to the city and finding opportunity. Maybe it *was* that—with a gay edge. I think she'd clocked me as gay long before I did; after all, I was a sensitive boy who clung to her and idolized her glamorous heyday. She delighted in hearing about the lavish meals I'd been enjoying at the decorator's table. She'd seek out the recipes and dutifully type them onto index cards, to file with her own.

One Sunday dinner at her house, I told everyone about the upcoming trip, and that we'd be visiting Amalfi. Grandma Helen swooned. "You have to take a lot of pictures, dolly…" (She often forgot my name and called me dolly.) On an index card, she typed out some addresses of relatives with whom she'd long ago lost touch, not sure they were still current. On my way out, she pressed a fifty dollar bill into my palm, whispering conspiratorially, "A little extra something for your trip. Don't tell your mother."

Our Italian sojourn was off to an idyllic start. Upon learning of my origins, the locals I met would proclaim that I was on *"un viaggio tipo*

Roots," referring to the blockbuster American miniseries. After a day of touring and an overnight at the Grand Hotel Vesuvio, an old-world palace on the Bay of Naples, we took the aliscafo to Capri. "I've been coming here for years, it's one of the chicest destinations, involved.... The people of Capri are *bellissimo*..." On trips past, he'd stayed at the Hotel Quisisana—the most exclusive resort on the island—but this time he'd booked rooms at the San Felice. He knew the owner, Pietro, from hanging out at his popular restaurant in Marina Piccola, and counted him as a friend.

Andrés and I were absolutely intent on seeing writer Curzio Malaparte's dramatic cliffside house, a meditative, modernist fantasy. At the time, the Casa Malaparte was in the hands of the Chinese government. We were repeatedly told that a visit was out of the question: *"Ma non è possibile..."* each and every Caprese answered with a fatalistic shrug. We tried anyway, trekking along the cliffside path to reach it. We explained to the young Chinese woman who met us at the entry gate that we were students of architecture from New York, that we'd come all this way just to see the house. She agreed to admit us for a quick tour. As we reached the roof, a ballet troupe was rehearsing under the bright sky, the sparkling Mediterranean laid out behind their synchronized figures.

One afternoon, we were driven to Anacapri, a village high on a hill, and toured the town's public garden. The gardener—a big, shaggy, rough-looking stud—cruised Andrés and I, and after some furtive signaling, led us both into a shed. I imagined his life in that small village on that small island as the shed filled with our mingled scents over the odor of peat. His only chance for sex was likely the occasional gay tourist, and now he had two. We matched his sexual heat in a frantic three-way while Greet wandered around the garden, no doubt wondering where we were.

As our stay on Capri came to an end, Greet announced: "Tomorrow morning, we take the ferry to Sorrento from Marina Piccola. A driver will meet us at the dock. I've rented a charming villa for the month, involved..." He'd sent Alvaro ahead to get the house ready. It was in the village of Massa Lubrense, an elegant, rustic country home: thick stone walls, hewed wooden beams, small but comfortable bedrooms, spotlessly clean. Poking around, we discovered a photo of the owners, a German couple. "Yasss, he's fine, tall and fit..." Andrés drooled over the husband. His wife was petite, with a bright smile. The house had long vistas of the surrounding terrain, over the olive and lemon groves of the neighboring farm. The neighbors raised buffalo and made mozzarella. The village was really just an intersection with a farm supply depot, a grocer, a small tavern that sold newspapers, cigarettes, and lottery tickets, and an open field.

We settled into the house. Greet had the master bedroom, Andrés and I slept on twin beds in the children's room, and Alvaro had the housekeeper's small bedroom, adjacent to the kitchen. Alvaro kept busy with laundry and coordinating with the caretakers, speaking Spanish to them, nodding at their replies in Italian, with Andrés jumping in to translate as needed. Surprisingly, Greet did not put any sexual demands on us during our stay at the villa. He seemed completely enraptured by the ambiance of the Italian countryside. His focus had retuned to me, as he fixated on my reconnection with my heritage, my acquisition of the language, my interactions with the locals. He came to treat Andrés almost like he did Alvaro—hired help, something between our translator and my private tutor. (In truth, we were all hired help.)

Over an amazing breakfast on the terrace in the early morning light—blood oranges juiced by the caretaker's son, home-baked bread, fresh cheese, and lemon curd—Greet outlined the first of our excursions: "Caserta has the most magnificent English Garden anywhere in the world, involved..." The baroque Reggia di Caserta was built in the eighteenth century for the Bourbon King of Naples. The travel agent had booked other day-long excursions to nearby landmarks. Though I was thrilled to be seeing these sites, I felt increasingly boxed in by how determined everything was; Greet often defaulted to astrology to explain his need to have every detail locked down: "I'm a Capricorn, we are planners..." My vision of overseas travel was unplanned vagabonding.

We were driven in a vintage Mercedes to the palace. Sunlight reflected off the pale yellow *madragone* stone, saturating the atmosphere with vivid warmth. If seeing Amalfi was my main goal on this trip, touring Caserta's English Garden, a high Romantic fantasy, was Greet's. Situated above the palace, beyond a series of formal terraces and fountains, it was a naturalistic sequence of grottoes, groves, and architectural follies, such as a ruined nymphaeum on a lake, and a tea house. It was stocked with exotic botanical specimens and redolent with lilies. I strolled these grounds with the air of a native son returned from exile—I was starting to buy into Greet's romantic fantasies. He snapped my photo in the garden, with Vesuvius hovering in the background.

We toured the ruins of Pompei on one excursion, and the village of Ravello, situated high above the Amalfi Coast, on another. "This view inspired Wagner, involved…" Greet rhapsodized as we looked over the sea from the gardens of Villa Rufolo. I must have had a puzzled looked on my face, because Andrés turned to me and said, "German opera… heavy on the drama." The thrall Greet was in as he guided us through Ravello and other picturesque villages like Positano (which he insisted on calling "Posi-tanto," a camp play on words suggesting that the town was "so much," *tanto* in Italian) revealed something about his sensibility. His love of Italy was embedded in Romanticism; fellow Englishmen Keats and Shelley both wrote and died on Italian soil, having articulated an aesthetic of nature, beauty, and ruin. Greet's interest in all things Italian stemmed from this aesthetic. It was a philosophy and a design sensibility, but it also had an erotic dimension. One afternoon when we were poolside at the Quisisana, he took an interest in a brooding, suntanned Italian teen boy with black curls, wearing a loose speedo. He turned to me and said, "He could be your cousin…"

We planned a day in Amalfi, a town with a sheltered port that spread upwards into a deep ravine. It had a storied past as the seat of the Duchy of Amalfi, its source of wealth maritime trade, particularly with North Africa. The people walking the cobbled streets reminded me of Grandma Helen and her brothers—their large, dark eyes, their thick hands, the gestures they made with them. I knocked on the doors of the addresses my grandmother had typed, but none of the people who answered knew anything concrete about my relatives. The Amalfi Drive as it enters town is called Via Matteo Camera, named for a nineteenth century historian, likely an ancestor—Helen's family name was Camera. I felt an ineffable remoteness from my kinship as a drop-in tourist with an overdressed Englishman in tow, hastily tracking down lost connections.

Making our way through the towns of the Amalfi Coast—Andrés and I typically walking a few steps behind Greet—I began to see him as a nineteenth-century figure. The whole of the Sorrentine Peninsula had a touristic infrastructure that targeted elite British travelers. He was retreading the path of the Grand Tour, a rite of passage for the British aristocrat since the seventeenth century. Seeing him in this context, Greet came to fascinate me clinically, as any living anachronism would. I often felt like I was along as his stand-in for the archetypal Italian youth. Every chance he'd get, he'd photograph me in gardens, framing me as his unspoiled discovery, the handsome villager he might have encountered by providence.

Aside from the hand-colored lithographs of the Arch of Constantine and the Pantheon adorning his bedroom walls, Greet had a stash of Von Gloeden's photographs of naked, brown, endowed Sicilian boys in staged historical settings locked up in an onyx box. This hidden stash of vintage porn signaled the erotic dimension to Greet's Italophile dreams, his Romantic longing for sublime, masculine, working-class beauty. Von Gloeden, the notorious gay German photographer who was active in Taormina in the early part of the twentieth century, enlisted local boys and young men as models. Their bodies, marked by their poverty and labor (irregular tans, leanness, rough hands) were somewhat incongruous in the photographer's classicist settings. In his more explicit photos— the ones Greet favored— these models display their oversize genitals, also incongruous in these settings. My own well-fed, pampered body was mostly unlike theirs— other than my cock. Greet was so enthralled by its size and power, going into a trance whenever I took it out. I suspect I fulfilled his fantasy of a cleaned-up Von Gloeden model, nature to his ruin, statue in his garden.

Then the Luna Park arrived. It was one of those popular traveling amusement parks with canned music, a Ferris wheel, spinning rides, test your strength, shoot a target and win a prize, zeppoli, a carnival tent with a bearded lady, and a cheap fireworks display every weekend. It set up in an open field in full view from the house and the terrace. It attracted teenagers from all over the valley who would yell and party all night. Greet's vision of a serene summer in an Italian countryside retreat was fully shattered. It became obvious why the owners had rented their idyllic home for the month of August. Greet fumed, his British animosity revived: "God-damned Krauts cannot be trusted…" The arrival of the Luna Park had turned quiet pastoral nights into an inescapable nightmare. He called the rental agency. For a brief moment, it seemed like he'd give in and accept the noise as part of the reality of summers in Southern Italy, but when the rental agency told him there was nothing they could do, he spiraled. Alvaro had managed to keep his drinking measured, but it quickly escalated, and he became increasingly belligerent.

Andrés grew restless, recoiling from Greet's sour mood. "Child, this is no fun, *andiamo via…*" He hadn't witnessed Greet's obstinance the way I had. Faced with the prospect of vagabond travel, I now worried about leaving the villa with no other place to stay and not much cash between us; luckily I'd held on to that fifty from Grandma Helen. Andrés was persuasive; we bailed on Greet and headed for Sorrento. He went into a bar and asked around for jobs, exaggerating my facility for the language. Amazingly, he found us positions as waiter/caretakers at a beachfront restaurant called "La Calcara," so named because the kitchen was inside a furnace once used for making cement. We were the hired hands and night watchmen, working in the simple restaurant that catered to boatloads of Italian vacationers who would drop anchor in the sheltered bay, la Cala di Mitigliano. It was run by a young couple with small children; she was Italian, a working Marquesa, and he was from the Canary Islands. It was inaccessible by land, except by hiking down through steep terraces planted with olive groves. Our new place was steps from the sea, and alongside a small grotto full of sea urchins.

On my first day at work, a customer waded to shore from his boat and yelled to me: *"Come salire?"* It took me a couple of repetitions to understand what he was asking; I finally signaled him towards the stone staircase. From then on, I picked up Italian quickly, immersed and working in a fully Italian-speaking context. We'd start the morning with a dip in the sea, mindful of the sea urchins in and around the grotto, then do prep work on the ingredients the owners brought by boat every morning. When guests showed up we'd work the ten or so tables for lunch and dinner. We'd clean up and close up and the bay was ours until morning. We slept on hammocks slung across the space inside the calcara, which by day served as the kitchen. It was rough but exquisite, and we'd escaped Greet.

Until one afternoon when he arrived in the bay on a hired boat. We had no idea how he'd found us. He waded ashore with the help of the boat's captain and sat down at a table for lunch. Andrés made himself scarce, busying himself with work in the kitchen. "I recommend the paella, it's the Spanish husband's specialty," I said, taking his order, hoping the situation would not turn dramatic. He'd sent Alvaro home, shut down the villa, and moved into the Excelsior Vittoria Hotel in Sorrento. "Please come back with me," he begged as I ran between tables, but I was indifferent. His hired boat took him away after lunch, and Andrés and I finished out our day, and the rest of our summer.

Back when I was a high school senior—on one of our trips into the city—Joy had brought me around to Scientology's Celebrity Center on the Upper East Side. They administered what they called a personality test, told me that the results indicated that I had "a hyper-critical mind," and recommended some courses to help with that. I scoffed at their offer, thinking: *That's all you can find wrong? You can't help me.* (Maybe that was hyper-critical of me.)

My early interaction with the Scientologists had stuck with me. From my defiance of their persuasion tactics, and my assertion of will at the tailor's, I knew that I had agency, but with Greet, it often felt like I'd miss the moment. That afternoon in la Cala di Mitigliano, when I told the old man that I was going wait tables for the rest of the summer, I finally felt like I'd taken back my power.

Or maybe my pimp was just working us both over. *È possibile…*

3. Garden Poses

Hung over from yet another bout of drinking and sexual labor, I rifled through the nightstand drawer looking for aspirin. One of those gray leather portfolios from the Concorde was hidden under some silk handkerchiefs. It was stuffed with photos Greet had taken on our travels. He'd drag me around, looking for just the right spot; by the time he'd find it I could barely manage a smile. There I was in the English Garden at Caserta, implacable as Vesuvius; in Kew Gardens, pouting among the bluebells; at Giverny, a snarling flower surrounded by bright ones; a sullen brat at the feet of Hercules, ensnared in baroque distortions. Looking over this hidden stash I was overcome with queasiness. It revealed the magnitude of his romantic obsession. I felt trapped in object status. All this time suppressing my will to sink into a role was laid out before me in wobbly snapshots.

Andrés and I flew back to New York after our extended stay in Southern Italy. We'd worked a while longer at La Calcara, then left the Cala in a borrowed rowboat. Our time drifting around the Amalfi Coast and Naples was a dreamlike suspension after Greet's over-determined itineraries. I felt untethered to time, place, English. Andrés and I had reached a certain equilibrium, our relationship re-cast as two thieves on stolen time. It came to an end when all that was left of our money was enough to buy cheap tickets for a return flight. Back in New York barely in time for the fall semester, I called Greet to let him know that we'd made it home. He expressed deep hurt over our abandonment, but invited me to lunch anyway, to my amazement.

Soon after, we resumed our routines as if nothing had happened, days of shopping and nights of dining and drinking—except that Andrés was entirely cut out of the picture. Greet unilaterally blamed him for ruining his summer, as if the Germans or the Luna Park had nothing to do with it. This fit his pattern of comparing Andrés unfavorably to me: he was a "Rounds boy," I was a "student of design." He was "flamboyant," I was "presentable." In Italy, he was the troublemaker, and I'd unfortunately fallen under his influence, according to Greet's narrative. I was back on a cash stipend, now up to ten bills; I let him have his narrative.

Even I found Andrés' attention-seeking exasperating at times, but he did animate the dinner conversation. His artistic self-absorption provided him with endless material for small talk. On my side of the table, an unspoken list of banned topics seemed to form: Andrés, the trip to Italy, school. The decorator and I would sometimes fall silent, making for an awkward stalemate between rounds of drinks or courses of a meal. At first, I felt that it was my job to keep the conversation flowing, and would scramble for topics; but after a time, I stopped rushing to fill the silences and would just sit composedly in them, cat-like.

After completing another year at Cooper Union I requested a semester off. The School of Architecture did not typically grant time off but my claim that I was advancing my education under the tutelage of a "noted interior designer" was convincing. I honestly couldn't deal with being torn apart for another year. Greet was making less and less effort to work around my class schedule and assignments. He'd call to insist I join him for dinner the same evening, luring me with reservations at the latest chic restaurant or the prospect of meeting important clients. He also expressed an eagerness to take me (alone) to Europe; he mentioned a buying trip to London and a long weekend in Paris.

He introduced me to his travel agent, John at Continental-American, whose office was next door to Gino. John had booked the disastrous Italian villa and now sought to return to Greet's favor. This was in the era when people really relied on their travel agents, when airline tickets were only printed (if you lost them, you were out of luck) and planes had smoking sections. I hurried back across town to give Andrés the news. He was endlessly staging and re-staging our apartment. Some days it would be a clutter of artifacts and street finds; that afternoon, I came home to find it stripped bare, the furnishings of our domestic life stashed out of sight. *Even my home is in his hands.* I sighed in resignation and handed him the itinerary.

"He's planning a quick getaway for the two of us. He wants to show me *his* London."

Andrés had been an airplane buff since childhood. He could pick aircraft models out of the sky and identify airlines by their liveries.

"Yasss, child…British Airways, flight 4…"

"Yea, and I got these new threads…" I added, sweeping my hand over a custom jacket.

His expression turned pained.

"You're taking the Concorde?"

"Yea, it's a quick trip, and…"

"I've always wanted to fly the Concorde. Since I was a kid! I had the model…"

After Italy, Andrés had simmered over being demoted, but he turned irrational over this latest slight.

"I mean, it's not that big a deal, there are flights every day…"

"You see? You won't even appreciate it…"

It was the angriest I'd ever seen him. He retreated into a corner, and I could see that his wheels were spinning.

"Ask him if I can come."

"Uhhh, okay, let me see what he says…" I already knew that I wouldn't be asking the decorator to buy him a ticket, but needed to placate him.

"Or maybe I can ask Joseph…"

I didn't realize that he was still in touch with his ex. Although I'd only briefly met him that one time, and under strained circumstances, Joseph had become a kind of marker for me. I remember him glaring at me from the threshold. At the time, I just thought he was a hostile person, but now I was convinced that he was trying to warn me. Finding myself entangled in Andrés' scheming, I wished I'd caught the warning.

Back at the workroom one morning, Greg offered me a warning of another sort: "This afternoon, you're going to visit the new client," he said. "It's sunny, so Mr. Greet will want to walk."

"Sounds great."

"Do yourself a favor–stay on this side of Madison Avenue when you pass Ralph Lauren," he said, gesturing left. "Or else you'll never hear the end of it."

"The end of what?"

"You know his new shop on the corner of Seventy-Second? Well, Ralph Lauren—Ralph Lifshitz, from the Bronx—was one of Mr. Greet's first clients, back when he was an aspiring tie designer."

"Oh, cool…" Greg was referring to the designer's recently opened flagship, inside an impressive French Renaissance Revival mansion.

"Well…he went on to build his whole fashion empire. Mr. Greet feels that it's based a little too closely on his personal style…"

"I mean, I do see the influence…"

"And now he's getting into home furnishings? It's a bridge too far…"

"Thanks for the heads-up. Anyway, the west side will be shadier…"

The new client had combined two apartments on a high floor of their Park Avenue building. Their Seventies era decor—Greet called it "Jewish Modernism"—featured earth tones, leather sectionals, and formica built-ins. All of that would be ripped out and thrown out, and in their place, they'd get a paneled library, an overstuffed living room suite, and crown moldings. Their art works and decorative items—the Chagall prints, the abstract metal wall hangings, the cubist-influenced paintings depicting life on the kibbutz—were sold or moved to the country house, to be replaced by Impressionist paintings and decorative antiques.

I found the image of the client's decor thrown to the curb a bit sad. It was as if every authentic affinity in their lives was to be severed and replaced with a suite of pretensions. Greet would stamp his style on his clients' spaces even when the spaces were not especially suited to it, like this apartment. The building dated from 1958—it was not a coveted Prewar—and the apartment had lowish ceilings. I worried that the big crown moldings he favored would look out of place.

Beyond the decor upgrade, Greet also provided his clients with social access. "I'm a Sherpa for the strivers," he once said of his services guiding them through the signifiers of taste and class. He could get them favored status with the maitre d' at the right restaurant. He advised them on where to vacation; he could propose them for membership to Mark's and Annabel's, his clubs in London, and refer the men to his bespoke tailor at Turnbull & Asser. I'd seen how he'd provided this side service in the field and watched his clients move up the chain. I compared it to my own family's assimilationist strides from immigrants to suburban homeowners. They'd firmly moved into the middle class; he gave his new-money clients a step-up into old-money appearances.

"Mom, guess what? I'm going to London next week."

"My world traveler! Don't you have school?"

"I'm taking this semester off, so I can work. It's a work trip. My employer, Mr. Greet, is taking me as his assistant. We're going to shop for antiques…"

I didn't mention the Concorde; it had already been a source of trouble with Andrés, and I worried that the extravagance of it would raise questions.

"Oh, is that how he makes his money?"

"Part of it…He's got a really good eye, and he gets a big mark-up. He's also going to see some old friends while we're there."

"That's wonderful, honey. Just take care of yourself…"

"I will, ma…"

As had become our habit, I gave her the date and the flight number, and hoped she wouldn't look it up.

In the days leading up to the London trip, we stopped by the travel agent for our updated itineraries. John let us know that Andrés had called him and asked him to book another seat on our Concorde flights, on Greet's account. I smirked a little over his nerve, but was also embarrassed for him. Greet was not amused, and it deepened the rift between them. Confused as I was by Andrés' irrational response, the London trip marked a turning point; I finally wasn't being led around by him.

In the car to JFK, Greet handed me the tickets. The travel agent had put them in a neat binder, and the cost for each was $2,999. Flush with the extravagance, I did math in my head: *that's about eight months of my rent*. Once on board, the other passengers seemed completely indifferent to the technological marvel. I tried to play it cool, too, but the moment fueled my unspoken fantasies of being desired at supersonic heights. The lavish meal, served on sleek china, was as good as any of the restaurant meals I'd eaten lately. I stroked the sleek gray leather portfolio, a courtesy gift. The woman in front of me left hers behind, so I quickly snatched it as we disembarked. We landed at Heathrow in just over three hours.

Upon our arrival at Claridge's Hotel, the rambling Art Deco palace in Mayfair, I was informed that our reservations for adjoining rooms had been lost and all that was available was a single suite. I immediately suspected that this was Greet's plot; he had the head of a big travel agency booking every detail. "You know, it's commonplace in Europe to share a bed, no one thinks anything of it, involved…" he said, justifying. I remembered how he'd insisted on the tailor making me a set of striped pajamas, even though I'd told him I'd never wear them. He'd packed them anyway. I refused to put them on, and instead paraded around the suite in my white briefs, weaponizing my body. Despite his romantic fixation, Greet could barely handle my body's hairiness. It seemed to strike him with clinical horror.

In the morning, we walked along Jermyn Street to Turnbull &

Asser, Greet's London tailor. In the mahogany-paneled shop, I noted the Royal Warrant hanging on a wall with stacks of cotton shirting—in my mind further evidence of Greet's nobility. His style came out in his love of striped and checked shirts, patterned ties, silk handkerchiefs, and brightly colored garters. "We're not matching, we're blending, darling," was a phrase he often applied to the curated mix of patterns and colors, both in his attire and his decor. This was way he publicly expressed *his* flamboyance—within the bounds of traditional haberdashery. Patterned shirts were made up with white cuffs and collars for a more formal look, and the cuffs were French, so he could show off his collection of bejeweled cufflinks. His tailor updated his growing waistline measurement. As the decorator ran through the options, he ordered dozens of items by eye within minutes.

  We walked around the corner to Mark's Club, which admitted members only and their guests for lunch. "I've kept up my membership all these years, may as well go…" It was a rush to enter that heavy blue door, feeling like an interloper crashing the gates of British exclusivity. After lunch, we toured nearby sights: Buckingham Palace, with a royalist's reverence, and St. James's Park to visit the duck pond. For our entire stay in London, we had bright, sunny days, which Greet considered something of a miracle for October, and attributed to my presence. We did not shop for antiques or see any of his friends, which I found odd. He mumbled something about them being out of town, and "perhaps on the next visit." I assumed he'd had second thoughts about presenting me to his London circle. I'd heard him joking over the phone with his old friend Milo about "kept boys," but couldn't tell if he was applying that term to me. *No matter how dressed up, is it that obvious?*

  Our return flight left Heathrow shortly after 10 AM and arrived at Kennedy Airport before 10 AM local time. We'd crossed the ocean faster than the sun. Back home, I gave Andrés a peace offering: one of the grey leather portfolios full of stationery. He was still fuming; he'd even sent Greet a spiteful, hand-written letter: "Your funeral will be very ugly because you will not be able to control the guest list." (This nasty prediction did not quite come true, but would come to reverberate over the actual circumstances of Greet's demise.) Andrés' irrational response towards our flying the Concorde still baffled me, but thankfully he didn't direct his anger my way; soon he was telling me about some new sugar daddy prospect he'd met at Rounds.

Greet and I settled back into our routine: days of showroom visits, evenings of rich meals, hazy nights at crossed purposes. One night, we gathered at the townhouse to have drinks with Greg. The decorator was upstairs getting dressed, leaving Greg and I alone in the living room, and Greg was in a chatty mood. He reminisced about headier times, when Greet had a shop on Madison Avenue and they had several projects going at once.

"This was before your time…the shop was busy, he sold to a lot of good customers, and design jobs just walked in the door…John Lennon and Yoko Ono would come into the shop to pick out antiques for their apartment at the Dakota."

"No way…"

"Oh yea, John Lennon and Mr. Greet had a real bond. They *really* got each other…" They seemed such unlikely friends. I would later understand something deeper about their bond.

"That's so cool…" This talk of the decorator's heyday got me feeling like I'd missed out.

"Mr. Greet rarely ventured across town in those days," said Greg.

"In those days? I don't think we've ever been to the West Side. Well, that changes tonight. We have a reservation at Café des Artistes…"

"Lucky you, that's a gorgeous room…well, Mr. Greet did cross town for John Lennon, but he usually sent the Hungarian to the Dakota, when it came to measuring, or overseeing deliveries…"

"Who? The Hungarian?"

Greg put down his drink and leaned in.

"Oh Jesus, whatever you do, don't bring up the Hungarian. It's a *very* sore subject…"

Another banned topic. We heard him coming down the stairs.

"I'll tell you later…"

Greet entered the room, and eyed us suspiciously.

"What are you two gossiping about, like old hens?"

On the drive to the restaurant, we headed down Central Park West, right past the Dakota. Greg's words came back to me: *"John Lennon and Mr. Greet had a real bond…"* I pictured him clapping Lennon's shoulder, the way he did with friends. I was a high school junior in 1980. The whole tragedy had been abstract and confusing to me: *What does Jodie Foster have to do with it?* Greet caught sight of the manned security booth casting its light on the building's front facade. It had been installed after the shooting. He shuddered, recoiling from the window. I couldn't think of what to say, so I just held his hand.

Alvaro pulled up to the restaurant, in the base of a Neo-gothic building designed for artist's residences. The owner, George Lang, welcomed us both like old friends. The room was decorated with murals by the artist Howard Chandler Christy, of the 'Gibson Girl' illustrations fame. They depicted scenes such as nymphs frolicking in a waterfall. The space was replete with images of playful, naked bodies, including a buff Tarzan on the wall behind us. The murals seemed to signal to Greet to forget his troubles; he clicked back into his jovial gentleman act.

"He's why I request this table," he said, leering at Tarzan.

Greet whispered reverently that Mr. Lang was an artist himself, a Hungarian Jew who had narrowly escaped death during World War II. I almost blurted out something about this being the second time a Hungarian had been brought up tonight, but held my tongue, remembering Greg's warning. The menu was classic bistro. We started our meal with oysters, followed by scallops sautéed with shallots and walnuts. The combined effects of the room, the lavish meal, and the champagne Mr. Lang had sent over seemed to have stirred Greet's romantic leanings: "You look very dashing in your new suit…"

All this tacking between pathos and romance inspired me to get drunk. Holding my head steady enough to look upon him I thought about how he'd fit into the London scene, and how out of place he appeared to me on the streets of New York. In this space devoted to fantasy, surrounded by the same nonplussed, rich crowd that flew the Concorde, something deeper and more complicated emerged than the romantic foolishness he was laying on me. He wouldn't put words to it, but he couldn't cover up his emotions. He lost his train of thought repeatedly, and trembled more than usual.

It was as if his turmoil had dislodged the mask he wore around me and in restaurants. From across the table, I sensed the contours of what he'd lost when Lennon was murdered: a connection, a precious thread to his authentic self. The evening's emotional undertow was too much for me to handle. As our dinner came to an end, I said, "I think I'll just walk home, it's just up the street and it's such a nice night…" but he pleaded with me go back across town for a nightcap. I relented.

On the drive back, we rolled down the windows to let in the crisp fall air, and take in moonlit glimpses of Central Park's naturalistic splendors. Greet was enraptured. Led to his bed, the resistance I'd held up for so long crumbled; he opened my pants and fondled my package. Drunk though I was, I had no trouble getting an erection. He marveled at its glory through his own drunken haze. He could no longer resist his urges, and overcame his germ phobia enough to take me in his mouth—not before swishing around some vodka. His body gave off the acidic staleness of heavy drinkers. I managed another spectacular show, which he cheered on: "Fly, boy, fly!"

Lying in that big bed, my head a drunken swirl, pants down, shirt and tie pushed up, I felt like I'd been led to this moment by an invisible leash. The way I'd been set up at the adult table as a precocious boy, the way Joy had brought me around as her pet to bait her friends, how Andrés had dressed me up, pulled me out onto the dance floor and into his hustle. On board a supersonic, there's no place else to be except your assigned seat and there's no exit. In his bathroom, I stared at the disheveled heap in the mirror, dabbing at a cum stain on my tie.

As a reward for my new degree of willingness, Greet proposed our next getaway, announcing with grandiose pomp: "One *must* visit the great palaces and gardens of the Ile-de-France before one dies, involved." I was quick to say yes but wary of his motives. Despite the way he presented it as an "inspiration trip," I suspected he was romanticizing it as taking his lover to Paris. In retrospect, I'd been too dense to see it as an obviously romantic gesture.

Upon landing at Charles De Gaulle, I was awestruck by the main terminal's expressive modernism. After making our way through its rotunda via one of the criss-crossing conveyer tubes, a limo picked us up and we were whisked to the Ritz. The hotel, on the Place Vendôme, had recently been acquired by Egyptian businessman Mohamed Al-Fayed (father of Dodi), and meticulously renovated. That this high-profile French luxury asset had been swooped up by a Middle Eastern billionaire with some dubious associations had me feeling swept up in a full fantasy of international intrigue.

Greet had planned a full day at the Louvre and two day trips outside of Paris: Vaux-le-Vicomte, a Baroque chateau with elaborate grounds, and Claude Monet's house and garden in Giverny. Every detail for these two trips—schedule, limo driver, tickets, lunch stop—had been attended to by the travel agent. Of course I wanted to see the Louvre, but what really excited me about Paris were its modern landmarks: train stations, the Centre Pompidou, Renzo Piano's massive 'inside-out' museum structure with exposed mechanical systems, the collection at the Musée Picasso. No train travel was planned, and the decorator had pronounced the Centre Pompidou "a monstrosity...who wants to look at plumbing?" I had little interest in being driven out of town to visit some dusty old castle.

Greet pulled the same stunt that he had in London: "What do you mean, our suite? My travel agent booked us two adjoining rooms, involved..." The hand-typed itinerary noted adjoining rooms, but I was now convinced that John at the travel agency was in on this gaslighting, too. I could tell the young woman at reception was gamely playing along as she apologized for the confusion. I was ready this time and caught Greet out by asking her about our options. He was startled to realize that I was actually conversant in French; I was smugly satisfied to have gained the upper hand. The young woman confirmed that adjoining rooms were available, but I relented anyway. It was enough for me to signal that I was on to his deception.

I plotted to get my revenge by shopping. I wanted a fancy pair of cufflinks to rival Greet's collection for all of my new shirts with French cuffs. I also needed a good watch. I never liked the idea of wearing one, but it was a token of status necessary to fit into his society. The men in his circle noticed your shoes and if you had a good watch peeking out from under your cuff. There was something a little homoerotic about the way they checked each other out, sizing each other up. The cufflinks I wanted were pure flash, but I considered a watch a must.

Our suite was classic French luxury; the living room was furnished with a chandelier, a sitting area, and an upholstered chaise by the window. This cocoon of comfort did not quell Greet's anxiety. I couldn't tell what he was anxious about, and it set me off at times. I swung erratically between fulfilling the role of docile companion and soaking in the luxury experience to wanting to run out of the fucking place and get into trouble in the "real" Paris. I felt penned in at how planned this trip was, too. We ricocheted between hungover hostile bickering and performed civility. After the first night, I would leave him alone in the bed and sleep on that upholstered chaise. This trip had triggered the rebellious brat in me.

Following breakfast in the suite, a limo arrived to take us to Maincy, about an hour to the southeast. The chateau Vaux-le-Vicomte, built by Louis XIV's Superintendent of Finances, was designed by the architects of Versailles. This was no dusty old castle, rather an elaborate working Baroque conceit of spatial effects, device-like in its precision. The garden behind the chateau was designed to disrupt the cartesian notion of coordinate space. From the rear garden facade, a statue of Hercules appeared just within reach. We trekked to find it was almost three kilometers away, its enormous size part of the visual trick. The terraced sequence of flowerbeds, lawns, and fountains we passed on our trek enhanced the effect. "It's an optical illusion known as *anamorphosis abscondita*, or forced perspective...from a certain designed viewpoint, the eye perceives elements to be closer than they actually are," I recited from the guidebook, as Greet collapsed on a bench: "I need a drink..." I identified with the silent figure, an object fixed in a singular gaze. "I know a thing or two about forced perspectives," I said as an aside to Hercules, as the decorator snapped a photo of me at the base of the giant, pouting.

Back in Paris that afternoon, we had an unplanned hour or so before our reservation at La Tour D'Argent—one of the Left Bank's oldest upscale restaurants—so I seized the moment and dragged Greet out shopping. Cruising along the chic Rue du Faubourg Saint-Honoré, we came upon the vitrines of the Baccarat shop, showing a set of cufflinks, little blown crystal domes studded with nubs, all in blue. They were expensive and out of the ordinary, the design suggesting a natural form, like a seedpod. We found a Swiss watch maker, Hebdomas, not too far away, and I picked out a Baladin style with a silver case, a crystal caseback, and a black crocodile strap. I opted for the black watch face, for drama, since I'd mostly be wearing it at night. With its black watch face and wandering hours display, it exuded a certain occult luxury. It was wild to waltz into these boutiques and pick something out guided by my taste and not once think of the price. Nor did he make any mention of it—he just paid. Though the links and the watch were my trophies, they were as much ornaments on my body for *his* pleasure. I flashed them at the restaurant that night.

We had clear skies the day of our trip to Giverny, I wore a plaid jacket that the New York tailor had made for me, at Greet's suggestion, "for country outings." The same brooding driver picked us up and drove us to the northeast, winding through the Seine Valley. We made it to the house where Claude Monet lived and painted for decades. He'd spent those years transforming his Clos-Normand, the traditional garden layout with fruit trees, into a tableau-vivant. The riotous growth and density of the flowers in this walled enclosure seemed to dissolve space into color, light, and motion. It was in this garden that I first understood the Impressionist project.

Greet dragged me up and down the narrow paths of the Clos-Normand looking for a just the right spot to photograph me. He must have been able to tell by my snarling that I was over it, so he reached out a finger towards me. This was how he referenced his favorite Kipling quote about walking with kings but never losing the common touch. I dropped the snarl and touched my index finger to his. He brushed the petals from my plaid jacket, and I managed a half-smile for the camera.

I retuned from the Paris trip triumphant with my gifts and treasures. Andrés had dropped his resentment over the Concorde, but amazingly was still scheming to get himself on board.

"Child, *très bien fait!* You're catching on," he said approvingly as I showed off my jewels.

"I just need to figure out where to stash the watch in case this place gets broken into again…"

Andrés found a spot for it above one of the ceiling joists, out of reach and out of sight.

"*Putain*, tonight we're going out, and you're buying drinks…"

Susanne Bartsch's parties, where freakdom and uninhibited fun ruled, had become my antidote for time spent uptown, where I had to conform to his vision and withhold my emotions. She ran a pioneering shop in SoHo that featured British avant-garde designers and had been throwing parties around New York. The latest venue was Bentley's, a midtown strip club which usually attracted a Black crowd. For the opening, she booked Lady Hennessey, one of Bentley's regular strippers, to entertain the club kids. She was known for her take on the standard magic trick of pulling an endless series of multi-colored handkerchiefs out of a hat, a bag, or the magician's mouth. Lady Hennessy performed the trick out of her pussy. She rounded out the assortment of lip-syncing drag queens, go-go dancers, and burlesque performers Bartsch had assembled as entertainment.

Lady Hennessy took the stage wearing a raincoat, a sea captain's hat, and a studded bikini, set the coat on the stage, and performed a series of erotic contortions. She then rose, opened her bikini top, and cupped her ample breasts. After soaking in applause on their behalf, she squeezed and twisted them, spraying milk out onto the gasping crowd. Those of us up front were drenched in her abundant streams. There was a stampede of partygoers ducking for cover in mock horror. Lady Hennessey once reported that she'd lactated for years after giving birth and just made it a part of her act. Her performance, a masculine display of spurting and projection from her motherly bosom, dazzled us. We danced on as her milk soaked through our outfits.

I went to Bartsch's next party without Andrés; I hadn't seen him all day. In the early morning, I stumbled up the stairs in my disheveled outfit. Andrés had gotten me into pricey Euro fashions for clubbing; that night, it was Dries Von Notten striped drawstring pants, a Byblos printed tank, gold chains, and a porkpie hat from Pat Field. I found him on the landing, struggling to unlock the door.

"Where have you been? You missed such a great party…"

"Yasss child, fabulous. You're getting into it. I just got back from Saint Luke's."

"Are you okay?"

"I was visiting Joseph…"

"What happened to him?"

"He'll be fine. Tell me about the party…"

I started running down all the antics, but he seemed to zone out.

"I really want to go out to dinner with you two. I need a nice meal…"

"I don't know…I think he's still pretty upset about the letter."

"Child, just ask. She probably forgot about it already…"

I promised that I would work on a reunion dinner and we went to bed.

I was awakened near dawn by some commotion; it was Andrés running through the railroad flat to the bathroom. I noticed that his sheets were soaking wet. I peeled out of bed and waited by the doorway. He flushed the toilet repeatedly, maybe to cover up the sounds his body was making. He emerged pale and worn. I looked over at him anxiously.

"Are you okay?"

Silence. He wobbled towards me slowly, squared himself, and looked straight back at me:

"Joseph is dying, and I have AIDS…"

I was dumbstruck. As my mind scrambled to make sense of what he'd just said, my core sunk. Panic thumped in my chest. This was my first in-person encounter with the disease. I'd heard about it, but up until this moment, it hadn't seemed relevant to me, only to older people. New York would soon after be one of two epicenters in the United States, but Andrés' stark pronouncement came well before the AIDS story would break open nationwide. We didn't have a television, and the newspaper coverage had been slight and circumspect.

"That fever I was running the day I moved in? That must have been the onset." He wrapped himself in a blanket. "My diagnosis—let me remember what she said—'rapid deterioration within a few months.'"

I felt the wind knocked out of me. My senses clouded, the dawn stalled, and I heard Andrés' next words rebound as if in a tunnel: "You need to get tested."

4. SUNKEN CARGO

In June 1990, the cargo of the wreck Vung Tau, which was approximately 15 kilometers away from the Hon Cau Island, at the depth of 40 meters and buried in the sand...was recovered. The wreck measured 32.71 meters long and approximately 9 meters wide. It was found to be the hull of a lorcha, a ship of combined Eastern and Western influence, and the first ever found.

The wreck has been dated to 1690. From an analysis of the cargo it seems that the ship was bound from China to Batavia (Jakarta) where the bulk of the ceramics would have been transshipped to a Dutch East India Company vessel for the onward voyage to Holland. The recovered cargo consisted of over 48,000 ceramics, mostly Kangxi blue-and-white porcelain from the kilns of Jingdezhen, and an impressive collection of white-ware...

The wreck was commercially emptied. Christie's, the British auction house, selected 28,000 pieces of porcelain for auction in Amsterdam in 1992. The Vũng Tàu Museum in Vietnam houses a representative sample of the artifacts. The remainder of the ceramics were divided between the recoverer Hallstrom and the Vietnamese government.

-UNESCO Silk Roads Programme

Greet entered the living room in an unusually subdued mood.

"Alvaro has disappeared…."

"What?"

"John says he doesn't know anything…surely he must, involved."

"Did you call him?"

"Of course, he doesn't answer. Perhaps it has to do with his papers…"

Alvaro, like Juan, was from Colombia; I wasn't sure about their respective immigration statuses, but had drawn inferences from their guardedness. I thought I could detect a pleading sadness in Juan's eyes, behind that impassive countenance. It echoed the carved features and high cheekbones seen in pre-Colombian gold figures of the Quimbaya. Alvaro's sudden absence cast a pall over the household, such as it was: Greet and the young men he paid. Though I'd never seen him treat Alvaro with anything more than gruff imperiousness—he'd never even learned to pronounce his name correctly, putting an errant emphasis on the second syllable—he seemed truly shaken. I counted out the steps it would take for me to disappear. The Jaguar sat in the garage unused, and Greet expressed no interest in hiring a replacement. Instead, he sold the car, and we began to rely on yellow taxis.

Soon after Andrés' diagnosis, I went to the city clinic in Chelsea and had blood drawn for an AIDS test. An agonizing week later I was called in back for my result. The nurse sat me down in a small office.

"Your test came back negative."

I felt the wind knocked out of me again. To my ear, unfamiliar with medical parlance, *negative* sure sounded like bad news. As I started to swoon, she steadied me and explained: "That means your blood *doesn't* show the antibodies…we are *not* seeing indications of the virus."

It was another kind of closet to keep anyone from school, our circle of friends, or Andrés' family from finding out. I became his sole confidante as his illness unfolded, while he served as mine in my continued trials with Greet. He faced a battery of opportunistic infections: thrush, intestinal parasites, shingles. He had ongoing night sweats and dramatic, worrisome bouts of diarrhea. He showed me a purple-black spot on his leg. Bearing witness to Andrés' medical horrors in such close quarters, I swung between clinical fascination and unfocused rage. Despite that test result, it triggered a subconscious fear that I was watching a preview of my own fate.

Soon after receiving his diagnosis, Andrés somehow managed to get himself enrolled in an experimental drug trial testing AZT, which at the time was unproven and controversial. He'd always been good at working the system, whether it was maxing out student loans or zeroing in on the prime sugar daddies at Rounds. This was the first trial for the drug, and luckily he was not in the control group; before the trial was even over, they stopped giving the control group a placebo because they were dying so quickly. Although AZT was hard on his system—it brought on cramps, nerve pain, headaches—it likely saved him.

He graduated from that first trial to another—"Child, I'm in the pharmacology pipeline…"—and embraced the role of lab rat, picking up yet another language, the lexicon of drugs, symptoms, and pathogens: Antiretrovirals, Kaposi's Sarcoma, neuropathy, Pneumocystis Carinii… We obsessively tracked his t-cell count, investing our slim hopes in various inhibiting agents, that they would stop healthy cells from turning his body into a virus factory. Each test result was a transmission from the front line drawn somewhere through his tanned body.

My primary role was to maintain the routines of our flat, absorbing new habits into our compact household. We were careful about what was left around when our friends came over. We got a lockable medicine cabinet. Boxes of Pedialyte stocked the kitchen cabinets. Andrés took to cleaning the kitchen and bathroom with bleach: "I like to do it, it's my therapy. Call her Mrs. Clean.…" He had some fairly normal weeks, alternating with bouts of symptoms and weakness, but none of it slowed him from carrying on. He threw himself into his art. While dutifully keeping the silence, tidying, and supporting his care, I steadily withdrew any affection. I didn't fear the disease as much as I resented Andrés for bringing AIDS into my life. I was a cold nurse.

Back on the East Seventy-Second, with the garage empty, Greet made another swift decision: He'd sell the townhouse and much of the contents. He rented a duplex apartment a couple of blocks down on Seventieth Street off of Lexington. It had a shady back garden, and on the second floor, a bedroom facing it and a large living room, which would double as his work space. His new living quarters allowed him to replicate the life and working style he'd enjoyed in the townhouse, and he'd profited nicely from the sale. My weekly stipend went up to twelve bills; I barely missed the townhouse.

Once they completed a spruce-up of the Seventieth Street apartment—new crown moldings, papering, painting—Greet was thrilled with his new digs. On a stately, tree-lined block, it was quieter and more exclusive than East Seventy-Second Street. Many of the block's single-family townhouses, including examples of Georgian, Palladian, and Neoclassical styles, were highly coveted for having wide frontage and full gardens. "Sette Mezzo is just around the corner," he proclaimed with excitement, though we never really seemed to fit in with the restaurant's regulars, a clique of serious elites. The Asia Society was on the corner of Park. Living on a block with a museum of Asian art and objects burnished his self-image as an expert on Chinese porcelain.

As he settled in, his contractors moved right over to the Park Avenue job. The client, Mr. Rosen, a currency trader, was raking it in with high-volume trades, and had finally pulled the trigger. after prolonged wooing. One reason he'd agreed to this extensive renovation was to make his home a suitable backdrop for his art acquisitions, mostly works from US Impressionists. Greet was charged with giving their apartment the full treatment: crown moldings throughout, a paneled dining room, marble bathrooms. He obsessed over the stone to be used in the guest bathroom. It was an expensive quartzite quarried in Brazil, Azul Macuaba. We visited the stone yard in Brooklyn to inspect the slabs as they were uncrated, until he found just the right one with enough blue. The gold-plated fittings were from PE Guerin, the venerable decorative hardware manufacturer in the West Village. The company still lists 'Greet Deco,' a hardware style with a radial sunburst pattern, 'named for beloved decorator Stuart Greet,' in its inventory. He'd used the style extensively on several projects; for the Rosen's guest bath, he picked an ornate, classical fluted style. He transformed that little bathroom into a sparkling blue chamber.

The living room was furnished with custom upholstery and drapery from De Angelis, a workroom established by an Italian craftsman in the nineteen-fifties. I drew the designs for the fruitwood-paneled library, collaborating with a woodworker on the hand-carved motifs. It was a major project with a substantial budget. Despite my misgivings about the aesthetics, I enjoyed working on it more than past projects. Greet was actually drawing on my skills; it was the closest I'd gotten to my vision of professionalizing our relationship. It also gave him a focus other than me, and the income to maintain his lavish habits (including me).

After a long day overseeing the job site, we went to dinner at Elio's, an old-school, pricey Italian restaurant on Second Avenue with a high-profile clientele. As we opened the door—both of us dusty and a little disheveled—we ran right into those former clients Greg had warned me about, who were on their way out. Greet made a show of bonhomie, then fumed once they were gone. "The audacity....I taught him *everything* he knows…" he muttered under his breath, after introducing me to Ralph and Ricky Lauren. "They seem nice," I said in an effort to placate him. Through it seemed clear that he was projecting his frustrations upon his former client, I couldn't get him to drop it. His mood was spoiled for the evening; I vainly tried to change it by praising his design for the Rosens.

Despite everything else going on, I somehow managed to graduate from Cooper Union. My thesis was a design for a secular chapel at JFK Airport, to replace the tri-faith chapels which had been slated for imminent demolition. I drew inspiration for the form from the pattern of a men's jacket. In the context of the project, the jacket stood as an emblem of the traveler. For me, it was an article of clothing I'd been straining at for years in my role with Greet, and the project represented a metaphorical release from it. I'd been wearing jackets for years to signal both class status and masculinity, and was driven to deconstruct the jacket and its signals for my thesis. The project is preserved at Cooper Union's archival site; in one photo, I'm standing next to the model in a black-on-black pinstriped Comme des Garçons Homme Plus suit I'd made Greet buy for me, despite his reservations about its styling: "You look like a baby mobster…" Its inky black boxiness shielded me like no other suit.

We completed the Rosen residence late and wildly over estimate. Greet's practice was hardly budget-conscious or timely, but Mrs. Rosen, whose patience had been strained many times over, was thrilled with the end results: "It is *everything* we wanted…" All eyes were on me as I carefully hung their prize acquisition, a pastel landscape drawing by the French Impressionist Pissarro, in the paneled library, the final touch to our work. Greet had turned an unremarkable unit into a classically inspired suite of rooms, the crown moldings sized appropriately for the space, a credible imitation of a coveted prewar.

Andrés was surfing from one drug protocol to the next, just as the last one had stopped being effective. With every new treatment, his prognosis improved slightly. There were side effects: gastric distress, a constant metallic taste; sudden nosebleeds, bouts of exhaustion. One day, I came home to find him on the floor, holding his nose while laying out a tarp and a sheet of thick watercolor paper.

"What are you doing?"

He let go of his nose, the blood flowed, and he quickly brushed it into the absorptive fibers of the paper. I swooned at the sight. He looked up at me with a maniacal grin:

"Child, I'm painting with my AIDS blood…."

I'd watched Andrés face the opportunistic infections that would break through his immune system with a nonchalance I found astounding. In the world outside, ACT UP was protesting the government, corporations, and pharmaceutical companies for access to drugs and basic dignity, but ours was a secret battle within the confines of our railroad flat. He did not once whine; instead, he clinically observed his body crashing, narrating the hospital interventions that would bring him back from near-death. I once looked down upon his camp flamboyance, but now he impressed me with his steadfast bravery.

Nothing about the past mattered. When we'd first gotten our respective diagnoses, it was no longer possible for us to be lovers; "safe sex" hadn't been conceptualized. When we were in Italy, we'd bonded as co-conspirators; operating in a furnace of our own once again, we reverted. Our relationship to each other had changed as did our relationship to the disease. Our language shifted, marking progress; we didn't refer to his condition as "AIDS" or "ARC" (AIDS-related complex) any more. Now he was "HIV-positive," which he transformed into "Hivvy." It was part of our AIDS Polari which allowed us to talk freely about his condition, since outsiders didn't understand it. "She look Hivvy," he'd say of a passing stranger who showed some of the same symptoms he did. The drugs he took were collectively known as "mama's Hivvy potion." Our burdens had become strangely equalized: I had Greet and Andrés had HIV.

Once it was clear that his trajectory would not be "rapid deterioration within a few months," as the clinician had once announced, HIV became just another character in his camp tableau:

"Child....after casting you in Lady Greet's period piece, now you're the nurse in the latest medical drama, *The Hivvy Files*."

"Who needs TV?"

Greet and I resumed our routines of lunch meetings at Gino and dinners around town. The tone of his table banter had shifted; he was cattier than ever. Entering restaurants, he gave a butch presentation, striding in assertively, demanding particular tables, barking orders. It would switch off once we settled in. For someone who operated in these dual modes he could be really bitchy about other gay men. He brought up a not particularly effeminate friend of Greg's we'd recently met: "He opens his mouth and a purse drops out." I'd clocked that same purse dropping out of his mouth.

For a creature of habit, he did something truly unexpected for my twenty-fifth birthday. First we went to dinner at Le Cirque, of the *singeries*—a stodgy choice, but I was given special treatment. The unexpected turn came afterwards: he took me to Rounds, a circus of a whole other sort, the bar where Andrés had first picked him up.

Surprised as I was that he wanted to bring me there, since he'd always taken pains to distinguish me from the "Rounds boys," I was more surprised to find it pretty swanky, a Halston-inspired lounge in taupe and smoked mirrors. There was a grand piano and a seating area for ordering food. As we took a place at the bar, I caught on to the game: the older men occupying barstools were potential customers of the younger guys standing alongside the mirrored wall opposite. It was pretty revelatory to see the mechanics of my relationship with Greet laid out before me in a spatial construct.

He whispered in my ear: "Pick any of them you like…"

"Really?"

"You only turn twenty-five once, involved…"

I tended to look down on escorts, drawing a distinction between my experience and by-the-hour escorting: "I never had to hustle. I caught a sugar daddy…" This revisionist view erased Andrés' role in my career and trivialized the real risks around sex work. I never had to worry about breaking the law; Andrés, who had truly "caught" Greet, had to watch out for occasional sweeps by the police while working Rounds, even though there was generally less scrutiny on the bar scene than on the street scene. Despite this bias, I'd idolized from a distance the ladies who worked the strip on Seventh Avenue just below Central Park for their seemingly glamorous lives. One night, I came upon cops throwing one of them against a car and roughly handcuffing her behind her back; her good shoes and fur coat could not protect her.

If I had any qualms about bringing in a third—after all, that was how Andrés had lost Greet to me—in the moment, buzzed on wine and adulation, I was game. When a handsome, dark-haired guy with a guileless expression approached, my bias dissolved and I gave Greet the nod. "Luca" was from Hoboken, also of Italian background. We talked about our origins and our families while devouring each other with our eyes. There was definitely a kissing cousins vibe to our pairing and Greet seemed as excited for it as I was. He flirted with Luca, launching into stories of his Italian travels.

Luca pulled me aside and asked, "So what does he like to do?"

"Oh, no…he's just going to watch. Today's my birthday and you're my present…" Luca lit up with relief.

The three of us headed back to the apartment; Luca and I groped each other in the back of the taxi. Once in the bedroom, we locked on each other, kissing passionately. I returned Luca's every move, as if to cancel out the transaction that had brought us together. We stripped each other of our clothes. I inhaled his briny ripeness, detectable under his woodsy cologne. Luca caressed my chest, and I stroked the fuzzy patch at his navel. Greet hovered over the action, muttering, "My regattis..." his drunken, mangled pronunciation of *"i miei ragazzi"* (my boys), prompting eye-rolls. With the ever-present crystal tumbler clasped in his wobbly hand, he goaded us on; but as our lust enveloped the room, he left in a dramatic huff. I felt a tinge of conscience.

"I should go see what's the matter..."

Luca kissed me again. He grabbed hold of the canopy and lifted himself up, offering his firm little ass.

"Fuck it—it's my birthday," I said, burying myself in his soft parts. We laughed and edged each other on. Greet was out of the room and I had a sexual equal, and my lust was finally unlocked. We burned that sturdy English bed to the ground.

Greet had Luca's envelope waiting for him. We kissed for the last time and he hastily scribbled his phone number on my hand before grabbing the envelope and saying his goodbyes.

The following morning, Juan woke me for breakfast with a silent glare. Greet was waiting at the table, and before I could lift my cup of coffee, he poured out his feelings. "It was unbearable seeing you with that...*boy*," he said. "Knowing I'll never inspire that in you, involved..." In Greet's highly constrained world–the strict code of dress, the unbroken routines, the phobias, the investment in social standing–I was the sole receptacle for these longings. He didn't lust after Luca, although he was definitely his type. I could only think about how much worse it would have been had he stayed and watched us fuck. I was hung over and short on patience for his melodrama.

Tears welled in his bloodshot eyes. He groveled for my sympathy, but the sight of this large, imperious man begging brought out a cruelty I didn't know I possessed. I scoffed, and examined my hand. The ink was smudged; I wasn't sure I could read all the numbers. I remembered the nerve charge as Luca's pen stabbed at the pads of my palm. I leaned over the table and hissed: "You're not in love–you're just looking for a rough scene." I laughed off his lovesick lament as I pocketed my weekly stipend. "I'm taking some time off for my birthday," I announced as I threw back some coffee, leaving him to his misery.

Carrying on with my birthday celebrations, I went out with friends to the latest Susanne Bartsch party, which had moved to the old Copacabana on West Fifty-Seventh Street. The parties at that location were peak Bartsch—wild, costumed blowouts, drag queens, club kids, burlesque performers, and now, showgirls in feathers and sequins. Andrés was feeling well enough to go and we danced until we were dripping. As we embraced on the packed dance floor I tasted his sweat; it had a metallic bite from his medications. Dancing was a needed release, a glittering moment to forget about the third and fourth wheels in our household.

My night with Luca had stirred some buried longings in Greet, apparently. Shortly after that drama, we retuned to his apartment post dinner and drinks at the St. Regis, both pretty drunk.

"I got you some of the larger condoms, involved…"

"Okay?…"

"I'll be out shortly," he said, disappearing into the bathroom.

Alone on that giant bed, I stared at the little gold-foiled packages, in a crystal bowl on the nightstand, still confused. Greet emerged from the bathroom, removed his robe, and bent over the side of the bed. Message received. His inert penis was buried under a mass of flesh. His large ass mounds settled, their pale skin dimpling. The skin stretched across his back flushed in incoherent patches; his ashen legs were still imprinted by sock bands and garter clips. Drunk though I was, I managed to slip on a condom and enter him, standing. His ass offered alarmingly little resistance. I pushed into this cavernous void, pretending it gave me pleasure where there was none, only bringing an end to this duty by faking orgasm, pulsing and moaning, pulling out and tossing the condom before he could turn around. Whether or not my performance fooled him or he just played along I'll never know; but with this long-avoided act, detached though it felt between the condom and the lack of feeling, I'd finally given in to him. Thereafter this performance in emptiness would become a part of our routine.

When we first met, Greet told me that he hoped I'd develop romantic feelings for him over time. That never happened, but there were moments like this when beneath the repulsion, I found pleasure in seeing his large body brought to prostration by his desire. As I stood there, hard dick in hand, looking down on his normally imposing figure, now a passive heap, I was turned on by my erotic power over him, beyond the money and the rewards. Through my twenties, this dynamic became imprinted upon me and would play out for years in both transactional and personal relationships. I became inured against demonstrating *my* desire for others as I had that one exalted night with Luca.

Greet was in a chipper mood at breakfast, while I was feeling fairly doomed. "Christie's has a major trove of blue-and-white," he enthused. He was an expert on the subject of Chinese export porcelain, especially those glazed with a cobalt-based pigment on a white ground. He could get a sizable mark-up placing important pieces with his clients.

"The Vung Tau Cargo," I said, reading from the catalog, seeking to take my mind off the wall that had fallen the night before.

"I'll call John to arrange everything. We'll take British Airways…. This time, we're staying at the Pelham. Isobel recommended it, and I think you'll like South Kensington, involved…The auction is Thursday, and on Friday we've got a car. We're going out to Wiltshire to see an old friend."

I was surprised that we weren't going back to Claridge's, or the Connaught, his five-star favorites in Mayfair. I asked his friend Isobel about the hotel the next time I saw her. "Some friends of mine opened it this year, it's charming. They are extending Stuart a courtesy rate." She confirmed my suspicion that Greet was watching his expenses. He'd actually cut back my stipend to the old rate of ten bills, but I couldn't complain.

"That's nice of them, it sounds lovely…"

"Can you imagine, South Ken is Stuart's idea of slumming it," she said, snickering.

"Well, I'm glad to be seeing another side of London…"

We flew first class on British Airways, a downgrade from the Concorde. The morning of the auction came and we didn't even attend. Greet had previewed the items while I'd slept in and had arranged to purchase a group of baluster vases. They had spent the last three centuries at the bottom of the sea.

He brought them back to the hotel suite and unwrapped one for me to see.

"Look at the color, the brush strokes, these are among the best," Greet enthused. From the photos, I'd imagined they'd be bigger.

"It's smaller than the ones you have …"

"Those are more commercial. These are older, far more valuable, and really impressive as a group, involved …"

He expected to turn a profit by taking them back to New York and selling them to clients. "Flying first class has its advantages," he said. I was struck by the desire for beauty and status that drove the transport of fragile, empty vessels, drained of their function, through perilous ocean voyages. Here was one in my hands, subject to the same cycle of longing, as if those three hundred years under the sea hadn't happened. They'd had a nice long rest, before the Swedish adventurer and the British auctioneers put them back out on the trot.

"I paid too much, but I already have a buyer lined up. I suspect she'll take one look and want the whole group for her mantle…" Instead of sitting through the auction, we went to Kew Gardens. At the Royal Picnic House, he was enraptured by a field of bluebells and photographed me in front of it.

The following day we drove to Wiltshire to visit Greet's old friend Milo, who lived with his lover in a modest cottage in Sutton Veny.

"We're the village pooftahs," announced Milo as he shook my hand. He was in a ratty bathrobe and hobbling on a cane due to recent surgery. Over the course of our visit, a young man stopped in with his wife and two children, to whom Milo was godfather. Milo's boyfriend whispered an explanation: "He's local straight trade Milo bedded years ago…"

"Really?" I replied, scrutinizing the young man.

"Milo's quite the soft touch. He has *dozens* of such godchildren," he said with a grim laugh. I loved it. I was actually relieved to find that our visit would be teetotaler dry. Milo was famously an ex-drunk, in a recovery program, and hadn't touched a drink in years. As the visit wore on, Greet became visibly uncomfortable, sweating through his collar.

The next morning, Greet called Mark's Club to arrange for lunch. "Lord Parmoor will be joining us," he said over the phone.

"Who's Lord Parmoor?" I asked as he hung up.

"You've just met. Milo is the Fourth Baron Parmoor of Freith."

At lunch I learned that Milo, "village pooftah" and Lord, was the owner of one of London's leading antiquarian booksellers and publishers, Bernard Quaritch. I was more inclined to believe Greet's wild stories about his London past and the hints at his own nobility. I was glad to be seeing Milo again; he didn't give a damn about appearances or formalities, between his parade of straight trade and his out gay status. Greet was so circumspect by comparison.

When it came time to return home, Greet packed the vases, interspersing them carefully between our clothes. His profit margin depended on him sneaking them back into New York in those understated Louis Vuitton hard suitcases of his, avoiding customs.

The smuggled vases sold to former clients, avid collectors who lived at the Beresford, a Central Park West landmark designed by architect Emery Roth. I could actually see the building's towers from my fire escape. The couple had upgraded from an apartment on a lower floor which Greet had decorated years ago into one of the tower duplexes, a lavish spread with a high-ceilinged great room, a terrace, and sweeping views of the park. They'd gone with another decorator for their new unit. At least on the vases, Greet turned a solid profit—although he'd likely spent more to take me to London. This calculation left me feeling submerged in the depths of his fixation. In the cab back to the East Side, I seized on Greet's good mood and persuaded him to host a reunion dinner for Andrés.

"Dress up, we're going to Cipriani tonight…"

"Yasss, child, mama's back in from the cold," Andrés replied as he pulled a jacket and tie from his rack.

My existence had long felt siloed, between the uptown luxury cocoon and the lives Andrés and I harbored in the railroad flat. I was tired of serving as a conduit for their hostility, of being bound to secrets on both sides. I was determined to reconcile my two polestars. We suited up and took the cross-town bus. Upon our arrival at East Seventieth Street I was relieved to see that they'd both put their hurt feelings behind them. As soon as they saw each other after years of estrangement, they smiled, embraced, and immediately fell into camp banter. This time, I joined in.

"So Mr. Greet, have you seen the new Louvre?" asked Andrés.

"Please, that ghastly pyramid! It's a goddamned shopping mall."

"Well, you didn't buy *me* anything there…"

"Next time, pick up a Poussin," suggested Andrés.

"Not the worst thing you could pick up in Paris," Greet replied, to our laughter.

It was reassuring to all of us. Andrés seemed transported back to the time before his diagnosis and Greet laughed like he hadn't in a while.

After dinner, we put on an encore performance on that big bed. I was happily complicit in concealing Andrés' condition from Greet. When the three of us had been in this bed before, I was the center of attention, especially the showy nature of my ejaculation, my headboard-hitting. This time Andrés was the star. Despite everything he'd been through, including another recent bout of opportunistic infections, he was lean, tanned, and radiating erotic energy. The latest trial he'd enrolled in was testing out a drug combination and he'd rebounded once again. We'd gradually learned more about how HIV was transmitted and I no longer feared his body. Instead, I took quiet pleasure in defying Greet's germ phobia.

By the time news of Joseph's death reached us, Andrés and I had been dodging loss for so long we were numb. The announcement that ran in The Baltimore Sun indicated that the cause, at twenty-eight, was 'complications from pneumonia.' This fit the pattern of major newspapers (and families) being unwilling to call AIDS deaths what they were.

On a recent late-night video call with Andrés from Santiago, he told me that there was more to his relationship with Joseph than I'd picked up on watching them break up at my doorstep. It had followed the sugar daddy/kept boy template, even though they were close in age. Joseph had family wealth, had given Andrés a credit card, and let him drive his late-model sports car:

"I was his trophy architecture student boy toy; he loved showing me off at high-end cocktail parties at Columbia and such. He was super generous with me…I'd go to Paris for weekend shopping trips on his card…"

How he had imprinted his hustle onto me and how unwitting I'd been. I wished I'd had some frame of reference for asserting agency in my relationship with Greet: a precedent, a menu, options. I couldn't ask Andrés for practical advice on how to handle him once it had become a sore spot. I just had to figure it out on my own.

Greet caught the flu during charity season and asked me to accompany his friend Isobel to a gala at the Waldorf-Astoria. Isobel, a well-preserved English beauty in Chanel, was the Director of Giving for Lord Hanson's company, a British-American conglomerate. It was a corporate title that basically meant she got to spend a rich man's money. I had designed a Neo-gothic inspired bookcase for her New York apartment. "You'll be her walker," Greet explained: a presentable plus-one for an older, wealthy woman. I bought a tuxedo and wore it to meet Isobel in the hotel lobby. While she networked, a man in a sharp tux, handsome like a soap opera star, approached me.

"I'm Bradley, " he said, running his middle finger through my palm while holding our handshake.

"Dale, nice to meet you…"

"What brings you to this shindig?"

"I'm here with Isobel," I answered, pointing.

"Ah," he replied with a wink.

I surmised that Bradley was also a walker. He was a florist who had come as the plus-one of a rich client. We clocked each others' good watches as we sniffed each other out. He'd perfected the art of flirtation, and deployed his skills on me, leaning into me, confiding in me. Feeling his breath on my neck as the back of his hand brushed against mine gave me an erection right there in the ballroom of the Waldorf-Astoria.

•

I'd figured out that there was gay cruising in the Ramble crossing the park on walks home from Greet's apartment. Living so close to the West Eighty-First Street entrance made the Ramble feel like our backyard. Gay cruising persisted in the area's naturalistic settings, and was even in something of a golden moment, despite the ongoing health crisis. There were established trails and plenty of places for men from all over the city to hook up: thick shrubs, crevasses in the outcroppings of Manhattan Schist, even a shallow cave. Andrés came home one evening, having spent the magic hour in the park.

"Child…I just ran into Juan in the Rambles…"

"Oh really? I've never seen him in there…"

"Well, he's seen you, Rambelina…"

"Okay…"

"You know how Juanita isn't much of a talker? Well, she had *a lot* to say." He paused. "About Alvaro…."

"What about Alvaro?"

"He got diagnosed with AIDS and died, fast. Juan's been too afraid to say anything to Mr. Greet about it. You know how she is, with her germ phobia…"

"Oh my god…Poor Alvaro."

Andrés raised his hands to the sky, proclaiming, *"Te bendiga Alvaro, y tu bigote!"*

(Bless you Alvaro, and your mustache.)

"Well, I'm not going to tell him either."

Alvaro's unexplained disappearance had destabilized Greet in ways large and small. Of course having an all-purpose servant and driver had made his daily life easier, but more than that, his reliably deferential manner seemed to ease Greet's anxieties. Handsome Juan was more stoic than deferential and I was a moody brat. I didn't like having to keep the secret of his death—yet another topic to be avoided—but it seemed like the best of bad choices. It must have weighed upon Juan until he was able tell Andrés.

I'd been smoking pot to unwind after my time with Greet was done, but the habit had crept into my so-called work hours. I started smoking just to be able to summon the courage to show up to our dates and drink with him. I'd take a last hit just as I swung into the restaurant, so I probably wasn't fooling anyone, between the lingering odor, my bloodshot eyes, and zonked-out manner.

•

In the Waldorf-Astoria ballroom, after that heavy flirtation with Bradley, I'd headed back to the table in time to overhear Isobel matter-of-factly refer to me as "Mr. Greet's kept boy." I was offended, but she charmed my anger away.

"Oh, don't blush! It's a good English tradition, gentlemen patrons, ahh, mentors, to attractive young men. In the manner of Socrates, darling!"

Isobel hadn't said anything I hadn't said myself, but hearing her offhandedly out me as *kept* hit me. I'd bragged to friends about having a sugar daddy. Often, the information would not land; they might have thought I was exaggerating, or joking, or just did not want to believe me.

Where was the agency I'd been able to assert before? It seemed to have died fast, like Alvaro—and Bradley, the handsome walker from the Waldorf-Astoria. Not too long after the gala, I asked Isobel about him: "Darling, Bradley has died. A sudden illness...." She held a steady gaze through this pronouncement, her eyes imploring me: *pick up the subtext*. "A sudden illness" was the other euphemism used by the press when reporting AIDS deaths, aside from "complications..." When Andrés had been diagnosed, and countable days away from dying, I'd just assumed I'd be next. This totalizing doom enveloped me, a fatalism which would only let me act out the one fucked-up storyline before me. Somehow the news of Bradley—a near stranger, his death buried in euphemism—had dislodged it. In that moment, I was done being kept.

5. MERELY DECORATIVE VALUE

> *Mr. Havadtoy…is at no loss for anecdotes. Born in London and raised in communist Hungary, he escaped through the Iron Curtain into Yugoslavia and on to Italy. From there he traveled to London. In the summer of 1972, he moved to New York to join a boyfriend and prospered as an interior designer until an encounter with Lennon and Ms. Ono steered his life in a new direction.*
>
> *The couple came into the shop where he worked and selected two chairs. "I was included in the price," he recalled with a laugh.*
>
> *"I am the kind of person that if I see a door, I want to open it…"*
>
> \- "A Hungarian Artist Comes Into His Own," the *New York Times*, June 2016

Some time in the early Nineties—after Isobel had offhandedly laid out my "kept" status to a table of her society friends—for a period which I apparently did not document, either in photos or diary entries, I tried to pull away from Greet, after years of seemingly uninterrupted servitude to his routines. As much as my body needed a rest from the marathon drinking, I was approaching thirty and wanted to imagine a life without him. I joined a gathering of my classmates, now alumni, in a loft in Williamsburg. These meetings were putatively about forging paths for ourselves in the professional world, post-Cooper Union. The esoteric education the school had provided us was not exactly grounded in the realities of the job market.

At one of these gatherings, one of my school mates introduced a small glassine envelope stamped 'NO JOKE' and containing a white powder. The ephemeral little packet was slipped onto the long industrial table we would gather around, among books, dried flowers, mismatched dishes from a shared meal, tobacco pouches, and little glasses of liqueur. The person who'd brought it had an innocuous little code name for it: they called it "mail," which they had picked up from the "post office." We started sniffing together. We intellectualized our use of heroin, talking up the artists whose work was inspired by opium, its fabled precursor: Cocteau, Picasso, Modigliani. Most of those in our group kept it within the bounds of our social rituals, but two of us fell hard.

Within a month, I had a weekend habit outside of that circle of friends. I mythologized heroin: it was *having a moment*. The supply in New York was *pure*. *Heroin was my boyfriend*—the best boyfriend ever. Once I counted out the steps I'd have to take to disappear from Greet's life entirely; heroin obliterated his gaze. On my cloud, I was in a relationship, but there was no small talk, no conflict, just a little casual puking and then all the hard edges would turn to vapor.

I somehow attended graduate classes at the New School. I was enrolled in the Liberal Studies program, which was intended for students who wished to forge an interdisciplinary path, and combined classes from the philosophy and sociology departments with design studios at Parson's architecture program. Not having the structure of a department made it easier for me to float through the campus on my cloud. I excelled at individual classes but could not put together a coherent thesis. I wrote pages and pages about the city, but none of it coalesced. There was a section on solar afterimages which I thought of as ground-breaking and experimental at the time, but re-reading it today, it comes off as the introspective ramblings of a low-grade junkie on the nod, eyes closed to the sun.

Weekends on heroin got longer, absorbing Friday and Monday. For most of my time in grad school, my stipend from Greet had covered tuition, until I came to find that being high on dope and spending time with him were wholly incompatible. It was as though the muscles I needed for the performance of companion had atrophied, or had never existed. I stopped showing up to his table altogether, putting him off with excuses—"I really need to focus on writing my thesis"—and coasted on whatever money I'd saved over the years. I never did submit a thesis or get a graduate degree.

I only kicked heroin when the person who'd score for us—braving the streets of the Lower East Side and walking into an abandoned building controlled by the local gang—got sent away to rehab. There would be no more trips to that particular post office since I was too scared to cop on my own. Without much planning, I got off of heroin by smoking a lot of pot, listening to Stereolab, and sweating it out. I was luckier than my friend who used to score; they'd developed sores on their face and had been caught nodding out at work. I didn't go through serious withdrawal symptoms, just a broken heart. Once my homespun detox was more or less complete, I realized I was out of money. Lacking any great ambition to find work, I fell back under Greet's gaze, nestling into the security of my stipend. He took me back like he had before.

"Oh, I remember this caper, the Vung Tau cargo," I said, flipping through the catalog from the Sotheby's sale a few years back. Once again at Greet's side, recalling the London trip, the auction we hadn't attended, I was transported back to our stylish suite at the Pelham, holding one of those vases in my hands. How impressed I'd been with it as an object and a story—at least until I'd been enlisted to smuggle it past Customs. Then it felt like a porcelain bomb. I'd related to the dumb, coveted object then, but related even more from where I now stood, on the other side of heroin. *Come to think of it, hadn't the British foisted opium upon the Chinese to exchange for porcelain?* My centuries submerged and sunken in its sands did not seem to change Greet's desire for me. The vases had resurfaced intact after a blip in time, only the glazing had dulled slightly. I, too, was fairly intact, although my body had been through alcoholic bloat, after years of drinking with him; at one point, my liver inflamed and raged like a furnace, and I had to stop drinking for six months, doctor's orders. Then the dope stripped me away to a more essential form.

For a third time, we resumed our routines of dining and drinking. Greet liked to be seen with me at his regular haunts above all else; whatever had kept me from appearing by his side was a yet another banished topic. Mario, now the maitre d' at Gino, acknowledged my return after a long absence with a solemn bow. The gestures of restaurant workers could carry multiple meanings. His bow seemed to say: *Welcome back, we've missed you, we're sorry to see you tied to him again, have some* Pasta Segreto. We drank and socialized at the bar, and when we made our way to his reserved corner table, Mario showed him that a little brass plaque with his name had been affixed to one of the ordinary fan-backed wooden chairs. Outwardly, he expressed a certain humble gratitude for the honor, hugging and clapping the backs of Mario and the waiters. One of the waiters proclaimed with awe, "Signore Greet, you put my kids through college!" Once Mario was back up front, he bristled: "What the hell do they think they're doing, memorializing me?"

We were visited at the table by his friend Eddie, an American who was roughly the same height and build as Greet, who dressed like him, and for some reason spoke in mid-Atlantic, theatrical English. Sitting between them as they twinned was far worse than being alone with the decorator. We'd once visited Eddie in his house in Hollywood Hills, when we flew out to Los Angeles and stayed at the Beverly Hills Hotel. The reason Greet had given for the trip was that he was to consult on the feature film project based on writer Daniel Farson's book *The Gilded Gutter Life of Francis Bacon*. The opportunity evaporated while we were there; it may have just been Greet's vague excuse to take me away. Eddie seemed to own the house for the sole purpose of chasing starlets. A self-described "pussy hound," he brought out in Greet a heterosexually coded performance of a jovial, naughty gentleman. I laughed at their jokes, but the way these two overdressed old men brought out each others' lechery made me cringe.

As we resumed our routines, Greet soon after faced another reckoning: the Rosen residence was complete, the Vung Tau vases adorned the mantle at the Beresford, and a new potential project had been curtailed. The final payments were in, and his income had not kept up with his overhead for some time. I'd eavesdropped on enough calls to his private banker asking him to transfer large sums from his investment account into his checking account to know what was up. There didn't seem to be any prospects for major projects, just some of his established clients inquiring about small add-on jobs here and there.

He entered into a downward spiral: when he had projects keeping his mind engaged and his body on the move, he drank less. Others who were close to him, like Isobel, openly discussed his escalating drinking with me. There were not just health repercussions, she said, but professional ones as well: reputation meant everything to Greet. He relied on the good word of his clients to get more work in their circle. He rarely sought publicity, and had a special disdain for design magazines: "Those nosy women from the rags, critics all! It's an invasion of privacy," he'd intone, pronouncing "critics" with a theatrical rolled *r*. "

Greg, who was busy with a project of his own, spelled it out: "You know these people. Only the contractors are worse gossips than the clients. Word has gotten around that he's not on top of his jobs the way he once was." I couldn't dispute it, having seen him on the Rosen's. "And it's true," Greg continued, "He's drinking more than ever…it hasn't been this bad since the Hungarian…."

"The Hungarian again…"

As his decor practice wound down, Greet saw little need in renting a showcase property on a prestigious block. He sat me down at his Regency table, mahogany with gilt lion's paw feet. There were neat stacks of paper between us.

"Frankly, darling, I'm spending more than I'm bringing in, and that includes you…" This didn't come off as him trying to blame me for his financial straits; rather it showed that he considered my weekly stipend a necessary expense. I was taken aback, but still willing to take his money.

Once again, he moved decisively, giving up the lease on East Seventieth Street and selling off more of his possessions, that Regency table included. He kept the Jacobean bed, a Louis XIV ormulu-mounted bombe commode, those Gothic Revival chairs, some blue-and-white vases, the Roman prints, and the academic painting of the sullen boy. He sold some investments and paid cash for a reasonably priced co-op with a large terrace on the corner of Fifty-Seventh and Lexington Avenue, on a high floor of one of those ubiquitous white-glazed brick buildings from the 50's.

He approached the whole move with an air of adventure, as if moving into this building were slumming it. He transformed the one-bedroom unit into sleek bachelor's quarters; a deep navy striped paper on the walls, plush carpeting from Stark, the small kitchen in beveled, blue-tinted mirror, like a bar. He bribed the super so that he could install a washer and dryer. The design reflected his personal style with a modern edge, which he believed could triumph over the obvious deficits of the apartment: the less-than-exclusive location and address. I wanted to believe it too.

"I had those boys carve back all the walls to make room for the bed, involved…" he boasted of his demands on his hunky construction crew. "They found a niche for the safe, too."

He turned the terrace into an outdoor dining room, with a retractable canopy and tall boxwoods in planters around the perimeter. When work on the apartment was complete, he settled into his retirement. In cringe-worthy moments, he joked that he was "semi-retarded."

For a time, he seemed happy in his new dwelling. It denoted a simplified life.

"I'm sure I'll walk a lot more living here, since everything's so close. I won't have to rely on those god-awful yellow cabs…"

He was just around the corner from Gino, and several of the other places he frequented were within his walking range. The D&D building, which housed many of the design showrooms he favored, was mere steps away, in case a project came along. Juan still came to clean the new apartment once a week.

We still went to dinner, too, though to a smaller list of nearby favorites. "I'm saving a fortune on taxis, involved…" he'd say, a remark that seemed stereotypically penny-wise and pound-foolish. He occasionally took me to Mr. Chow, an upscale Chinese restaurant just a down the street, more for the elegant decor than the food. Soon after moving in, he "rediscovered" the 21 Club, on West Fifty-Second Street, an ambitious evening stroll away. The restaurant's exterior was hard to miss—it was adorned with dozens of lawn jockeys, cutesy emblems of the served class—and once Greet made it through the door, he'd sink into the boozy men's club environment. He was rarely able to walk home from a night at the 21 Club.

His happiness in the new apartment was a short-lived mirage: "I can't sleep with the noise coming through the walls, involved…those tacky people next door blast their television all night…" He became increasingly reliant on prescriptions–Xanax during the day for his anxiety, Halcion to sleep. His doctor had urged him to cut back on his drinking while taking these pills, but he scoffed. The combination of pills and alcohol made him erratic and moody.

Some time after moving in, Greet learned about what had befallen Alvaro, and was furious that the news had been kept from him. I'm not sure how he found out; Juan was as inscrutable as ever. Greet seemed mortified that an infected body had been in his home, had handled his belongings, even helped him dress. He became absolutely manic about cleaning, doubling up on Juan's chores. Increasingly paranoid about careless restaurant staff, he went around sanitizing his table settings with vodka.

"Vodka kills everything," he'd intone, wiping down a fork. After that period when I'd checked out our relationship and sniffed heroin for a long winter, and he'd taken me back, I'd mythologized his forbearance: "He's always so forgiving of me..." More likely he'd taken me back because he approved of my slimmed-down build, as if my dope stint was diet camp for alcohol bloat. When we first met, I was Greet's romantic ideal: a slim, sullen Italian youth, even if I was Long Island Italian. Now I was spoiled, bloated once again, and aged-out. Our exchanges were increasingly hostile; we hadn't been on the same frequency (or the same drugs) for some time.

His health declined, and he was forced to cut down on his drinking, although he still consumed way more alcohol than most. I shifted into the role of cheerful home-care attendant. He really disliked this shift; I think he would have preferred the dignity of cruelty. I enticed him with sugar, having read that alcoholics craved sweets as they weaned off of drinking. He upped his dosage of Halcion at night, leading to troubling nocturnal bouts of sleepwalking and binge-eating. One morning, Juan preserved the evidence of an overnight ransacking of the kitchen for me: torn-up packages of cookies and crackers, half-eaten ice cream containers swimming in melt.

He became withdrawn and morose—and what was worse, he became cheap, doling out what was once a weekly stipend every nine days, now ten, now attaching new conditions. He'd made a decision that he was going to spend his days dining and drinking in his accustomed manner, calculating that his remaining money was enough to finance that plan; but as his bank account dwindled, he seemed to look upon me as an investment with diminishing returns.

Even though Greet no longer lived directly across town, I still took every occasion to cross through Central Park. In the Ramble, I felt unkept, an equal among guys from all over the city. We would stalk the paths, throw hard stares, do circling dances towards one another, and signal with head nods towards secluded spots in green-hued shadows. One afternoon on my way through the Park I got cruised by a compact Latino stud in a Fila tracksuit. With his eyes on me, he sprung over a metal rail in one swoop; I followed him down to a shallow cave below. He neatly hung his jacket on a branch outside the entrance and we got down to business, sucking each others' cocks in turns until he pulled me in tightly to make out and stroke each other to furious completion.

I got to the apartment high and sweaty and reeking of sex, slyly pulling twigs out of my hair. Greet was immediately on guard. I told myself it was fine; after years being his pampered pretty boy, I knew how to keep the edges just rough enough. Through the doorway, I could see that the safe was open; it was usually hidden behind one of the nightstands. It was stuffed with cash, good watches, yellowed stock certificates, and that binder full of photos of me, pouting in European gardens.

We argued about money; he was being obstinate. I hadn't seen my stipend in two weeks. Enraged, I tied him to the Gothic Revival chair he was sitting in, using a handful of his silk ties I'd grabbed off the dresser. At first, he looked at me with mocking disbelief; then his brow knitted with increasing alarm as I tightened the ties that bound his wrists. I helped myself to a roll of money from the safe. His alarm turned to anger: "What do you think you're doing?" I flaunted the roll. Wrapped in brittle rubber bands, it was the most cash I'd ever handled. It seemed to turn in on itself, like a serpent eating its tail.

Tying him up seemed like my best and last option. What I really needed was to break through our crossfire-riddled haze. Once the satisfaction of seeing him bound wore off, I was at a loss, and a fury of unspoken resentments took over. I did what I'd dared myself to do because I couldn't think of anything else; I punched him in the face, a real closed-fisted punch, not a slap. His dental bridge flew out of his mouth and blood spurted from his nose. He slumped in resignation.

Blood sprayed on one of the upholstered arms of the chair and on the roll of bills in my hand. His blood hardly clotted anymore, it just poured out watery red in a stream. What had made me desperate enough to tie him up and punch him in the face? Something about seeing this aristocratic British man bound to his throne with his own silk soothed me: *Behold my colonizer!* I laughed maniacally at one point, followed by a flash of confused remorse: *I don't really need the money this badly.* What I really wanted was assert some dominance over my withholding sugar daddy.

After landing the punch, I broke down at his feet.

"I can't do this anymore, " I said, sobbing. I untied him, and he retrieved his bridge and stuffed a handkerchief in his nostril. He steadied his trembling hands with a swig of his cocktail.

"I understand, I quite understand..." he said, patting my sweaty head.

He understands? Maybe I'd finally given him the rough scene he always wanted but didn't know how to ask for.

Even after that amateurish bondage scenario, Greet took me back, and our routines resumed, such as they were. I hadn't seen Greg in a while, so I invited him to lunch to catch up. Our conversation soon turned to Greet's drinking, which was again compared to his previous low point: the Hungarian, that ghost who'd been stalking me for years.

"But *who* is this Hungarian? Isobel started telling me once, but she cut herself off..."

"He was Mr. Greet's lover, before he met you," said Greg. "He worked at the shop on Madison. Another bisexual," he added, implying quotation marks with his emphasis. "This was when John Lennon and Yoko Ono would come into the shop. You know, John Lennon and Mr. Greet had a real rapport. They bonded as expats Brits in America."

"I know he's very sentimental about John Lennon..."

"I'd just started drafting for him around that time. You know Mr. Greet, he does not like to cross town. It was the Hungarian who would go to the Dakota, to measure, to oversee deliveries, and so on. As soon as he heard about the shooting, he left the shop and immediately ran over, right to Yoko. He never came back, not even to explain, not even to pick up his things."

His words hung in the air for an overlong pause.

"I was still in high school..."

"Don't remind me." We laughed. "The Hungarian stayed with Yoko. Mr. Greet was *devastated* by John Lennon's murder. It was just senseless...but the Hungarian's vanishing act? That nearly killed him."

"It's all so unbelievable..."

"I'm not even being dramatic, that's Mr. Greet's forté."

"No wonder...I wish I'd known sooner."

"To lose your lover to Yoko Ono, of all people...his friend was killed, he lost Sam, he lost his shop assistant, not to mention a good customer...Afterwards, his drinking really took off. I tried to talk to him about it, but he yelled at me: 'Don't ever mention that man's name in my presence again!'" Greg's imitation of Greet was pretty solid.

"What's his name?"

"Sam, Sam Havadtoy. He and Yoko are still together, if you can believe it."

I've since turned the tables on the Hungarian and become his stalker, at least on search engines. According to the press he's granted over the years, he met Greet in London as a young man. Greet brought him back to New York, and put him to work in his Madison Avenue shop. His anecdotes seem to glorify his time with Greet. Greg and others described him as Greet's boyfriend and employee, approximately the same role I'd been in. Havadtoy referred to this period as one during which he 'prospered as an interior designer.' I wouldn't begrudge anyone a little resume-fluffing, but he seems to have boosted Greet's credentials.

Following that terrible day in 1980, Havadtoy stayed with Yoko Ono for twenty years before resettling in his native country, purchasing an apartment in Budapest. He's had a varied career as a gallerist and an artist. Although we have never met, the figure of the Hungarian has been with me for all these years. How I'd come to admire my predecessor with the quick exit.

•

Although he'd had warning signs here and there, the first thing that really scared Greet about his health was when the bleeding started. After sleeping through the night on Halcion, he woke up to find the bedsheets stained red. That got him to see his doctor. When I asked him about it, he mumbled an explanation. I couldn't make any sense of it, but one takeaway was clear: The doctor had ordered him to stop drinking all together.

"So are you going to quit?"

He nodded in reply, answering with a barely vocalized "Yes," while looking like an admonished schoolboy.

That afternoon, I took him to an Alcoholics Anonymous meeting at St. Bartholomew's Church on Park Avenue. I thought he'd relate to the crowd, and enjoy the church's opulent Byzantine Revival structure, its beautiful, multi-hued stone, tile, paint, and stained glass finishes. The location was a lovely walk down Park Avenue away. "Maybe we can get lunch after at the Four Seasons," I said, reaching for enticements. The meeting was held in a sunny and stylish room right off the street, no dank church basement. Sitting in the front row was a woman in a Chanel suit he seemed to know. He was mortified, and signaled me to get up and leave with him. We slowly walked back to the apartment and he poured himself a vodka-and-tonic. He raised the glass with a little toast and looked straight into my eyes. He never went back.

Instead of sticking with AA, Greet called the travel agent and booked a "restorative" visit to the Sonoma Mission Inn in California's Napa Valley. We'd spent a few days there once before, with the intent of getting away from his daily routines and all the drinking they entailed. "Of course he picked a health spa in wine country…" was what I'd said returning from our first trip, not feeling terribly restored; we'd drunk less than usual, but still daily. Given Greet's present condition, it seemed unwise to fly across the country. In a somber moment of clarity, he announced over breakfast: "Darling, I'm afraid I have to cancel our trip to the spa…I'm just not feeling up to the travel."

Greet had made his decisive move and I'd decided to do the same, out of the Upper West Side walk-up where I'd lived with Andrés for years. Andrés spent very little time in New York any more, and I'd been longing to relocate to Brooklyn. Besides feeling that I'd be removed from Greet's gaze, Brooklyn appealed to me because it was the borough of my birth. I mythologized moving there as a "return" to my origins. Like many, this myth was built upon a dubious foundation. I was really only born in Brooklyn on a technicality; my family had long before relocated out of Bay Ridge to Long Island, part of the postwar suburbanization fueled by the GI Bill. My mother was only sixteen when she'd gotten pregnant with me, and she'd continued to see the family doctor in his office. She later told me the story: "When the contractions started, your grandmother drove me to Doctor Mussio's office, and he delivered you, just like he'd delivered me."

I had a circle of friends who had moved into Fort Greene, a pretty brownstone district which had suffered a decline into the 80's but was being reclaimed and restored by Black artists and professionals, notably filmmaker Spike Lee. I rented a parlor floor apartment in a brownstone with a rear yard and a basement. It had seen some rough times, but the crown molding, plaster medallions, and parlor doors were still intact. I only realized later how I'd replicated the spatial conditions of the Seventieth Street apartment: a formal living and dining room suite, a basement workshop, a garden, and a large bedroom.

I also had a boyfriend. His circle called him "Machito," with a hint of irony. He was a bull stud of compact body and easy smile, and I fell hard after catching sight of him during a crawl through the East Village's gay bars. I stared at his reflection in the bathroom mirror until he turned around. He was a brown-skinned Venezuelan with a nearly incomprehensible accent, but I wasn't much interested in talking anyway. We lunged for each other right there and it got pretty intense, as the bar's jaded customers came and went. Walking out of that bathroom over strains of "Rhythm Nation," we were in an instant relationship.

How I'd judged Greet for years for way he'd projected his romantic notions upon me, how his expressions of emotions felt unearned. Now I was shacked up with a guy after cruising him in the toilet at Crowbar. There was sexual heat but not much substance. Maybe I was on a bit of savior trip. In hindsight, it was an earnest but misguided attempt to embark upon a "real" romantic life after operating under Greet's fixation—and Andrés' manipulations—for another twelve-year cycle. I was not ready.

Machito, who was working as a cook at a cozy Italian restaurant in the East Village, had one urgent problem; he was about to overstay his tourist visa. I hastily arranged a flight to the Dominican Republic, using the voucher from that cancelled trip to the Napa Valley. I'd earned enough trust with the travel agent—and Greet was so out of it—that I was able to pull off this stunt without his knowledge. It seemed the easiest way to leave the country and re-enter. I pictured a long weekend at one of those all-inclusive resorts–sunbathing, Caribbean waters, elaborate meals–and upon our return, Machito's visa would be renewed for another ninety days, giving us time to figure out a more long-term solution. At least this was the idea. I told the decorator that I was going to Miami for the weekend.

Landing in Santo Domingo without an itinerary, we hailed a taxi driver. Machito asked him where were the gay clubs in the city. He replied *"No los tenemos aquí,"* ("We don't have those here.") A troubling answer, since we couldn't be sure whether he meant gay clubs or gay people. Machito then asked him to recommend a place for us to spend a few days at the beach. Possibly to punish us for the first question, he took us to Boca Chica, a popular resort town close to the capital. We checked into one of the town's upscale hotels, which promised a trouble-free stay and elaborate meals. Our room had a view of the beach from the balcony. On our first night, we strolled down Avenida Duarte, the main pedestrian strip; it was overwhelmed with drunk tourists, pushy vendors, and teenage girls hustling for foreign tricks.

Creeped out by the vibe in town, we returned to our room, only to find a break-in under way; the thieves jumped off the balcony and disappeared under the palmettos. They hadn't gotten away with much but had succeeded in rattling us. Since the thieves had broken the lock on the sliding door to the balcony, the resort moved us into a suite on a higher floor. We spent the next day at the beach, whose sweeping vistas were marred by an oil tanker stranded offshore. We enjoyed the sun and the sea for a while—until we witnessed the crowd abuse and beat a Haitian trinket-seller who had strayed onto resort property. I railed against the injustice, and fumed at the oblivious tourists carrying on with their vacations. Machito had seen worse. In my aggrieved state, our immigration plan was hardly front of mind when we boarded the return flight. "Let's just get the hell off this fucking island," I said to Machito.

Once we were instructed to form separate lines at Miami International, the import of our plan came back into focus. From the line for citizens, I watched as an immigration officer went through Machito's bag. She had a round, pleasant face, a plump body, and salon waves in a short bob. She looked comforting, like a suburban mom, except for the uniform. I was sure she'd be sympathetic. She pulled a postcard from Machito's carry-on. The thoroughness of her search surprised me; I really just figured she would stamp his passport and move on to the next. Machito had written to his sister, but we couldn't find stamps or a post office in Boca Chica, just underaged hookers and cheap liquor. She read his scrawl:

'Estoy trabajando en un café, esta bien.'

Her pleasant face fixed in vindictive triumph. She yelled, "We got one!" and high-fived her male associate. Machito had all but confessed to working on a tourist visa. As the customs agent reviewing my documents waved me through, I watched, horrified, as Machito was shuttled off to an interrogation room. He glared back at me with a mortally wounded look. He looked so small next to their wide bodies, like they could crush him with one coordinated turn. "Sir, you can't linger here. Move it along," the customs agent barked. I made my way through the area, then doubled back to find an official.

After facing some stonewalling, I learned that Machito would be sent back to Caracas, his passport stamped barring re-entry for ten years. *My government has taken my love away,* I lamented. The official gave me the location of the facility where he'd be held overnight. "They're taking him to Krome," he said with a certain fatalism. I took a taxi to the Krome Detention Center–this concrete bunker built on top of an unused airstrip and surrounded by a tall chain link fence. A crowd was gathered outside the fence. One person yelled a name, and got an answer, so everyone else let them talk. A older lady, the despairing mother of one of the detainees, explained to me that it was the only way to talk them. I waited my turn, then yelled "Machito! Machito!" but my cries just bounced off the concrete. I flew back to New York alone in total despair. I was pissed off at Machito for the avoidable mistake of the post card, but also felt some responsibility for the fuck-up. I didn't really know him all that well, and didn't know if I was really in love, but resolved that whatever journey we were on was not going to end with that mean mom-lady in beige.

Back home, I went to see Greet, withholding any information about the drama which had befallen me in Miami International. He was happy to see me after my long weekend away. "You're very tan," he said when I showed up at his apartment; I covered up my angst with friendly chatter. Machito was back with his family, and we were talking by phone every week. I was determined to show up for my caretaker job and pocket my weekly stipend, so I'd have the resources to plot his return to New York.

Between the grim task of caretaking an alcoholic in decline and my despair over Machito's immigration crisis, I was smoking a lot more pot. It was easy to come by in Fort Greene. The bodega on the corner sold it; a customer just needed to know the code, which was to reach into a non-working refrigerator case, pull out a warm can of beer, and bring it to the register. They would slip a nickel bag into the paper bag along with the warm can and charge you for both. In retrospect, pot had clouded my judgment on the trip to the Dominican Republic, witnessed by the lack of any real planning or attention to details, like don't incriminate yourself upon re-entry.

To get myself to a lunch date at Gino, I'd leave Fort Greene with a joint and a bottle of eye drops in my jacket pocket and take the 6 train. I'd light up on the short walk from the station to the restaurant—wheeling past uniformed cops, amazed at what I could get away with it in a suit and tie—sucking back my last toke as I wheeled into the restaurant. Greet loathed being kept waiting by anyone, but at this stage, I was usually running late. "There was a delay on the subway…" I'd lie. He'd acquiesce because he didn't have much choice at that point; he was in no state to break in a new boy. The waiters would notice that I was high, Greet would notice, but I'd be too baked to care.

At our last lunch there, I sought to take attention off of my stoned state and make Greet smile: "Do you remember our trip to Venice? The gondola ride to Guidecca, our dinner outside in the garden?"

"Oh my boy, it was magical." We toasted our cocktails, an ordinary ritual now with a fatal edge.

"One of the most beautiful places you've taken me."

Despite my stoned state and my motives, there was a genuine moment of appreciation between us, beyond reach of our conflicts. We'd traveled to Paris and London several times; we'd returned to Southern Italy after the ill-fated summer in the Villa with Andrés and the late Alvaro; we'd visited all the major attractions on the island of Sicily, along with a stop in my grandfather's home town; we'd spent a month in Nice, and from there taken a tour of northern Italy in a rented sports car, hitting Monte Carlo on the way, then Portofino, Milan, Verona, and Venice; we'd toured the Vatican, stayed at the Hotel Baglioni in Rome, and the Villa San Michele in Florence; we'd traveled to California, once to the Beverly Hills Hotel, another time to Napa for that spa retreat; we'd stayed at the Ritz in Madrid, and toured southern Spain; we'd been through Quintana Roo to see the Mayan sites. He'd educated my palette. He'd taken me to Café Carlyle for an unforgettable night seeing Eartha Kitt perform; she twinkled with recognition upon seeing Greet enthralled to her talents, then came over to our table and vamped and did a backbend over my lap for him. Usually when I looked back on this extensive history of posh experiences, I'd tally up the costs and think: *I paid the fare with my body.* In this moment, I was genuinely grateful for the wild ride.

The good vibes didn't last. Greet picked a fight with Mario over a perceived slight. Mario had committed the sin of seating customers at the table Greet expected would be waiting for him, the one with "his" chair, the one with the plaque he'd been pissed off about. There was an equally good table in the other corner, but Greet could not be assuaged. It was vanity that fueled his dislike of the offered table; it didn't show off what he thought of as his good side. We left, and on our way to Isle of Capri—another old-school Italian stalwart one block over—he said, "I'll never set foot in that dump again…"

Gino had been the nexus of his social life in New York for decades and now he'd estranged himself from it over some pettiness. Though it was troubling to see him so unmoored, I didn't think to try taking him back to AA. I just showed up for our lunches at places other than Gino. We'd have cocktails beforehand at the apartment, but he wouldn't order them out any more. He would pick a bottle of wine "for the table," and we would share it. I tried shorting his pours, but other than that, I mostly let him kill himself in front of me. If I broached the subject of his health or of not drinking, he'd shut me down: "Don't worry, you're still in the will…" That would end that.

His death came not too long after and was ugly: He'd started bleeding from his mouth. The diagnosis was esophageal varices along with a host of other ills. I pressed his doctor to explain. "Essentially, the veins of his lower esophagus are hemorrhaging, an effect of his alcoholic cirrhosis. So first we need to stop the bleeding—but there are other challenges…" He was admitted into Lenox Hill Hospital. He did not want to die in a hospital, but here we were. I visited him every day, and he just looked at me with pleading eyes.

The bleeding wouldn't stop, his liver was shutting down, and all these infections popped up. Blood tests revealed that he was HIV positive on top of everything else; he must have found some other trade. The doctors had no other option but to induce a paralytic coma and insert a balloon tamponade down his throat, the intent being that the balloon, once inflated in place, would exert pressure on the esophageal lining and stanch the bleeding. Comatose, mouth spread open, with a contraption inserted deep down his throat: It reminded me of something medieval torturers would devise for sodomites.

The balloon tamponade was left in place for several days but didn't work. Greet had effectively burned away the lining of his esophagus with alcohol: *Vodka kills everything*. His decaying body gave off only a faint antiseptic odor, as if it had been truly pickled. He never woke.

His death went unnoticed; there was no obituary in the *Times*, though they had once raved about his shops. There was no service; instead he was cremated. He'd left instructions for us to take his ashes to Capri and scatter them into the sea. After his death, articles came out warning of the dangers of taking Xanax and Halcion together, especially in higher dosages and for long periods. If that weren't bad enough he'd been combining these co-addictive, round-the-clock benzos with alcohol. My drugs were street, his were prescribed, but his killed him.

Milo sent me a letter of condolence on understated pale blue stationery printed with his address in Sutton Veny.

> You were kind to keep me informed over the last weeks. It will have been a harrowing period for you and although, in a sense, it might be a relief that the worry and uncertainty is over.... Stuart had so much charm and was such fun and was so deeply generous...I knew him for over four decades...

He went on to invite me for a visit, and to warn me about fulfilling Greet's last wish: "At lunch the other day a woman friend told a story about a woman she knew who'd taken her husband's ashes back to Florence & was told by the English consulate that it was exceedingly illegal to have anyone's ashes in Italy..." His ashes wound up stashed in Greg's closet for years.

I reached Milo by phone after receiving his letter. He apologized for being so absent, explaining that as an alcoholic in recovery, keeping

Greet at a distance was an act of self-preservation. Then he opened up about Greet's past:

"You're a lovely young fellow, but no match for a man brought up on secrets…"

"What do you mean?"

"In our day, England was an inhospitable place for homosexuals. We were subject to criminal prosecution and worse. So, when he was young, Stuart married a woman."

"So she was his beard?"

"His *beard*…" He seemed amused that I knew the term. "Except the poor dear wasn't in on it. She became vengeful after finding him with a man. To avoid scandal and arrest, the marriage was annulled and Stuart fled to America…"

"I never knew about any of this…"

"I'm not surprised, he did not speak of her."

"I wish he'd told me…"

"But you see, my title has provided me some cover. The village pooftahs and such. Not so for Stuart…"

"I thought he had some sort of title?"

"He did play it up, didn't he?" said Milo, chuckling. "His father was a groomsman. He worked in the stables for a family at their Cornwall estate. It was a good Georgian house, which young Stuart admired…from outside."

"How did you meet him?"

"You probably don't know this, but Stuart was strikingly handsome in his day: tall, blond, blue-eyed, an athlete. Cricket. But you wouldn't know that either. He'd been picked up by an old friend of mine, who left him a modest fortune after his death."

I absorbed all of this new information.

"But they all seemed to know him at Claridge's…"

"He stayed there for a time while arrangements for the annulment were made. They knew nothing of the scandal—or at least they didn't let on. Proper British, soul of discretion and such…"

"Although I was surprised that they lost our room reservations," I said, archly.

Milo laughed. "He pulled that old ruse?"

"Yea…."

"You know, I was his last touchstone here, sadly…"

"I understand your reasons, Milo."

Greet had created a fiction of status in New York; perhaps the spurned son of England longed for the protective cloak of nobility. I remembered his hostility to Ralph Lauren, who he insisted on calling *Lipschitz*, spitting it like it was a curse exposing his pretense. Greet apparently had long ago bought into his own fiction. I'd had a hard time understanding his bond with John Lennon, based on what I knew of him and Lennon's public persona; now it was clear that they both had roots in the British working class. If he'd been honest with me about any of this maybe things would have been different between us. We could have been co-conspirators. There were many times he seemed to want to come clean, when the contours of his secrets would push against the surface of his illusory existence. I think that was what I'd punched at the day I tied him up in silk: the deceptions. He drank expectantly, like the next round would give him the courage. Instead, the façade he'd built long ago just crumbled.

Milo continued: "It seems dear Stuart fairly re-enacted his own history as a kept boy to an English gentleman…"

"Except that I couldn't be kept…"

"…and he was no gentleman, bless him. He was an enigma in a good suit."

According to the magazine coverage of his shops, Greet arrived in New York in 1960. I looked into the context of his exile: Homosexuality between men had long been outlawed in England. It wasn't decriminalized until well after he'd left, in 1967, under Prime Minister Harold Wilson, part of a raft of liberal social reforms few British observers had seen coming. Unearthing these long-buried secrets softened my take on him. I'd lashed out against what I didn't even know were his lifelong deceptions, but now found that I could recover the good of our relationship. He loved me, in his flawed way. He provided me with a guided tour of European art and design, and through it, had imparted his refined sensibility, his admiration for exquisite craft, his impeccable eye for color. He'd shared his deepest passions with me, vague though his transmissions sometimes were through the haze of alcohol. It's a queer legacy entangled in damage.

The lawyer handling his estate called to notify me that I was a beneficiary and to schedule a meeting. Greet had told me this many times—and had even shown me his latest will—but I never trusted him. Greg and I ran into each other in the lobby of the lawyer's midtown office building, each of us in black turtlenecks and sunglasses.

"Couldn't figure out what to wear either, huh?" I asked.

"I think he would have approved of our understated widow looks…"

Up in the lawyer's office, the executor reviewed the appraisal of the contents of his apartment. "Some of the items are not true antiques, but have merely decorative value," he said, looking up from the document. I was sure his eyes lingered on me as he rolled into the phrase "merely decorative value." *Of course*. The lawyer's bright-eyed children smiled at us from silver-framed photos, a reminder that this was a rite normally reserved for blood relatives. I was a gay cat burglar pulling off a heist in broad daylight. Greg and I enacted a solemn kabuki of mourning. We agreed upon which items we each wanted to keep and which to sell. Greet had left each us half of what remained of his fortune. He'd burned through a lot of it but there was still a good chunk left. His family in England—surviving next of kin was a young cousin in Cornwall—had been cut out entirely. There was some uncertainty as to whether she'd contest it, but she signed whatever she had to sign.

THIS GAY MONEY, I told myself, as a shield from the lawyer's disapproving glances and the unseen family's claims. Greet's death felt less abstract in that high-rise office space than it had standing before his sallow body shrinking into the hospital bed; there was an established process, and there were witnesses. The apartment and the unwanted items sold quickly and the proceeds were split between us. His death was a relief to me and everyone else in his orbit, and whatever sadness we felt sprung from this stark fact.

After a return visit to the lawyer's office, walking to the bank with a six figure check in hand, I startled a passing Madison Avenue matron fresh from a salon visit by blurting out: "My sugar daddy's dead and I'm free."

6. VOLUNTARY DEPARTURES

Each time we don't say what we wanna say, we're dying.
-Yoko Ono, "Yes, I'm a Witch," 1974

I was whooping about being free but in full turmoil the day I walked out of the lawyer's office with that fat inheritance check. The decorator's death had flooded me with the relief of finally being out from under his relentless, objectifying gaze; but like a Gorgon's, that gaze had already hardened me. I'd been dependent on his money and his adulation for most of my adult life and now he was irretrievably gone. Had I squandered my twenties by his side? What direction would my life had taken had I kept on Broadway, had we never met on Fifth Avenue, or had I not seen him again after our first night out? Though it was never easy, I could have said *no* to Andrés that one time. I had to admit that I missed the decorator's soft oppression, at least its comforts. More unsettling was the sense that I did not know how to live in my unscrutinized body.

Putting that sum into my bank account should have brought me security; instead I was terrified that I'd squander it all and humiliate myself. I had the presence of mind to seek professional advice. In line with my notion that it was gay money, I contacted the city's one openly gay financial planning firm. They sent a blandly handsome Midwesterner with all the right credentials. I sensed that his deadpan professionalism masked a core greed, so I next interviewed the firm's only lesbian, figuring that a woman would have to be better and tougher to thrive in personal finance. She read between the lines of my story: "I recommend moving half of your funds into a ten-year annuity." It didn't promise the highest returns, but it was an investment that I wouldn't be able to touch without penalties for a decade. The rest would be mine to spend how I wanted.

The decorator had been absolutely disdainful of design magazines; his business was driven largely by reputation. That meant there were no photos of the projects I'd worked on. The only proof that I'd done actual work was a scant few process drawings. I hit a roadblock when I reached out to photograph our last big project retroactively; The client was facing legal scrutiny for his high-volume trading practices. "Sorry, the last thing I need right now is any kind of attention on this place," he said of his lavish, art-filled residence. My attempts to salvage the twelve years under the decorator failed, compounding the feeling of having been stuck in a dead end. I may as well have spent those years doing nothing else but drinking and shopping.

Word of mouth and cachet may have worked with his old-money and aspirant clientele, but it left me out. Greg had taken care to document the projects to which he'd contributed. I remembered him offhandedly asking, as we were sorting through the late decorator's possessions: "You don't mind if I keep his address book, do you?" I'd shrugged. Now he stood to add the decorator's clients to his already established practice. On the other side of his death, my past under his gaze felt almost completely untethered to the world beyond, no footprints, no evidence, nothing more tangible than the cone-shaped trap of his fixation.

Though I didn't want to follow the decorator into his profession, I was determined to prove that my time under him was not wasted. I dreamt up the idea to design, build, and operate a photo studio; it was the best I could do to envision a future out from under his influence. I was advised from all corners to think through it carefully, to seek out a partner, and to write up a full business plan with projections. I had no prior experience running a business, and zero in this field, but the money I not long before had feared went to my head, giving me the confidence, however false, that I could do anything. After all, I'd gotten an old man to leave me half his fortune. I got part of the way through the business plan before jumping in, signing a commercial lease on a loft in the DUMBO section of Brooklyn, at the foot of the Brooklyn Bridge. It was in a former manufacturing complex known as the Gair buildings, named for the Scottish industrialist credited with the invention of cereal boxes. I latched on to this bright and shiny new thing, desperately invested in it coming to define me: I'd be a kept boy no more. There were parallels to the decorator's reinvention after coming to New York, but to my mythical thinking, they were blotted out because I wasn't running away, like he had: it was a homecoming.

The loft had spectacular views of the bridge, New York Harbor, the downtown skyline, and Miss Liberty. Seeing the Twin Towers from the windows sealed the deal for me; They'd been a beacon since childhood. On clear days, the tower's beveled corners would catch the light and shine so brightly that we could make them out on the distant horizon from miles away, where my family spent summers on the beach. As a disaffected boy growing up on Long Island, those gleaming chamfers beckoned to me. I claimed them as navigational markers. Now they'd be a talisman for my impetuous business decision.

An emotional attachment to a skyscraper was no substitute for sound thinking. By the time I signed that lease, I had a daily pot habit. At first, I smoked just to be able to tolerate sitting at the decorator's table, but by the time the inheritance hit my bank account, I was a roached-out stoner, still scoring nickel bags from the bodega, but instead of every weekend it was every day. It eased the worry about squandering the money, but also left me too baked for boring details like cash flow or financial projections.

When I wasn't planning my reinvention, I was despairing over the whole mess with Machito. At dinner with my friend Josh, a contractor who was fabricating some casework for the loft, and his new girlfriend, a designer from Vancouver, I poured out the whole story. I couldn't keep it to myself any more. When Josh said, "Dude, just bring him back through Canada," like it was the most obvious solution in the world, I was thrown into more despair: *He just doesn't get it.* Josh persisted: "She can put you in touch with some people…" His girlfriend was evasive with details but assured me that they could help. We'd have to meet up with them in remote British Colombia. "They will show you the path," she said, smiling. My skepticism about my friend's flip comment slowly turned to hopefulness.

Machito was back living with his middle-class family in Maracaibo, an oil-producing Caribbean port in western Venezuela. At eighteen, he'd moved to Caracas for school. Like Atila, his best friend growing up who was also gay, he'd come to New York to escape his country's oppressive homophobia. They'd both risked arrest, humiliation, and endangerment from the police for cruising in the Parque Los Caobos, not far from the Caracas Hilton, where Machito used to work. *"Tengo mucho vergüenza, sabes…"* he told me about his unexpected return on one of our weekly calls: "I'm so ashamed." Whatever part I had in his being stranded, I felt compelled to fix it.

I called him with the good news and walked him through the logistics of our next travel adventure: "Ok good, so first we have to figure out how to get you into Canada without passing through US airspace…" We landed on an expensive but surprisingly uncomplicated solution: Machito would first fly to London, visit with an aunt who had married a British man, and then from there fly to Montréal. That's where we would meet, and after a few days, we would fly across Canada. My inheritance would finance this wild scheme: Machito's new passport, without the incriminating stamp from US Customs, all the airfare, my travel to Canada, the rental car, and more. I convinced myself that this was some valiant form of activism. You could not tell me that there was a better use of the decorator's money than breaking US immigration law in the name of gay love.

After his visit with his aunt in England had come to a close, I headed to Montréal on Amtrak, meditating on the vastness of Lake Champlain as the train chugged northward. Machito's flight had landed by the time I got to Dorval Airport; we nearly ran into each other on a crowded concourse. Once we recognized each other after a year of separation, the black pools of his eyes flooded with tears. We embraced, and I started crying too, which made me worry about attracting attention, but no one seemed to notice or care about our reunion. I bought tickets to Vancouver right at the Air Canada counter, and we spent a long weekend in Montréal dancing in gay clubs and fucking, both amazed and elated that the plan had worked so far. Our raucous reunion weekend over, we boarded our flight; after a couple of days touring around Vancouver,

I rented a car and drove us on the Trans-Canada highway to meet my friend's girlfriend's mysterious friends.

Our rendezvous point was a clearing at the head of a trail. They were three—all sons of US-born Vietnam-era draft evaders and Canadian women. Their friendly, laid-back manner put me at ease, though they did not offer their names. They were basically white Rastafarians, these strapping guys who kept their blond hair in dreadlocks and grew marijuana in the woods. I offered to take them out to dinner and they gratefully accepted. Due to their fathers—who had never been granted amnesty—they were themselves stateless in the view of the US. Over vegetarian burritos, we took each other in across the gulf of our differences, knowing that we had this one thing in common: the eye of the state upon us at the border. They'd figured out how to sneak across—to visit relatives, but also to conduct business.

After dinner, the time came for our instructions: "Machito, you're going to walk through this dry river bed. No flashlight, there's plenty of moonlight," one of them explained. It was a half-moon at most. "You walk about three miles, until the river goes under a road. That's where you hide, in the drainage ditch." Machito was shaking. Another gave me my directions: "You drive through this checkpoint, then go a mile or so down the road. You'll see a guard rail on your left…that's where you pick him up." I quietly freaked out at the prospect of dealing with another US border agent. Then the third said to Machito: "Oh! And if you see a bear, just ignore him."

With this, Machito started crying, and threw himself into my arms. "I can no ignore bear, we no have bear in Sud America," he wailed. I tried to be strong: "You can do this. Just follow the river. I'll be waiting for you." Then the guy who mentioned the bear said, "You guys seem really stressed–wanna smoke a joint?" We all smoked together, their potent strain ritually bonding us, and we mellowed out to the point where Machito and I were actually laughing about our situation—until the paranoia kicked in, and then we worried about forgetting our instructions.

At sunset, we dropped Machito off at the trailhead. I had to push him down the trail to get him walking. I drove to the checkpoint; the border agent asked me routine questions. It seemed to be going fine until she noticed some stray pot seeds in the ashtray. *This is what I get for getting involved with stateless drug runners*, I thought to myself, panicking, although the seeds were entirely mine, from a bag I'd scored in Vancouver. She had me step out of the car, and went through absolutely everything looking for contraband. Of the two big suitcases in the trunk—one mine and the other Machito's—she asked, "Why do you have so many clothes?" I played the gay card: "I just never know what to pack," I replied, throwing up my hands. To my amazement that actually seemed to work, and she waved me on with head-shaking disapproval. As the checkpoint got further away in the rear view mirror, I heaved a sigh of relief.

It was a clear night; trees swayed in the breeze. I slowed to a stop as I came upon the culvert our guides had described. I heard a rustle as Machito popped his head up from behind the guard rail; his scared eyes reflecting the headlights as he scrambled to the car. "Did you see a bear?" I asked. "No, I run all the way," he replied breathlessly. His heart was racing, his jeans soggy; that river bed wasn't all that dry. "You did it!" I cried as we hugged awkwardly in the bucket seats of the rental. The relief that flooded through me was measured; we still needed to make it to Seattle.

Our guides had given Machito someone's Canadian driver's license, but it was hardly a match: a fair-haired guy with an Irish last name. "There's no way anyone would believe this is you," I said. Machito hesitated and checked his appearance in the visor mirror. He seemed to be trying to style his closely cropped, tight black curls to match this Irish kid, but it was futile. After staring at the driver's license, he relented: "It's true." I was eager to get moving, conspicuous as we were in rural Washington State: a gay New Yorker and a brown man with fake ID.

We were tearing through this hamlet outside of Spokane when we got pulled over by a police cruiser. I quickly handed Machito a ball cap and said, "Pull this down over your face and pretend you're sleeping." An impossibly good-looking officer approached the car: black hair, blue eyes, broad chest, broad smile. He looked like a superhero and seemed mainly interested in small talk.

"Oh, you're from New York?" he asked as he checked my license. "I've always wanted to go...What brings you out here?"

"We're on vacation," I replied, adding, "just doing some hiking." This wasn't entirely untrue.

I held it together against his superhero charms, while Machito shuddered under the ball cap, tears tracking down his cheek. I started running through what the charges against me would be: *Harboring a fugitive? Human trafficking?* My heart thumped audibly in my chest as I tried to keep smiling at this hot cop fantasy figure standing outside the car door. Amazingly, he didn't seem to notice my nerves or Machito's trembling. After some more friendly chitchat, he said, "Well, you *were* speeding, but I didn't have my radar gun on, so you're free to go," and flashed a thousand-watt smile.

Tweaked on relief and adrenaline, I drove cautiously through the night to Seattle, where we were to be put up by my friend Gwen. She had recently relocated there from New York after a break-up. "You're our Harriet Tubman!" I cried as we group hugged—fairly cringe, but my relief was real. Machito and I slept long hours in her guest room, hung out in coffee bars, and smoked lots of weed with her Seattle lesbian riot grrrl clique. Walking around the diverse, crunchy, queer Capitol Hill area, we felt safe and free together for the first time since that fateful day with the mean mom-lady at Miami International. After bestowing our gratitude upon Gwen and her friends, we took a return flight, with a layover in Houston.

When we got back to New York, we had some celebratory dinners with a mixed group of my friends, Machito's friend, and his former co-workers at Caffe dell'Artista, a West Village hangout also owned by his former boss, Stella, an Argentinean restauranteur. These were joyous nights, filled with good food, wine, smoke, live tango music, and occasional drag performances by Tenté, a beloved queen from the Canary Islands. Mostly everyone knew not to ask too many questions about Machito's unexpected return. When the celebrations subsided, he learned that he wouldn't be able to go back to his old job as he'd hoped. Stella was already going through some immigration issues with her employees: "I can't take you back, *cariño*, not after you got deported. It's too hot right now…" Technically, the United States government did not consider Machito to have been deported. They called what he had been through a "voluntary departure." He was not given any choice, but Immigration did bill him for the flight from Miami to Caracas. The technicality didn't much matter; in the eyes of everyone in the know, he'd effectively been deported. Still out of status, it was harder for him to find work than before; there was increasing scrutiny on the gray labor market. As he struggled with this changed reality, I was stumbling through my days overseeing the loft build-out. At home, I'd get stoned and morosely trace the spiral of his journey on a world map. His stopping points formed a jagged spiral around New York: Caracas > London > Montreal > Vancouver > Seattle > Houston.

Once the business opened, Machito took on the role of Operations Manager. He was capable, but his English was still fairly incomprehensible. It was like he talked with a mouth full of marbles. His visit to England had strangely made it worse; he'd picked up an affected lilt from his aunt that made no sense in Brooklyn. Clients who interacted with him would sometimes look to me after he finished saying something for a translation. His old friend Atila, who was proficient in English, once said to me, "Honey, it's not just English, I can barely understand him in Spanish…it's his thick tongue." I didn't sweat it at first, but after a few confused interactions with high-profile prospects, I started to think I'd make another emotional decision.

The loft had some initial success: landing a booking with the renowned fashion photographer Peter Lindbergh and another with the creative director Fabien Baron on a shoot for the Italian luxury brand Bottega Veneta. These were figures of the highest status in the status-obsessed arena of fashion photography, and it was validating; my vision of the loft business was working. I'd heard so many naysayers: "The good photographers will *never* travel to Brooklyn," but sensed that those Manhattan-centric attitudes were shifting. A seasoned operator told me, "You're getting the newcomer's bump," and warned me that there may follow a slump.

After the initial glow wore off, it was more work than I'd imagined to keep the operation running day-to-day. The parts of the business plan I'd blown off were now painfully apparent: cash flow, overhead, payroll. I'd sometimes draw parallels between the way I ran my business and the way the decorator had run his but this was pretty uncomfortable to think about, a dread that despite my resistance, I'd been shaped by him in unknowable ways. The main problem as I chose to see it was that all the pot-smoking had left me unmotivated. I needed to do something if I was going to make it work.

Machito knew another Venezuelan with a supply of "excellent" cocaine. I bought an ounce and broke it down to sell, a little criminal sideline to prop up my start-up. I don't even know who I thought I was, some sort of low-level Guido Don? "This shit is very pure, you only need a little at a time," I'd warn my buyers when they came around for their eighths—advice I was not taking myself. I'd do a line in the morning as if it were coffee, and bump throughout the day. I told myself I was doing it correctly because I wasn't chasing a high so much as using it for work. In my mind, I was taking after the Venezuelans, who knew how to moderate. For all the rationalizing, I craved the burn in my nostrils and savored the drip like nectar. I congratulated myself on my finesse and the drug's purity. I couldn't see it at the time, but cocaine had become my business plan.

Running an event was a long night of work. Sometimes there was a shoot going on during the day, and we had to remind the clients that there was a hard out due to an event booking. This often led to a crisis, since photo shoots typically ran late. The event load-ins of rentals and liquor would start, and then the turnover and set-up for the event would happen just as the photo crew was leaving. Vendors would arrive—the caterer, the florist, the deejay, the waitstaff—each with their own needs. Guests would arrive, the event would take place and go late into the night before we'd turn on the overhead lights for load-outs and clean-up. It was exciting and I was in charge, everything I'd hoped for when I opened. My new business supplied me with not just a new identity, but also a storeroom full of leftover liquor that I could hit at the end of the night to take that coke edge off, a perk I felt I deserved.

I had a contract for an art department project—to make up a couple of simple upholstered benches for a photo shoot—and was scrambling to get it done in time. I did a mess of coke and worked through the night. The project was done, barely on time, but I was completely frazzled. The client's disapproving glances burned into me; I knew he'd never hire me again. Despite this clear sign, I kept cycling between stoner lassitude and cocaine-fueled manic bursts. Now that all constraints had been removed, the addiction I'd nurtured at the decorator's side was unleashed. I drank because it had been part of the job; I started getting stoned when I could no longer stand that job, and I'd checked out on heroin for a brief euphoric period. Years of drinking at crossed purposes had led to getting high just to show up for my drinking job, and that had now brought me to getting higher on the pretext of working. The decorator had cycled between booze and benzos; my cycles were cannabis and cocaine. I was still drinking too, but in my mind, it somehow didn't count because it was mostly out of leftover bottles.

As the business skittered along, my drug-taking became more routine. I had a fortress of justifications for my coke use; one rampart was that I needed more than Machito because of my bigger size—he was 5'-8" to my 6'-2". I didn't even stop to enjoy it; I thought of it almost as an office supply, like the coffee for the espresso machine on the kitchen counter or the shiny marketing materials I had designed myself. How much of the "product" we were snorting up was our secret, or so I thought. Today I'm pretty sure the people around us back then would say, "Oh, gurl, we knew…"

Things between me and Machito fell apart before long. Once the celebrations were over, we found that we didn't really know each other all that well; the biggest thing we'd shared was being separated at Miami International. We were constantly bickering; he faced the strain of coming back to an unwelcoming city and my lingering resentment over his role in the whole mess. The fighting really erupted when we started working together on top of living together. Making it worse, our escalating drug use put us both through patterns of payback bitchiness. Outwardly, we were happy to be reunited, but when we were alone, we locked in dysfunction. Beneath it all, I think we just reminded each other of our respective trauma.

Machito agreed to go to a couple's counselor at the Gay & Lesbian Community Center in the West Village. I looked forward to having a captive audience to talk about everything I'd been through with the decorator. I'd already ended it with Machito, but he was in denial. I thought that by bringing in a third party I could make him understand. During our sessions, I'd normally talk over him, outlining how he was to blame for our problems. The counselor—a handsome, friendly gay man—would normally listen to my grievances with forbearance, but during a recent session, he'd cut off my complaining: "Ugh, when are you two going to stop enacting this tired stereotype of a drug-addicted gay couple?" I was momentarily gooped, but resumed bullying Machito soon after.

At our next session I was struck dumb. My neural network was so fried from all the coke that I couldn't form words. The counselor took note of my misfiring synapses. It was almost a year after the decorator's death, and I found myself in full neurotic despair. I'd just turned thirty-four. Though long a lapsed Catholic— at thirteen, I'd walked out of Catechism class and vowed never to return—I couldn't help but note that I'd just made it past my Jesus year. Despite my drive towards self-destruction, I found that I wasn't dead, just really fucking impaired. I couldn't count on myself or my dwindling inheritance for answers.

The counselor asked, "What are you feeling right now?" After a pause, I answered, "I feel alone." Without missing a beat, he replied, "Go to an Alcoholics Anonymous meeting right after this session. There's one starting soon at the clubhouse on Perry Street." I just stared at him with my mouth open as humiliation washed over me. I knew he was right, that I was an addict and needed help, but I was so deeply embarrassed that he had figured it out before me. I'd prided myself on being smarter than everyone and here was proof that I wasn't. At least this was a form of acceptance; I did what he said. Machito went home, and I walked over to Perry Street in the rain.

It was raining hard. By the time I got to the clubhouse it was already full, so I wound up standing in the vestibule. The crowded space was suffused with the odor of damp wool coats, and I could barely make out the speaker's voice, so I had to listen intently. This would be my first lesson from the program, since I was never a sincere listener. Before that night, when someone was trying to tell me something, I'd be calculating what my answer should be while they were talking instead of really listening to them. This tendency to tune out was exacerbated when I was with decorator, whose words I could not trust. Dumbstruck, mouth hanging open, I was able to listen, possibly for the first time in years.

That session with the counselor would mark my bottom, and I was desperate enough to hear him. Over the next nine months or so, I detoxed off of the coke, pot, and alcohol that by then made up daily habits while sitting in the East Village meeting of AA, still mute, often fidgety. The room had metal folding chairs that were painted beige, and during the course of my detox, I picked out one and methodically peeled all the paint off of it, stripping it to bare metal until my fingertips were raw. I was slowly being stripped bare, too.

In that room, I found a group of fellow travelers who were also getting sober. They were there waiting for me once the drugs were out of my system and I could accept their embrace. I stuck with them and with AA, and have had what was wished for me many times: "a long, slow recovery." Some changes came quickly; aside from being willing to listen, my ego was immediately deflated. One night at a post-meeting meal at the Tiffany Diner, an older queen said to me, "Honey, suggestions are free—except for the ones you don't take. Those you have to pay for," and that lodged in my head. Being put on a pedestal by the decorator had been ruinous to any sense of humility. I went for program's secular notion of a higher power as being an ineffable something I did not need to name or describe, only accept that it was not me. I eventually came to use the ">" symbol as a kind of shorthand for my faith. This went a long way towards ending my self-centeredness.

Other changes took years, like building trusting relationships. The damages incurred being the object of a delusional, alcohol-fueled romantic obsession dissipated in half-lives, like radioactive isotopes. It's taken me at least as much time to recover the dozen years I spent in his wobbly orbit and work through those alcohol-soaked resentments. Looking down on a lovelorn drunk had diminished my compassion, while living under a chintz-lined canopy of deceit had eroded my trust; I had to reconnect with these capacities. Though I hadn't known at the time what I was being deceived about, I'd sensed the contours of the deception and lived in a state of active suspicion. Sitting opposite an obvious alcoholic/addict had made my own drug and alcohol use seem amateur by comparison. Then there's nothing like spending your formative years as an ultimately fatal lust object to harden the heart.

Milo's revelations were important to my recovery of that lost dozen years. The letter he'd set me after the decorator's death, in which he'd explained that he'd had to keep him at a distance for the sake of his sobriety, hinted at the secrets which had poisoned our relationship. It was newly resonant. Without knowing that I'd been raging against buried deceptions, Milo had taken the initiative to seek me out and tell me the truth in plain terms, which had finally brought me some closure. Milo was my first real contact with the principles of our recovery program.

Once I sobered up it was hard not to see the parallels between my relationship with Machito and the decorator's relationship with me. There was the power/finance imbalance: He was rich and established while I was a student; I had citizenship and money that Machito did not. I'd taken him on trips—one with a far worse outcome than being abandoned in a villa. Apparently, I'd sought out a relationship in which I could re-enact the power dynamics of what I'd been through, either as a way of processing or simply because I didn't have any other template. This was what the decorator had done with me: as a young man, he'd been in a relationship with a wealthy older man. He'd kept this history from me while keeping me—I only learned of it from Milo after his death. *Is this what I want to carry forth? Patterns of gay exploitation?*

These were the broken boundaries of selves which ultimately separated us. I'd gotten sober and he had not; we'd spent a lot of our time together as two drug-seeking individuals pooling our resources. I'd fallen in love with how his bullish demeanor belied a fiery tenderness, but as cocaine fed our resentments, I saw little but hostility and recrimination in his eyes. I'd shifted all the blame onto him and wouldn't recognize my part in our dark spiral until years later.

Our pairing may have brief and fraught, but his not-deportation and our crossing the 49th Parallel has trauma-bonded us for life. It was the most consequential journey of either of our lives—and one we could hardly talk about. In the years since, I was compelled to write out our story, first as nonfiction and later in as a short story—a protective fiction—but it had to stay secret. It might have burned the path or triggered the scrutiny of the post-9/11, reactionary, militarized Immigration and Customs Enforcement agency. Even with name changes and misdirecting details, I didn't want to risk subjecting anyone to a fucking ICE raid.

Our three guides at the border were children of Canada and the US who'd first been estranged from one homeland because their fathers did not want to fight in a senseless war. Thereafter they'd been pushed further underground for cultivating marijuana. Machito had been kicked out of the country for working in a service industry job, and only got caught for trying to keep in touch with his sister. In spite of our volatile conflicts, I probably would have married him—but gay marriage wouldn't come to Massachusetts for another six years, and wouldn't go national until 2015. We may have been hapless fuck-ups but Machito just wanted to work and live freely as a gay person while maintaining family bonds, and I just wanted to help him do all that. Yet our actions were crimes against the state.

Once Machito spiraled into New York he was safe but out of status. He landed like a shipwreck on my shores. In the ensuing years as he's pursued a fix, the antagonism between the United States and Venezuela has deepened. There's been a steep decline in the Venezuelan people's safety and security, resulting in a global diaspora. Machito—though greatly relieved to have made it back here—has been unable to return home, even for a visit. He'd faced federal detention at Krome and the disruption of the voluntary departure process, only to helplessly witness the dissolution of his country and the endangerment of his family from afar. Venezuelans were once buoyed by affluence from oil exports but of late the country has devolved into an isolated, corrupt, violent, crisis state.

Machito was stateless in a city with no direct flights home. I was living a few miles from where I was born, carrying my own isolation and helplessness. Compounding this, I counted myself among the causes of his isolation, if not the US government's immigration and foreign policies. In a narcissistic spasm, I'd loaded his tangible estrangement onto my own intangible sense. Machito had lost his freedom to travel freely while I suffered in my autonomy. After the decorator's death, I'd been cut off from the social realm in which I'd once moved and alienated from my own free body. I'd come back from my own voluntary departure only to surrender to despair.

7. GUIDO STUD FOR HIRE

Experience: OK...*Dominick is the real deal. I was looking for an aggressive top...and boy did I find one! Dominick is an Italian Stallion dream cum true. He says he's 35, and I think that's about right. If you are looking for a boy, he is not for you. He showed up on time, looking awesome, and ready to go. I'm not going to go into great detail, but I will tell you that this guy will rock your world. As nice or as aggressive as you want him to be, he totally tuned into my needs and delivered. He kisses like a man, fucks like an animal, and then treats you like a human being when it's over. A rare combination of nasty and nice...and did I mention a cock that is to die for! I only hope he will save a little time for me after this review is posted. Treat him well guys, there aren't a lot like him out there...*

- Hooboys Reviews, 2004

In the decorator's final weeks, I'd watched his body sink into a hospital bed and fail from the effects of alcohol and prescriptions. Less than a year later I myself had bottomed out on bodega weed, New York's purest cocaine, and leftover bottles. Walking beside such a large figure who was so obviously and publicly an alcoholic pulled the attention away from my own growing addiction. After all those years of adoration and privilege I was more than a little brought down by the realization that I was an addict/alcoholic like him. *Behold his legacy.* We just liked different drugs.

After detoxing in the rooms of AA and finding my sober circle, I threw myself into the loft business, booking fashion shoots, television and film productions, and corporate events. I picked up creative work, too, collaborating with photographers, art directing shoots, landing film and television work, and graphic design projects, all handled on my new Bondi blue iMac. I art directed a (low-budget and chaotic) feature comedy helmed by a SNL alum, produced a fashion show, and even produced a compilation album of down-tempo tracks. I faced those maddening freelancer struggles to be compensated fairly and on time, and nagging doubts that I was compromising my creativity, but enjoyed most projects, stayed sober through it all, and scraped out a living. The loft was fulfilling that hazy dream of boundless creative work, one I once thought lost. I accepted the long hours, erratic pay, and some dubious assignments as part of the cost of redeeming my creative life after having it hobbled under the decorator.

I had help: a sober photographer friend partnered with me on many of the bookings, and though we'd broken up, Machito was still on board. He focused on the logistics of turning the space over for each new booking while I stepped forward to handle prospects. Our lingering resentments would occasionally flare up in hostilities, but we were better off having our own lanes. I'd also entered into a new relationship: John was a tall, striking, mixed-race guy a few years younger than me with a goofy streak that belied his soulfulness. We'd found each other in different corners of the East Village scene, bonded over a shared love of Blondie, and developed real intimacy in his nest of an apartment. At least that was how I'd seen it. On many nights I'd slept in the dressing room of the loft, but as the space got busier, I spent more nights with him.

That's where I woke up one late summer morning in 2001 to unusual noises filtering through the rear window: overlapping radio and television newscasts at full volume, people yelling. John turned on his tiny television set and we watched the replayed footage of the first plane hitting the tower; then the coverage cut to the live feed of the second plane. Thinking of how many people worked in those towers, I felt sickened, and suddenly very unsafe in John's small walk-up, just a couple of miles from the attacks we were watching on television: *They wouldn't target the East Village, would they?* I'd only recently started to feel a real part of the neighborhood, and now we were possibly under some grave threat. John and I looked at each other, unsure of what to do, until he said, "We should go donate blood."

"I thought they don't want *our* blood?" I asked, referring to the ban on gay male donors.

"I don't think they'll care about that today…"

By the time we made it across town to St. Vincent's Hospital there was a line of hundreds of like-minded New Yorkers. After a few hours, they started to sort us by blood type. As news filtered through of the buildings' collapses, word traveled down the line that the hospital didn't really need any more blood: "There's no one to save."

Once the phone lines were open, John got a call from his estranged half-sister. She'd been at work in a downtown office building when the planes hit and debris started crashing down. As the assigned safety marshal of her floor, she'd led her coworkers out onto the street, zig-zagging uptown to avoid the bombs they were convinced were falling. They'd run as far as the Corner Bistro on West Fourth Street, where we joined them. Their dust covered-figures filled the bar. They sat shell-shocked, getting steadily drunk, watching the news, piecing it all together.

A few days later I made my way back to Brooklyn. There was no subway service, so I biked. Canal Street—normally of cacophony of commerce and culture—was a police checkpoint. All of Southern Manhattan was a restricted area. In the face of this uneasy development, I showed my business card to prove that I wasn't some ghoulish curiosity-seeker. As I cycled across the Manhattan Bridge, I was struck with a dreadful certainty that the Brooklyn Bridge, visible to my right, would be targeted too, probably while I was over the river. I was a wreck by the time I got to DUMBO and broke down in tears on Washington Street. One of my neighbors found me and helped me into the building. I stumbled through an excuse for my breakdown, but he just held me and said, "You don't have to explain…"

Standing at the loft's windows, we stared in silence at a brownish line in the sky, the smoke trail from Ground Zero carried across the East River by prevailing winds. My friend Dean Johnson, who lived in Carroll Gardens, later told me: "All of this World Trade Center debris dropped from the sky onto my street: computer printouts, letters on company stationery, business cards…"

The creative work that had been coming through my door dried up entirely. A location scout told me: "Productions have fled the city. They can't get insurance, and anyway it's just too sad…" We'd recently started booking more events at the space; now I wondered if anyone would ever want to look out those windows again. I drew the curtains closed and they stayed closed for a while.

What followed was wholly unexpected. Post-9/11 human interest stories ran about a surge of marriages; it may have been more of a media angle than factual, but the loft was suddenly in high demand for wedding receptions. The all-white space—its industrial edges softened by flowing curtains—was large enough for parties of about one hundred. The evening view was still cinematic: traffic twinkling as it crossed the bridge, the illuminated skyline, the tranquil East River. The absence of the Twin Towers was somehow more bearable by night. Those weddings kept me afloat, and it was genuinely touching to host intimate celebrations in the aftermath.

Having somehow fallen backwards into the role of wedding planner, I soon learned it was a fraught, high-stakes enterprise to which people sometimes brought emotional baggage. A couple of years in, I was closing out one such reception when the bride's mother—who had paid for the whole event in cash—burst through the doors, shoes in hand, angrily demanding her pocketbook. As we turned the place upside down, I overheard her mutter to her son, in Spanish, "I'm sure one of those faggots took it," referring to the catering crew. I threw her and her son out. She called the police. Seeing how drunk and hostile she was, I was furious at how they deferred to her, until one of them pulled me aside and explained: "She's a 9/11 widow…" It turned out that a relative had her bag the whole damn time, but the damage was done. She'd solidified a looming suspicion that market forces under disaster capitalism had conspired to pigeonhole me into performing a gay stereotype. Engaged couples had pounced on the space after 9/11 had driven away the film and photo clients. The business I'd started on that dream of boundless creative work had come to this.

Not long after that mess, the condo boom forced me out of the loft; the building was slated for a luxury residential conversion. Soon after that, W's recession brought my freelance work to a standstill; then John kicked me out. I'd entered the relationship openly, an effort to counteract my toxic past with the decorator and a step forward from my recklessness with Machito. Though he wasn't typically prone to drama, John was apparently fed up with the long hours my business demanded, among other complaints: "You're too emotionally unavailable." My sincere reply—"This is as available as I get…"—didn't go over too well. He knew something of my history with the decorator, but couldn't appreciate the damage it had done to my capacity for intimacy; I didn't fully appreciate it myself. In a shouty scene, he shredded my clothes, including some of the decorator's silk ties, and threw them down the stairs, along with a collection of mid-century glass. Homeless and on the street after cascading losses, I picked through the scraps and shards and took over a cheap sublet around the corner from a food blogger.

I was thirty-nine. I was alone, unemployed, and facing a rent bill along with the outstanding SBA loan that had carried over from my now-closed business. I may not have deserved being thrown out but on some level respected the finality of it. My nascent sobriety hadn't sheltered me from what I look up now as an emotional and financial bottoming out; at the time, I'd almost welcomed it coming all at once. I had a few low-dollar freelance gigs lined up, but not nearly enough to live on. I hadn't burned through my inheritance entirely, but that big chunk in the annuity was still years out of reach. Having been my own boss for the last five years, I was unaccustomed to supervision, so working for someone else seemed implausible. I needed a fresh start.

Like a lurker of my former life, I'd moved just a few blocks away from my now-ex. I didn't want my messy history figuring into how I handled this break-up. I tried playing the grown-up: sober, accepting my part, avoiding melodrama. That said, I couldn't help but seek passive revenge on him by getting buff. I quickly stripped off those relationship pounds running around Tompkins Square Park and waiting my turn at the pull-up bar with the local chulos. Dinners on those late nights at the loft had consisted of fat-laden hors d'oeuvres and leftover wedding cake. Now I was cooking my own meals with produce from the Union Square Greenmarket. I'd handle this break-up without any fights, defensive posturing, or character assassination; I'd say goodbye with a bicep flex and a big smile.

Soon after moving in to the sublet, I realized that one of my less tech-savvy neighbors had an unprotected Wi-Fi signal, so I was online for free. I'd held on to my America Online account from the days of dial-up and my iMac from the loft. AOL was still in its glory days, having recently merged in a news-making deal with Time-Warner. There were hundreds of user-created chat rooms, and at least a dozen specifically for gay men in New York City: for chatting, for dating, for out-of-towners, for hooking up, for hooking up NOW, an S&M 'dungeon,' for bisexual guys, for masseurs, and at least three rooms for escorts, coyly called "Companions." The vibe was so evident snarky users had started calling the platform "gAyOL." It gave that upbeat announcement by an anonymous vocal actor a new inflection: *Welcome, you've got mail (male?).*

I posted photos of my newly buff body and was getting a good amount of play in the chat rooms. I set out to take on the neighborhood one Internet-mediated conquest at a time. Through the dense web of NSA ("no strings attached") hook-ups, fuck buddies, and romances, it seemed that just about every guy in the chat rooms was one degree of separation from the next, a sexual ecosystem I now wanted in on. Word would get back to my ex, no doubt.

'HornyUWS' was a guy I'd encountered in the chat rooms, one who I'd passed on mostly because he lived uptown. He was more persistent than most: After dozens of chats in which he'd attempted to arrange a meeting, he sent a last-ditch message: 'R U $ure?' Given my circumstances, it was easy to agree. I assumed it would be a one-off. No one need know; after all, he lived on the Upper West Side, a universe away. I hadn't had a reason to go back uptown for years. His insistence was flattering and validating in light of my recent break-up. *This john was willing to pay for what that other John had kicked out.*

I took the subway uptown and met the guy, who I found pleasant and by no means unattractive: a solidly built, middle-aged antiques dealer with a dog, a lover, and a house in New Hope. He definitely lived up to his handle: He'd kept his old apartment after moving into his lover's' larger place and called it his *garçonnière*.

"I'm the top in our relationship, but every once in a while I want to, you know, flip the script…" he confessed.

"Ok and your partner?"

"Oh, he can't be bothered..."

After getting to it, I could understand his partner's reluctance. It was a real chore—he was super hairy and had a tendency to tense up completely at the first hint of penetration, but I persevered, like a trailblazer through dense jungle, and got it done. HornyUWS was thrilled. I didn't really know what the going rate was, so when he asked, "How much do I owe you?" I stammered. He emptied his wallet—just over two hundred dollars—and said, "Here, you deserve this, you're better than those other guys..." For a half hour sexual encounter I might have had voluntarily had the winds been blowing differently, I had cash for the week. Andrés' glib comment on the crosstown bus after our first date with the decorator—*You just turned your first trick*—echoed back at me. This time, instead of confusion, it landed with the thrill of new possibilities. I headed home with a stack of twenties and a new business plan.

HornyUWS was hooked and dangled the prospect of regular income: "I have a big crush on you. Can we meet next week?" He liked that I wasn't an escort per se and took some odd pride in having turned me out. He related his agency in my first by-the-hour transaction to his work as an antiquarian: He'd recognized the value in something before anyone else did and brought it to market. He'd been dissatisfied with most of the working boys he'd hired before. Other than one guy who lived out of state and traveled only infrequently to New York, none had ever satisfactorily topped him, or so he claimed. "The local boys just won't go that extra mile..." was how he'd put it. He assured me that I could thrive as an escort if I wanted to.

Could escorting really be the road forward? Signs pointed the way. That pirated wireless connection gave me access to the bustling chat rooms. There were even days when I'd have to slam my way in, holding down the return key for repeated entry attempts upon receiving the message: 'The room you have requested is full. Please try again later.' That these rooms were hosted by the user-friendly platform of AOL provided me a cheap, low profile, corporate-approved forum to test the waters right from the shelter of my sublet. My newly buff body brought me lots of sexual attention, and after years in a mostly monogamous relationship, I was feeling mighty unconstrained. The little villain inside of me loved the idea that it would be the ultimate rebuke of my ex: *Emotionally unavailable, you say?*

I'd lived the kept boy fantasy, nights of drunken sexual performances with the decorator. I was still wresting myself from the harms of his deceptions: his stilted pose as a British aristocrat, his romantic obsession for me which had recapitulated his own unexamined personal history. Even after he'd worn down my resistance his sexual demands on me had been limited both by his impotence and his germ phobia. Since he'd paid me to be in a relationship, I once considered by-the-hour sex work beneath me. My situation with him had pedigree, or at least that's what I'd told myself: older, accomplished men had provided patronage to attractive youths since the days of Plato, as Isobel once framed it. Since his death, my sex life had been my own—at least that fraction of it I'd managed to recover. The prospect of putting it back in currency was daunting on one level, but it also held out the promise of clear terms, terms I might prefer to the unstable realms of love and romance.

My time as a kept boy was a closed chapter. I'd fallen out of touch with everyone I'd known through him, except for Andrés, who had gotten into a supportive housing apartment in an Art Deco building in Gramercy Park run by the Quakers and had turned it into a chic artist's atelier. Witnessing him battle opportunistic infections and surfing from one clinical trial to the next following his 1986 AIDS diagnosis felt like a lifetime ago. He'd gotten on a regular course of meds, his health had stabilized, and he was thriving. He was still really good at working the system, still painting, and still traveling extensively.

I was even estranged from the decorator's possessions. I'd lived with them for a while, but had lost or destroyed some through carelessness, or some other underlying motive: a mirror smashed by a falling stage set, a group of Mughal-era portraits left unsecured and stolen. The last of his money was out of reach, and the remaining loot wound up in a storage unit in Brooklyn when the loft shut down. There were few visible traces of that twelve-year period of my life. I hadn't ventured into any of his haunts, or even uptown, in years.

I was also sober, which had not been the case those drunken nights of falling into his bed. I'd been in recovery for about four years; I'd enter this new experience clear-eyed and fully present, not groping at reality through a haze. I felt—or at least hoped—that I had a strong enough foundation in recovery to step into this world and not be tempted by alcohol or drugs. The apartment I'd sublet was minimally furnished, on a quiet block, in a small building, and on the second floor. It seemed ideal for in-calls.

One lingering doubt was my age. At thirty-nine, I was at least ten years older than most of the escorts I'd seen in the chat rooms, although a few listed their ages in the thirties. From my experience with HornyU-WS, I gleaned that my maturity could be an asset: "Too many boys out here trying to do a man's job..." he'd once said to me. He tended to lay on the praise.

I set up a screen name: 'BiMuscItalPackn.' With this, my first shot at marketing, I was transmitting a somewhat mythical sexual persona, one I thought I could fulfill, at least for an hour or two. *Bi* was for bisexual; though at that point in my life, I was only having sex with men. I'd been sexually active with women into my twenties, a bit of a stretch, but permissible license by most marketing standards. It telegraphed to prospects that I did not present as overtly gay. It would also bring me occasional requests from women and male/female couples.

Musc was for Muscular. Many of the escorts and porn stars were really buff. They had thin waists, ripped abs, massive pecs, and huge guns. Some overbuilt the chests and torsos, but paid scant attention to the lower body, resulting in a top-heavy, rooster-like effect. Many of the headless bodies I was seeing in profile photos were only possible through the use of steroids. I cultivated a more natural physique, and kept a little extra padding. My paradigm was the build of a construction worker, a man who uses his muscles on the job, eats heartily, and maybe throws back a few after work.

Ital was for Italian. I developed a baseline identity, a bisexual Italian guy from either Brooklyn or Long Island. The customers, locals and tourists alike, ate it up. I modeled my speech on blue-collar types, mechanics who drive in early from Long Island in their vans and go from one job to the next, men who fixed things, men who had the right tools for the job. It wasn't so much that I put on an accent; I just summoned the speech patterns of my hometown, which I'd spent years trying to erase. I thought of myself as one of these laborers, a fixer, a technician, a mechanic, or maybe even a utility worker on the night shift. The decorator had been an Italophile, so sexualizing my heritage was familiar ground. He'd projected his fantasy of a dissolute Italian prince upon me, but for escorting, I went for more of a blue-collar persona.

I refused to conform to the then-prevalent notions of male body hair grooming, the trimming, the shaving, the waxing. I personally found it very unsexy, even infantilizing at times. It was one area in my relationship with the decorator where I'd always defied his wishes; he'd have been a lot more comfortable around my body had I cleared the forest. In that suite at the Ritz in Paris my body hair had acted like filaments of armor against his gaze. With escorting, I had an intuition that I'd have a better shot with a little counter-programming in this department. There'd be no manscaping for me. I kept my chest hairy, held on to the thick stand of pubes, and even the fuzzy patch on my lower back. It tracked with the ethnic identity I was selling, too.

Packn, for 'packing,' had developed as chat shorthand for well-hung. The decorator had been enthralled with my cock, but I'd since come to realize that his reaction was not that unusual. There were qualities most gay men and tricks alike valued: length, girth, hardness. I'd soon learn from another escort that there was little tolerance for exaggeration when it came to representing size. Over a late-night phone call, he talked me through the established way to measure length (from the root to the tip) and girth (the thickest part of the shaft, not the head), and emphasized that if I didn't represent myself accurately, it would lead to disappointment: 'They're all experts, able to size you up like that…' he said, snapping his fingers.

I christened myself 'Dominick.' The name had an odd history in my family. It was my father's given name but he'd always been called by his middle name. He was born during World War II while my grandfather was away fighting the fascists in Italy. I once asked my father about it: "My mother was pregnant with me when my dad shipped off. He'd insisted that his first-born son be named after his father, Domenico, but she didn't want me to have such an ethnic name. When he came back from the war, everyone was calling me by my middle name. He was furious." Since my dad wasn't using it I figured I would. Sometimes I'd worry that I'd face a reckoning with the ancestors about it, but I'd reason: *Pimping out our heritage is the American way. When we're not assimilating by effacing our identity, we're enlisting ethnic caricatures as sales mascots.* This was a pretty flip take on my Italian-American identity, but it felt like an antidote to the decorator's fetishization.

The name 'Dominick' certainly sounded Italian, but it also suggested dominance, an inflection that would come to serve me well as an escort. The persona I developed was that of a dominant, verbal top, without veering into leather or S&M. Identification with those scenes wouldn't have jibed with my blue-collar, 'bisexual' persona. I posted an AOL profile:

> Name: Dominick
> Gender: Male
> Location: NYC
> Marital Status: available for yr pleasure.
> Hobbies & Interests: top MAN. Hung & hard. ALWAYS ready. Shoot big & FAR.
> Favorite Gadgets: bi, tall, worked out, natural, masc hairy bod.
> Occupation: Outcalls to all boros, NNJ, LI
> Personal Quote: what you crave

I didn't use the words 'escort' or 'for hire,' hoping that the mentions of being 'available' and doing 'outcalls' were enough of a dog whistle to guys in the know. With a personal quote filched from a White Castle commercial, this was the extent of my marketing. I sat in the 'NYCM4M Companions' chat room for nights on end. I didn't want to place ads on sites like the recently launched rentboy.com; that seemed too overt. I worried that I wouldn't get any more business; I still didn't have next month's rent. As it would turn out, this short paragraph would ultimately earn me more money than any other writing.

Men contacted me mostly via instant message (IM's), and occasionally by email. I developed a specialized style of communication, Internet shorthand I'd picked up in the chat rooms, by measures direct and obtuse. Andrés had always been the polyglot between the two of us, but this language quickly became my second tongue. The lingua franca of online sex work was a clipped, coded, computer-mediated slang:

> BuffaloBiff: Hey hot man! great profl pics? X? R U very dom? In midtown hotel here on biz, avail?

Entering these chat rooms, I'd pulled up a front seat to witness the radical transformation of sex work in the digital age. When I was with the decorator, hustlers and escorts were out in force on the streets of New York City. In Times Square, I'd seen the action in and around the Port Authority, the Gaiety Theatre, and notorious bars like Hombre. There was a stretch of Second Avenue downtown that brought out a pretty rough late-night scene, lots of junkies. There was East Fifty-Third Street, home to Rounds, the upscale bar where Andrés had first picked up the decorator, which had been shut down by the NYPD under Giuliani in 1994. Then there were the fur-draped women I'd long admired who strutted along Seventh Avenue just below Central Park.

With the popularization of Internet access, much sex work had moved off the streets and entered virtual spaces. I'd jumped into a universe of specialized sites, message forums, and chat rooms. The way seduction had become text-based brought to mind the days of scheming French courtiers and their perfumed letters portrayed in de Laclos' *Les Liaisons Dangereuses*. Chats and emails were supplemented by photos. Closing the deal, of course, remained the same, but that initial encounter, which had once taken place on the street or in a bar, had been digitized. It required certain writing skills: the ability to communicate obliquely, and to draw out desires from people who often could not name them. What Andrés had done at Rounds, what the street hustlers had done outside, had been face-to-face; now the pick-up had been reduced to abbreviated texts and emoticons. That escorting had become so text-based often made it feel like extended field research. It had become a project in written persuasion.

From the outset, I kept a diary. I was embarking on something new and possibly dangerous and thought I should chronicle my experience. Entries would describe each call, sum up my weekly earnings, and touch upon some larger theme. Reviewing the earliest entries, I was mainly interested in making my sales goal, upping my average take, and watching overhead. The first weekly goal I set for myself was $1,500. I tended to average seven calls a week. I tried to up my take by booking longer calls, but most were for an hour. What counted for overhead was travel expenses and some supplies. I filled a hip pack with condoms, lube, gum, wipes, aspirin, bandaids, mouthwash, zinc tablets, and a bag of pepitas (I'd read that the last two items were good for sperm production). I was driven to prove to myself that I could earn my living as an escort. My first ever customer had promised to be repeat business, and I quickly learned the value in cultivating regulars, guys who would re-hire me, some weekly, some monthly, some sporadically. For one thing, a regular was a known quantity, safer than opening the door to a stranger. Being able to count on regulars also meant that my income would be more predictable.

I'd advertised that I was willing to travel to the outer boroughs and the tri-state area, and lots of guys took me up on the offer. In the first week, I went to Brooklyn twice, to the Heights and Bensonhurst. The guy in Bensonhurst, who planned to bring me back for a three-way with his fireman partner, told me: "Most of the other working boys won't even come out here." I also traveled to Hackensack via train to meet "Jeff," who was so happy I'd come that he tipped me generously. From the beginning, I claimed the greater metropolitan area as my territory, relying on google maps, mass transit, and my capacity for travel logistics.

There were plenty of calls within Manhattan—uptown, downtown, hotels—but in the first weeks I went back to New Jersey (a young tweaker in a cheater's motel in Secaucus, a theater queen in his Morristown condo), back to Brooklyn (a retiree in a Park Slope townhouse), to Long Island (an elementary school principal by day, by night a depraved submissive, in a hotel in Farmingdale), and to Mamaroneck (a kinky medical resident in his attic lair). I met a gay couple in Stamford, Connecticut; the younger partner picked me up at the Metro-North station. He'd given me detailed instructions, including on my attire:

> Can you wear your jock? You have a "wife beater" shirt and tight jeans? and if you have ripped up 501's having them unbuttoned to show off pubes is even hotter...Can you wear work boots and a ball cap too?... My partner LOVES a man in a ball cap!

I also booked my first overnight, with a young submissive in upstate New York who had been vouched for by another escort. I took the Trailways bus on a two-hour ride. I worried that I might get stranded up there if it didn't work out, but it was the first of what ultimately would be many trips to Ulster County.

I also did select in-calls in my apartment and it worked out for a time. My door was one flight up at the top of the landing; the foot traffic my visitors generated differed little from that of the civilian tenants. The only real precaution I had to take was making sure my visitor wasn't allergic to cats. I'd send my cat out onto his private terrace (being the roof of an adjacent one-story building, accessible through the window) during calls. I barely knew or saw any of the upstairs neighbors. I marked my buzzer with a simple 'D,' which worked for both my names. As discreet as the apartment was, I eventually decided to keep in-calls to a minimum. I didn't want to ruin my chances of taking over the lease, and it felt too exposed. After putting in the time and effort to do six to eight calls a week, plus a strict workout routine, I needed a space, and especially a bed, that was all mine. That meant I was traveling to most calls.

If I had the leisure of an appointment scheduled in advance, I'd walk to it. Before there were bike lanes, biking around New York City meant risking life, limb, and sanity in a combative jostle for territory with drivers and pedestrians. Biking long distances got me a little too sweaty and hostile, so I mostly biked to calls downtown. Otherwise, I relied on buses, subways, or taxis. As I'd seen, some out-of-town calls required a ride on a commuter rail line: the Long Island Rail Road, Metro-North, New Jersey Transit. I could catch up on my diary entries on train rides back, just another laptop warrior returning from the field. When I couldn't get there by public transit, newly-formed car-sharing service Zipcar became my last-mile solution. Out-of-towners, who accounted for about a third of my business, were almost always happy that I'd deigned to travel to them; I got as much of a sense of power mastering the travel logistics as I did being a hired stud.

Closer to home, I was taking calls with both locals and visitors. My second ever call was someone who I'd identified in my diary only as "a Grammy winner" and "well-known entertainer." I met him at his swanky midtown hotel. Although usually terrible at recognizing famous people, I knew who he was right away but didn't let on. He'd just played a big deejaying gig. Thereafter he'd call me any time he had gigs in the city. I saw HornyUWS every week, and at some point he started bringing in other escorts. Working with other escorts—doing "double-ups"—was fairly common, and would get me through a lot of calls. I also met an accountant who went by the handle "HeadMaster" and lived in the Flatiron District. He would come to hire me dozens of times, usually providing me with a young escort to fuck while he recorded videos for his private use.

After a couple of months, I was approached by another escort, a handsome Egyptian, and met him in his West Village apartment. I was the new guy and he was sniffing me out. He suggested to me that I was riding the newcomer's bump, to be ready for slower weeks ahead; this rang familiar from my days operating the loft. He explained how prices were set: he had different rates for hourly, extra hours, and overnights. He was busy enough in Manhattan that he didn't have to travel much, but when he did, he charged: "I count travel time and round-trip transportation costs." I'd been absorbing the cost of travel. He also told me that I should lower my stated age by five years. "Everyone does it. It'll just be confusing if you don't…" He welcomed me into the fold with his deep-set brown eyes and a sadness I thought I could fuck out of him. It didn't work, but setting my age to thirty-four did, and my worries about being too old dissipated. Having given up drugs and alcohol—and my fraught, dysfunctional relationship with an alcoholic well behind me— I looked better now than I had when I was *actually* thirty-four. My libido and staying power were still going. No one ever objected to or questioned my stated age.

I'd already gleaned from the chatter in the companions rooms that escorts charged by the hour, not by the act. This was a dodge to avoid any overt criminality. The reasoning went: *I'm a paid companion, any sex which may happen is entirely consensual.* After my Egyptian colleague clued me in, I had a better feel for the whole price scheme. I settled on a rate of two hundred and fifty dollars for a one-hour call, which was pretty much standard. If you could get a client to extend, an extra hour was two hundred; a prearranged three-hour session was six hundred. A three-hour booking was usually seen as a "date" or a "boyfriend experience," starting with drinks and dinner. There were also varying rates for overnight calls and couples. I implemented this menu and went straight to work, comforted by the existence of agreed-upon terms.

The first time I went to see HeadMaster, I rang his bell at the appointed time, and over the intercom, he answered: "Oh! You're actually here..." He was so used to other escorts showing up late, when at all, that my on-time arrival surprised him. I came to understand that I was operating with an uncommon level of professionalism for a hooker. When I went on a call, I'd show up on time and freshly showered (unless otherwise requested—some guys wanted me to show up ripe). I'd heard from more than one of my new regulars that some of the younger working boys would show up late and high. *This is how I will distinguish myself in this business*, I told myself.

I faced occasionally scrutiny from my online host. AOL content moderators would sporadically shut down all the 'Companions' rooms. Some of my fellow escorts complained that their handles had been deleted as well, for TOS (terms of service) violations. I tried to rally them to enter a replacement 'Companions' room that I'd started, only to find them wary; this would be my first of many lessons to come in the frustrations of trying to organize sex workers. I worried more about AOL's erratic enforcement more than I did getting caught by the police. None of the other escorts seemed to worry much about cops, either. Warnings occasionally circulated about NYPD stings operating out of hotel rooms, but they were fairly infrequent. It seemed that the police were mostly relieved by the fact that hustlers were less visible out on their beats. Reading about what other sex workers were dealing with in media reports, it seemed that men were far less scrutinized than women or trans workers.

Because of my insecurity around my age I thought I had to try harder than the others. A younger guy I'd worked with once told me, "I'm just dabbling, you know? If I can get over on a trick I will." He clearly didn't share my careerist approach. I carried over the ethos that I'd developed in my stint as a business owner and found that many practices were applicable to my new trade. It all came down to a performance at a designated time and place. A wedding reception was by contract providing a couple with a space and an array of services, but there was also an unwritten compact for intimacy and trust. Yes, there's a throughline from wedding planner to sex worker. Making a space available for someone else was my prior gig; now I was making myself available.

A few weeks in, I was chatting with a short (5'-2") guy with a stated interest in size difference. He carried on with pulpy, descriptive messages about what he wanted me to do: "Big sexy giant, you come to my door pick me up and take me into my bedroom…Throw me on the bed and peel off your size 14 boots (not my size…) I can't wait to taste you… Maybe we can make this a regular thing." I replied in kind, while trying to steer our chat towards setting a date and time to meet. I indulged him for a while with replies in my best giant persona before really pressing him to schedule; he disappeared entirely, his profile deleted. This happened enough that I figured that this guy and others were getting off on the chat. I became wary of users with elaborate scripts. Most were time-wasters with no interest in booking, but there were exceptions, like that couple in Stamford. I accepted that dealing with time-wasters was just a cost of doing business.

In the photos I'd posted, I was wearing a jockstrap, so clients would often request that I show up to their call wearing one. On one such call in Gramercy Park, the shy older submissive who had spent most of our session worshipping my body asked, "Do you think I could buy your jock, sir?" More of these requests came in, so I ordered every style I could source, and added a back-up to my kit. Eschewing the super gay fashion brands, I stocked the wares of traditional athletic manufacturers: Duke, Bike, SafeTGard, McDavid, Wolf. It was easy enough to run this little sideline, though I didn't love it. It wasn't a sense of exploitation creeping into my sweat glands with every sale; it was just sometimes hard to part with a favorite funky jock.

After being around the decorator's large and failing body for years, I wasn't squeamish about the work. I was sober and fully present, not one to keep my eyes on the wall. I once found myself at the door of a skeletally thin man. His strange appearance—enlarged jowls, a hardened pouch, a sunken ass—was evidence of lipodistrophy and other effects of a long-term antiretroviral drug treatment. His legs were bandaged from recent surgery to fix his varicose veins. I didn't shrink. I dropped the macho strutting, put on a big smile, and told myself I was doing God's work.

A trick in Chelsea answered the door when I rang with flipper-like, partially formed arms. I assumed it was thalidomide-related but didn't ask. I was startled—he'd sent me a carefully cropped photo concealing his condition—but sucked it up and took it in stride. I silently counted my blessings, starting with my two functioning arms and hands. I pictured other escorts in my situation freaking out and leaving. He asked me very directly if he could fuck me, and I found myself impressed with his nerve. Not wanting to be seen as anything less than professional, I mounted his perfectly formed cock and rode him as I held on to his shoulders. It was the first time I bottomed on a call. I think I gave him my ass because I couldn't give him arms or hands.

I carried over some of the business practices I'd developed operating the loft. I kept an Excel spreadsheet to document my weekly income. I identified clients using a fairly elaborate color coded system of my own logic, so as not to incriminate myself should it fall into the wrong hands. My spreadsheet broke down how they had found me, tracked repeat calls, and the rate they'd paid. I used abbreviations to notate preferred sexual activity and any kinks.

Within a few months, I had a good number of regulars. Servicing regulars was like being the completely trouble-free boyfriend to a dozen or so guys at a time. There were no arguments; I'd be sure to notice a new haircut or weight loss; I'd remember to ask about their sick mom or their health condition. I was kind to their pets, and of course, I never withheld affection. Business was brisk: *I've monetized the internet*, I'd think, patting myself on the back. I netted an average of sixteen hundred dollars a week in that first year. I did the math: *Eighty grand a year in cash, that's the net equivalent of a six-figure salary.* I was on call twenty-four/seven, had no health insurance, no 401K, but it was a living. I could cover my rent, the business loan I'd carried over, a gym membership, and keep myself in fresh food and jockstraps.

Like with the decorator, when the money wasn't enough incentive to perform, I could get turned on by my own erotic hold on the client. Unlike with him, a call had a set beginning and end; once the hour was up and I had my rate, the spell would be broken and I could slip off the performative masque. Lots of other escorts worked hard to extend into a second hour, but I preferred hour-long calls for this reason: they were easily shed. It was so much less wear and tear on the psyche than being stuck in the kept boy role.

The first year I filed a tax return after being a full-time escort, I didn't claim the income, only the few legit jobs I'd done. Those jobs were my cover story: *I'm getting by on freelance event work* was my answer to anyone who asked: *What are you up to these days?* It was true enough. The actual event gigs that did come in paid less than one call for a full day of work and took at least a month to pay out. One of those gigs made me really appreciate sex work: overseeing dinner presentations for a pharmaceutical company to tout the benefits of their latest sedative. Had any of those doctors once looked up from their steak dinners they would have clocked my doomed expression. That cover story worked for as long as I needed it.

When I had my own business, whether it struggled or thrived, I paid taxes. I thought of it as the entry cost of being an entrepreneur. I had guilt pangs over not paying taxes on the thousands I made hooking until I looked upon the ineptitude of the Bush administration. I hadn't been tuned in to politics as a half-baked kept boy, but being an independent sex worker fixed that right up. I was fighting to reclaim my bodily autonomy the only way I knew how yet I was now considered an outlaw. Working in the gray/gay economy and keeping money out of their coffers lent my work an air of righteousness, at least in my head.

That first year on the job was a master class in desire since I was fairly naïve about kinks. Often as I was agreeing to do something I was googling to figure out how to. I'd learned to tie a square knot in Boy Scouts which came in handy for my first bondage scene, not counting that sorry episode with the decorator. Luckily, the client, a media executive in Tribeca with an amazing modern art collection, had soft cotton ropes. I'd come to find that they were easier to tie than nylon; he seemed happy with my amateur work. As I bound his ankles and wrists, he whispered, "You can go a little tighter," before I hogtied him and gagged his mouth.

Calls from submissives shifted my focus towards the nature of longing, how all of these forms of submission were efforts at ego reduction, and its disinhibiting effect on the sub, effacing shame and fear. Working through this while learning the ropes distracted me from my growing isolation. Escorting via Internet—like much work in the digital economy—put me alone in front of a blinking screen for long stretches. I'd be out on a call for an hour or two, interacting with a single person, in a private setting, inhabiting a role, in transaction mode.

I said yes to more and more calls for kinks and fetishes, things I'd only ever heard about, more things I had to google. A running list of the kink/fetish calls I took in the first year: foot worship (size twelve, high arches), bondage (not wanting to invest in heavy gear, I preferred to use a client's own socks, underwear and t-shirt to tie him up; but I also used ropes, handcuffs, tie-wraps, and leather cords), spanking (bare-handed, paddles, strops), tickling, watersports, domination, exhibitionism, blindfolds, leather, spandex, Speedos, wrestling gear, smothering, verbal abuse, role-play, humiliation, smoking (cigars, cigarettes), wrestling, toys, gooning (mutual edging), raunch, and fisting.

I marveled at the way the sexual drive differentiated into ever more specific desires. I had a working theory that the more complex our society, the greater the urge for such specialization. I tracked the patterns that emerged from all the requests I got, looking for correlations of geography and real estate. I could almost predict the type of call I was in for based on the address. Homeowners were generally stingier than renters. Uptown calls were usually more work. Downtown calls liked to get to know me first with a little conversation. Porn addicts with unkempt apartments and large televisions would barely register my presence. Men with opulently decorated homes expected a deep emotional connection. The suburban calls tended to be married men with fetishes.

Hotel calls gave me a buzz for the anonymity and the amenities, while seeing people's homes gave me a voyeuristic thrill. I was amazed at how many of my johns would play the Buddha Bar compilation of trippy lounge world beats. It became my soundtrack, the chords of track two triggering a Pavlovian response of cash hunger and blood flow. More patterns emerged: Long Island had more than its share of married subs, Brooklyn brownstones were home to many thrill-seeking gay couples looking to spice up their sex lives. Too many of the calls from Central Park West addresses came from a kept boy at the behest of *his* sugar daddy, triggering some rueful recollections of the decorator. A heat map of urban desire was soon imprinted on my brain. Figuring out the complex overlay of desire and real estate kept my observational mind engaged; I was back to being a researcher in the field, like I had been with the rich and aspirant on the Upper East Side.

For all the exotic requests, many of my calls had me receiving oral sex, in the trade called a "blow-and-go." I'd come over, whip it out, get sucked off to completion, get paid, and leave. I welcomed the few inquiries I received from women just for the potential to mix it up. Over three years, I went on exactly one call with a female client: an attractive older woman in Murray Hill who seemed to be working through some intimacy issues. She held her body so tightly even her skin was contracted into gooseflesh; just when she seemed to relax, she patted me on the back and whispered, "Thank you," bringing the session to an end.

I was up for just about anything short of blood, the sight of which had always made me queasy. I advertised as a top because it I found it easier, not as risky as bottoming and way less preparation. Sometimes with regulars, roles relaxed. Even though no one posed it directly to me—no one knew what I was up to—I considered a question that seemed to hang in the air around me, shaped by moralistic views of sex work: *How could you sell your body?* Wheeling into a second call on a busy Friday night, my bills paid, my pocket padded with cash, my refrigerator stocked, I formulated my answer: "Eh, it's more of a rental."

I got to know the city and its environs like a postal carrier knows their route. I got an extensive tour of the tri-state area's residential interiors, from Section 8 housing to elegant lofts to brownstones to split ranches to prewar classics to walkups to duplex penthouses. I left my mark in just about every hotel in Manhattan. I preferred the Carlyle for its old-world elegance, but the Pierre was a bit more discreet. There was nothing quite like a corner suite at the Plaza, but those floor-to-ceiling windows at the Mandarin Oriental were bomb. I developed a sixth sense for how to glide past security guards and reception desks in hotel lobbies.

I took the Long Island Rail Road to Farmingdale to the Hollywood Inn, a cheater's motel on Route 108 with Eighties décor. In the room with red ultrasuede walls, smoked mirrors, and black lacquer furniture, I met that married, depraved submissive. He'd been drinking beers and watching porn, but he snapped to obedient attention when I walked in. As he unpacked his sex toys—dildos, butt plugs, alligator clips—he droned on about the wearying demands of his work as an elementary school principal. When I couldn't listen to his soliloquy any more, I started verbally abusing him, pushing him around and roughly working over his ass with his toys. He groveled at my feet for a while: "I am unworthy of your presence, sir," his dialog provided by porn, then begged me to spit on him. I finished off the session by administering a piss enema.

I traveled to a business hotel in Englewood, New Jersey to meet a slender, attractive, married executive, a tickle fetishist. First he pulled a feather out of his kit, and I held him down and tickled his feet, under his arms, and his ass as he squirmed around, giggling. Then he tickled me. Next he pulled out a 2" sable paintbrush, and I worked him over with deft little strokes. Though I hadn't done anything like this before, it seemed to be going fine, until his big reveal: with a mischievous grin, he pulled out an electric toothbrush. The contraption recalled oral hygiene and dentistry—profoundly un-sexy images for me—but he was so desperately invested in it. He looked like a lost little boy with it buzzing in his hand.

A very prominent type-A attorney—short of stature, hyperactive, a real Napoleon, a guy I'd caught barking orders at his underlings over the phone—would regularly come over to my apartment early in the mornings. He'd first quietly stock my refrigerator with groceries from a list I'd emailed him. Then he would prepare coffee and gently wake me. I'd drink the coffee while he bowed his head in submission. Ignoring him, I'd go about my business as he cleaned the kitchen and the living room. After I'd showered and shaved, he'd clean up behind me in the bathroom. He'd be down on his hands and knees obsessively scrubbing the bathroom floor and I'd step on his head with my bare foot and nudge his groin a couple of times, and he'd shoot off in his pants. Bossy in his daily life, his submission to me was apparently cathartic. With that said, he was paying (in groceries) and would always find a way to assert his will—to top me from the bottom.

Franco, an Italian guy living in Stuy-Town, would invite me over to fist him. Advanced fisting bottoms liked me for my large hands and long arms. Fisting didn't really turn me on as much as I found it morbidly fascinating. In our many sessions together, we explored his physical limits and developed mutual trust. He'd take one arm nearly to the elbow, or one hand and my cock, or both my hands pressed together, like an overhead dive. Fisting sessions were physically challenging and visceral, with all the mucous and veterinary lube; it was the uncanniness of having my arm inside a pulsing, living being that kept me coming back.

I met a man from Ohio at the Marriott Marquis in Midtown. Calling himself "Bad Wet Sissy," he set up this elaborate role-play scenario in which I was the hotheaded next-door neighbor: "Is that my daughter's dress you're wearing? Did you steal it off the laundry line, you dirty little thief?" I played the part to the hilt, railing about my daughter's purity, scolding him for his perversion, punishing him for his transgression with a firm hand, forcing him into subservience. I was undaunted by the sight a middle-aged man wearing wet diapers, a pink button front-dress, and a bad wig, but the stench of stale piss nearly choked me. When the scene was over, Bad Wet Sissy quickly stripped himself down to a clean towel and wrapped it up with me in his normal speaking voice; the spell had been broken. That this happened in a room with a view of the theater district made me feel like just another show for out-of-towners.

After a year or so working hourly calls, I began getting more overnights. My first overnight had been the young submissive in Ulster County; he called me for a return visit. He picked me up from the bus station in a vintage Cadillac El Dorado, and took me back to his simple, comfortable house, where he lived with six cats. He was twenty-seven with a frat boy vibe and a country strong, doughy physique. The house had quaint country charm and a study full of Nixon memorabilia—as I walked through the rooms, it had the feel of a sitcom stage set.

We got to know each other with a little chat while he smoked a bong. He'd been living this solitary existence in the house his parents raised him in; they'd retired and moved to Florida, and he'd barely changed the décor. He boasted that he was the youngest alderman ever elected—on the Republican ticket—as "Forensic Files" played on the television. The show prompted him to tell me about his work at one of the town's two funeral homes. Adding this disclosure to his politics, the absent parents, and his blandly pleasant demeanor, I was suddenly alarmed: *I am in the house of a serial killer.* Survival mode kicked in, adrenaline rushing inside, cool demeanor outside. I was on high alert for more signals, but then he got so baked I reasoned he couldn't get away with murder.

After my shower and all those bong hits, the Undertaker's submissive side came out. He liked to be put on his knees and throat-fucked, and he liked verbal abuse: "Take that cock down your throat, you dick whore. Open wider, so I can spit in it and get it all slick for my cock. Open your throat boy. I'm gonna grab you by your neck and skull fuck you. Then I'm gonna put you on your back and grab your ankles and mount you. I'll bang out your fuck-hole with my big tool. You want that? Huh, Pussy boy? Beg me for it." He was a demanding and energetic sub, goading me into ever more dominant behavior. One of the cats came into the room and swiped at me while I fucking his human; I snuck the cat some pets, like the diligent, full-service escort of my self-image. He got back on his knees and took a facial to end the session, spilling his own seed puddle onto the carpet. In the morning, he woke up hungry for more: *He's really making me work for that overnight rate*, I thought as I fucked his face and throat again. He'd take me to a diner for country breakfast, then I'd get on the bus back to the city.

The Undertaker would call me once a month. We got to know each other some more, and despite my earlier misgivings, I found him kind and likable. His political views seemed to have evolved as we spent more time together and he started to decompartmentalize his existence: living a public life in a small town, dwelling in the realm of the aged, dying, and dead, and being a bossy slut bottom. Or maybe not: he's since run for Mayor, still on the Republican ticket. When I was seeing him, much of his days were spent driving around his somewhat depressed hometown in his vintage Caddy waiting for calls that someone else has kicked off, a country grim reaper. Despite his politics, I came to feel compassion for his need for a vigorous, life-affirming fuck every now and then.

There were bad calls. I got an IM from a certain MuscleJuicer, a bodybuilder escort who'd proposed we work together. He had a two-to-three hour call on the Lower East Side. The john, Revolutions, was willing to pay a lot of money for a gang bang. We set up an appointment. I got to the building and it was an assisted-living facility for the disabled. The guy had told me that I would need to bring ID but I'd forgotten, so I ran back. When I returned, Revolutions told me that MuscleJuicer was running late. I didn't see any money on the table, but seduced by the possibility that I might see some big bucks and get to work with Muscle-Juicer, I stayed.

Revolutions, a heavyset man, was an advanced fisting bottom. He was doing lines of coke and even having me put coke in his ass. This should have been a red flag to me—along with the fact that he was living in public housing—but my morbid fascination kicked in. As we were getting into it, Revolutions explained, "I like you to turn your hand around inside...that's where I get my screen name...." *Okay, whatever, butt puppet...*

The time came for me to end the call. I'd been there way too long already, and MuscleJuicer was a total no-show. According to Revolutions, he'd texted to say he'd been in a taxi accident. I still hadn't seen any money, and started thinking that MuscleJuicer was actually Revolutions and he'd catfished me. I said, "If you want to see me get off, you need to come up with some cash." He anxiously pulled together a stack of bills. I counted the stack; it had couple of twenties with some fives and singles underneath.
"Where's the rest?"
"I have to go to the ATM for it." I quickly gathered up his wallet and his coke.
"Let's go."
As we walked to the bank it became obvious that I wouldn't get any more than the $75 or so in the stack.
"It won't dispense cash for some reason."
"Could the reason be you're on public assistance and don't have any?"
I began to walk out, his wallet and his coke still in my hand. Strung-out and cornered, he started after me and sprayed mace in my direction. I ran down the street as my eyes grew red and irritated, swelling so much I could barely see. I spitefully threw his coke vials down

the sewer and ran all the way home. This guy had my information—I'd signed in at the building—but I had all of his ID, and the camera at the ATM likely had some interesting footage. When I got home, I called him.

"I'll exchange your wallet for an apology, my pay, and an admission that you lied to me about Musclejuicer." He refused.

"Fine, I'm going to turn your wallet in to the police. You figure it out from there."

"Wait please! I'm sorry." I hung up and brought the wallet to the local precinct, having taken whatever cash was in it and left in its stead a card printed with the twelve steps of AA. He called while I was in the precinct. I thanked the officer and dashed. Once home, I expected this whole sorry episode to be over.

My phone rang; it was the police, requesting my address.

"I don't want to give that out."

"I understand, " she replied. I thought I detected a note of falseness in her tone. I wondered what Revolutions had told them; I'd counted on him not talking, or being low on credibility, owing to the fact that he was strung out on coke. I decided to get the hell out of my apartment, thinking the police might be able to find me. I showered, dressed, and hastily prepared for work the next day; I had booked a freelance event gig.

A squad car was idling in front of the building. In a panic, I ran to the back garden, and jumped the fence to the adjoining property. Adrenalin coursed and I scrambled to my employer's car, which luckily I'd parked on that block. Once in the car, relief flooded in. It was 3:00 AM and the freelance event gig—at the Meadowlands Arena—started at 7:00 AM, so I went to get a bite at Florent. It was open, and always had a comforting air, and it wasn't far from where I'd have to pick up my boss. Luckily, Andy Butler, a very cute guy I knew (who would go on to a fabulous musical career with Hercules and Love Affair) was working the overnight shift. I laid out the whole sordid mess to him over eggs and boudin noir, relieved to have someone I could process with.

I laid low for a couple of days after I finished that gig, and didn't hear back from the police or Revolutions. I did get a message from MuscleJuicer, who was mad at me for "robbing his client." Fictional or not, his whole set of excuses was so improbable that I blocked him. Soon enough, I was back at work, faking my way through a call for an erotic massage.

After a year or so, I picked up a new semi-regular: Arnaud, a trim, forty-something Belgian with a pied-à-terre in Chelsea. He was strictly a bottom and made no bones about it. He had impeccable hygiene, was polite, and tipped well, too: a dream client. I genuinely enjoyed fucking Arnaud; he would pulse his ass on my cock, which felt amazing. I speculated it was some Old World practice he'd picked up in a dark alley in Brussels, but that didn't make much sense. Once I complimented Arnaud on this ability and he replied: "Ahh, this is thanks to Kegel exercises." I looked them up once I got home. Named for a gynecologist from California who'd developed a protocol for "educating" the muscles of the pelvic floor, the exercises were designed for women, but are beneficial to men. For me, I found that after a few weeks of training, I had a stronger erection, an ability to pulse my cock while fucking—which my clients *loved*—and even more impressive money shots than when I was in my twenties. I went out into the world for another season of hustling with my well-conditioned cremaster muscle.

In year two, the list of kinks and fetishes I would figure out on the job expanded to include cuckolding (two different married couples, both from New Jersey), scat, double penetration, and sploshing. For all of those outlandish calls, there were also guys who wanted nothing more than a jacking scene, like naughty schoolboys, and guys who were most turned on by frottage, or non-penetrative sexual rubbing ("sword play"), or intercrural (between the thighs). I found these low-stakes calls comforting—as did the clients, it seemed. The only category I'd learned to avoid was the foot fetishists, only because I found most of them to be cheap. Those who contacted me gave various reasons why my rate should be lower for them:

"I would really only be renting your feet…"

"Foot worship isn't really sex."

"I won't even take off my clothes."

That cornerstone of escorting—that we charged by the hour, not by the act—was somehow lost on these guys. It pushed my constant, low-grade feeling of being objectified towards a gruesome limit the way they fixated on a body part.

I learned about a new fetish from two married men, which involved their consenting wives. The first was staying at the Renaissance Hotel near Newark Airport. When he asked me about "a cuckold scene," I quickly hit google and bluffed my way through his questions. Much of the available porn depicting cuckolding I found was racialized; the alpha was a Black man, the couple white. I texted Dick, a tall, lanky, dark-skinned actor/escort with a picked-out afro and a ten-inch cock, what he knew about it. "I get a lot of inquiries, but not too many calls…but, yea, they're out there, white men who get off on watching a hung Black dude fuck their wives. The wives are into it too." The man at the Renaissance watched from the corner as I fucked his wife while quietly touching himself. She put on a noisy show for him. Going in, I was focused on how versatile a professional this call would make me. For such a tame scene, I didn't expect to feel so diminished afterwards, being the rented buck for the eyes of a straight man.

The second call for a cuckolding scene was an elaborate role-play scenario in which I played a thief breaking into the couple's home (I made sure to get the wife's consent). I followed the husband's instructions and entered the house through the open garage door. We performed a struggle while his wife looked on, and I wound up tying him to the banister, gagging him with a handkerchief, and fucking his wife on the floor just a few feet away from him. All the while, his wife yelled at him: "You useless piece of shit, he's fucking me," and "His cock is so much bigger than yours…" When it was done—the wife whispered in my ear, "Okay, that's good…"—I waved my cock in his face and taunted him with its size, and even made him smell his wife's pussy on it. Once his wife removed the gag, he begged forgiveness for not protecting her, and whimpered about his weakness, how she was "ruined," how he would never satisfy her again. She answered: "Just shut up and finish me off," and then mounted him. Having serviced a married couple as completely as in my wedding planner days, I ducked into the kitchen and had a Fresca while watching *Inside Edition* on the small set.

One Upper West Side trick wanted nothing more than for me to throw pizza, burgers, and pie at his naked obesity, whereupon he would pick at the mess and devour it. For all the visceral kink calls I'd done, this "sploshing" scene was my least favorite; I was repulsed by mingled fast food smells and the waste.

It was not all extreme or repulsive. There was a young marketing associate, just out of college, who would come over on his lunch breaks, with a sandwich in a paper bag, so I could break in his virgin ass. He was nervous and shy, and professed to having no experience with gay sex, but had willed himself into taking this step. I undressed him and he was a sight to behold: a lean, beautiful, nearly hairless body, like a Greek kouros. He had close-cropped hair and a halo of innocence that made horns sprout from my forehead. I made some gentle advances on him in an attempt to put him at ease, but his rare and fine beauty made me feel like a clumsy brute. He was determined to get fucked but had the tightest little ass this side of adulthood. I asked "Are you sure you want to do this? My goods are not exactly a starter set…" I thought I might get a laugh, but he was resolute. He came back to me over three lunch breaks; each time he lasted a little longer, but always with a resolute grimace. Our last session happened one night in December when he called me after his company's holiday party, a little tipsy. He finally broke free and allowed himself to enjoy the sex. As we lay in a sweaty heap, I said, "You just graduated," with a hint of pride. It turned out to be true; I never saw him again.

There were moments when I surprised myself with my fortitude: As I looked up into the smoked mirrors of the room at the Hollywood Inn, I watched myself squat over that married elementary school principal. While he spun himself into some fusion of ecstasy and revulsion, yelling, "Give me that treasure," I pushed out a firm dump on his chest. He reveled in its weight and its warmth, and inhaled its dense odor until he puked. The porn fantasy apparently did not match the reality. I stared at my reflection, in awe of both how far my limits had stretched and how quickly, and what he was willing to pay for.

Although we were all very much lone wolves, if not by temperament than by habit, I did develop a real camaraderie with some of my fellow escorts—and a friendly rivalry with others. I bonded with several over our shared experience. On such guy was the late Arpad Miklos, who had been recruited from his native Hungary to be a porn star. A client I had seen before, a prominent agent/producer from Los Angeles, asked me to arrange for a double-up. I asked him what he was looking for, and he answered, "Someone as hot as you." I'd heard that Arpad had recently started escorting, so I contacted him. The client immediately agreed; he seemed to know his work. We convened at the client's duplex suite at the City Club Hotel. Sitting in the living room for a flirty chat, he was immediately charmed by Arpad's Hungarian accent and dry humor, and so was I.

We took the client upstairs to bed. Arpad, well-formed in every respect, was my same height; his muscular body pulsed with true athleticism. I almost lost myself in his ruggedly handsome face, his devilish grin. His rock-hard, torpedo shaped cock was meticulously formed, as if lathed from steel. The client was in such a happy place he was practically levitating. We bookended him, and he exclaimed, "It's like being in bed with twins!" This was terribly flattering; Arpad and I might have fit the same police description, but he was in every aspect the bigger stud. His carried his sinewy build like he was born to it; I was one of those skinny kids who'd reluctantly hit the gym. Arpad's body hair shaded his muscled frame in soft, inviting clouds; mine was patchy and rangy. His cock was a precision instrument, mine a blunt club.

Arpad and I put the client through every position we could think of; we played with each other, too, making out and stroking each other's cocks. As we got into sixty-nine, the client got thrown off the bed; he stood up to admire us from above. *This is one tough gig*, I thought, as he looked upon us wide-eyed. When he wasn't looking, Arpad would make silly faces at me, trying to get me to laugh. It was charming, but was also a subtle assertion of his dominance.

The evening wound down; Arpad tallied up. We've been there for just over three hours, and his rate was three hundred an hour. I tend to round down a bit, discounting time spent chatting, but for Arpad, the meter was running. The client was little stunned, but went to the safe. He had just enough to cover Arpad's fee, so he quietly asked me if we could meet tomorrow, and I agreed. Escort rules will tell you that this is never a good idea, but I trusted him, knowing the situation. The following afternoon, I met him in Union Square Park, and he handed me an envelope: "I don't feel right giving you any less than I gave Arpad…" The envelope contained twelve hundred dollars, way more than I expected. He thanked me profusely for making his unspoken fantasy come true as we reviewed the night; on that park bench, we were both fans of the spectacular Arpad Miklos.

Weeks later Arpad called me, and I walked over to his apartment off Tompkins Square for some off-hours, recreational sex. This was the usual arrangement when another escort brought you in on a call, kind of an informal commission system. He was playful and charming as before. He told me about how busy he'd been, flying around the country for regular overnights. He told me about his advanced degree in chemistry, and a little about his family in Hungary. I got the impression that much of his income went to supporting them. When we were sucking each others' cocks for the client, it was more of a performance; alone together and off the clock, we fed each other's hunger. He wasn't the public, Alpha top version of Arpad, he was a man with desires and longings, not just an object of longing and desire. For one night at the City Club Hotel, I'd measured up to this monument of a man; that gray afternoon, we simply comforted each other. When it was all said and done, ever mindful of the difference in our hourly rates, he deadpanned: "Okay, now you owe me fifty dollars."

Just like I'd done with the decorator's stipend, I got into the habit of stashing ten percent of each take. Now it went into a shoebox hidden under my platform bed. I thought of that money as an emergency fund in case I had to stop working for any reason. Nothing really interrupted my work once I started except for a single case of gonorrhea, which kept me home for a week. That would turn out to be the one time in three years I had to stop working. Another escort gave me a stash of Zithromax so I could treat another case at the first signs of symptoms. I added it to my call kit but never needed it.

In New York City, rates of HIV infection and illness were on a decline while I was working. Still, my practices were risky; I hadn't kept to the plan to always use condoms and only top for very long. Many of my regulars wanted me to fuck them raw. I did what needed to be done and got myself tested regularly with newly available rapid tests; that was the best I could do. My inner dialog with HIV was fueled by multiple delusions. There were nights of righteous indignation: *I'm not a vector of disease, I'm a vector of love!* There were nights I told myself that the Norman invaders reputedly in my dad's lineage had made me immune. There were mornings when I was convinced that the trace of blood I'd been in contact with on that last call had finally gotten me.

After topping and dominating for years, I myself yearned to "flip the script," as my first regular had put it, off-hours. I sensed that some other top-only escorts—like the handsome Egyptian who had guided me through my early days—had the same syndrome, because more than a few wanted me to fuck them. With some, we'd start conversations about taking turns fucking each other, but often our schedules were impossible to sync up. Because I'd been performing at a professional level, any old slacker wouldn't do. I wanted a rock-hard ass master to dick me down. I wanted all the punishing I'd given out back in one single fuck. Ass masters being hard to come by was why I was pulling the equivalent of a six-figure salary. So I resigned myself to renting out my sex life, inhabiting the role I'd advertised, and relishing those rare occasions when the stars aligned. In the meantime, I sat on my own hunger while doing Kegel exercises.

•

By the end of my stint as a sex worker, I'd paid off that outstanding SBA loan. My shoebox stash, transferred to a bank, totaled $24,000. I'd never managed to save much when I was collecting the decorator's regular stipend and haven't since. How I'd managed be so disciplined in sex work when I'd never before shown a capacity for discipline, especially around money, is a mystery. That stash went toward the down payment on a run-down place in Cherry Grove with Tony, a member of my sober East Village circle, on the easternmost walk in the Grove. We described the location as "Meat Rack-adjacent." We rebuilt the interior by hand and rewarded our hard work with decadent summers in the dunes. Tony had earned a share of his down payment with a stint in porn; we came to refer to it as the house that sex work built.

The decorator had enveloped me in a world of wealth and privilege. I had memorable moments with him: flying the Concorde, a gastronomic tour of the south of France, being measured for custom suits, the summer in a rented villa on the Amalfi Coast, jewelry shopping in Paris. I longed to be my own man, whatever that could mean. I hadn't done too much deep self-reflection while immersed in sex work. Even when it had an emotional component, I thought of it as physical labor and focused on the condition of my body. It found it a respite. When I did look back upon my years of architecture school, design work, and creative projects and wonder how it had all culminated in sex work, I could not solely blame the decorator for poisoning my engagement with the field of design. The best I could do was square it with my studies of urbanism: As I practiced it, hustling was a kind of field research in urban desire, while renovating the house in the Grove gave me a hands-on outlet for my years of design training.

Sex work also gave me another creative practice: writing. When I look back upon any writing I'd done prior to my hustler diary, whether it was my incoherent graduate thesis or sketchbook marginalia, it comes off as littered with pretensions. It tracked with my prior inability to listen when others were talking: I was unable to listen to myself, and was instead writing what I thought people would want. I attribute my inauthentic pose when writing to the gay shame that shadowed me well into my thirties. If I couldn't accept who I was, I'd write myself into *some* acceptable identity. My words rang false because they were self-deceptions. My sex work diary was the first honest writing I'd ever done and would prove foundational to all of my creative output to this day. Our creativity is mutable and persists.

My foray into sex work in the protective space of AOL's walled garden (now dismantled) occurred at something of a golden moment. The way I had to duck AOL's moderators seems quaint in contrast to today's conflict between corporate control and individual expression. I've watched many of the freedoms I enjoyed in the early Naughts be taken away from today's users, mainly around the passage of SESTA/FOSTA in 2018. The law was supposed to facilitate the prosecution of child sex-trafficking rings but instead has endangered consenting adult sex workers by shutting down their trusted platforms while collaterally curtailing all user's free speech. Every time another friend gets suspended for a mild or artistic depiction of nudity on Instagram, I shake my head at how a moral panic organized around the avatar of a helpless, exploited child has had such chilling effects.

Being a full-time escort was a spellbound, underground period. Off a pirated signal I conjured up an income out of pixels. The work was about as glamorous as a plumber's but it was mine. It spun out of me and left a web of desire. It was a decent living (or an indecent one if you prefer) in which I conducted myself ethically. I can think of far more dishonest and hurtful things people did for money in the Naughts; my own freelance gig hustling pain meds to doctors, for example. As an escort, I offered satisfaction of longings, pleasure, intimate touch. I provided value.

For all my emotional detachment, I sought to instill my work with a sincere measure of love, and this helped to redeem that capacity after my fraught time with the decorator. Our relationship had not been wholly devoid of love, but it was too hard to be loving through the deception and the impairments, his and mine alike. I practiced love on my clients—and I needed the practice, after all those years with a man at the bottom of a crystal tumbler. I loved them for their strange and specific longings, I loved figuring them out when they couldn't, I loved them for inviting me into their homes, I loved them for their libidos, I loved their hotel rooms.

It has taken me longer to reclaim my sexuality from the effects of the decorator's obsession. One night with my tribe in AA, I launched into a qualification, going over my past with him. I called him "my sponsor in alcoholism," as I had many times before, which was good for a laugh. Over the years, I'd sensed that when I used those handed-down terms "sugar daddy" and "kept boy" to describe the relationship, my listeners would shut down. Even with this thoughtful group, those terms were too loaded. At this meeting, I put it another way, the way I'd seen him when I had him tied to a chair: *He was my colonizer.* The room shuddered. I remember first thinking this when I'd tied him up and punched him, but it was something else to profess it to a roomful of people. I'd named the dynamic and could start to reclaim my borders after a half-life of confusion.

Those delicate miniature portraits from the Mughal era—painted on elephant tusk sections—now watch over me in my apartment, among a few remaining artifacts from my past life with the decorator. It's no wonder they'd attracted his imperialist eye; the Mughal princes had been supplanted as rulers of the subcontinent by degrees. The armed, seafaring British Empire colonized India, a vastly larger state, first by establishing trading posts, then entering defensive agreements with local rulers, and finally with the incursions of a corporate apparatus, the East India Company. British historians often use the term "cooperation" to describe the Empire's success, while their Indian counterparts are more apt to describe the strategy as "coercion." The decorator was my East India Company, I was his coopted/coerced local prince, and my body the exploited laborer beneath us both. Hustling represented my return to home rule.

During their twenties, my peers blossomed sexually, whether through hook-ups or romances. They were figuring out what they liked, exploring kink, and getting practice, while I was reporting uptown and turning my body over to the decorator's fixated impotence. I'd been ensnared in his Romantic ideal of a brooding Italian male for too long. Hustling was the only way I could find to dislodge it. After Andrés compared me to the black-curled youths of Caravaggio, I'd sought out his works and those of his followers. I most identified with Guido Reni's depiction of Sebastian: hanging by his bound wrists, glancing towards the sky as arrows pierce his luscious body. Sebastian might have been an avatar for my kept boy reality, the arrows the decorator's obsessive gaze, but as a hustler I caught arrows in my hand. In my twenties, I'd ransomed my sexuality for cash payments; in my back-dated thirties, I set my own terms and took back agency over my unimpaired body. In prevalent depictions from pop culture, sex work is a cautionary tale or a dark chapter from which one must heal or seek redemption, but not for this hustler. Sex work *was* my healing and my only redemption.

8. R U AVAILABLE?

Money can't buy you love, but the rest is negotiable. —Dean Johnson's slogan for rentboy.com

I had a sole confidante for the years I was a full-time escort: Dean Johnson. Everyone else heard the cover story. We'd become friends after a single back-room encounter at the Cock, the notoriously frisky bar run by Mario Diaz which for years defied Giuliani's moralistic assaults on queer nightlife. As we sized each other up like competing alphas, sniffing, grunting, throwing looks in the dark, eyes in the room shifted towards us, and our sex became more performance than passion. He was an exhibitionist, on that night with me and for the rest of his days, and I'd played along.

Afterwards, he proposed that we go to Odessa for a late-night meal. The Ukrainian diner was a regular hangout for the cool crowd, who affectionately called it "slow-death-a." I was flattered. On our way out, he turned to me, his deep and resonant voice that would rise into camp flirtation carrying over the bar noise, and said: "I have a feeling we will make better friends than lovers." And so it would be.

In the back room, he'd appeared to me as a tall, pale figure with a massive cock; I only realized who he was on our way out when his face caught some light. That's when I saw both stars and red flags. I'd seen him around downtown for years, a drag queen and party king with his own band. He hosted "Foxy," on Saturday nights at the Cock, where I'd watched as guests competed for prizes by doing outlandish things for the stage show. As we slid into the booth at Odessa, he asked me my birth date, and when I told him, answered, "Oh, another gemini, I knew it. We could *never* be lovers." Whether he was protecting himself from possible rejection or truly believed it, I went along.

The decorator's ashes were still at the bottom of Greg's closet the night I met Dean. I'd moved into the city in 1982 to attend Cooper Union, and by the time I found my way into East Village nightlife, Dean was already a New York landmark, like a tall tower or a tourist attraction. Seeing him go-go dancing on top of the bar at the Pyramid in his signature look—bald head, a cocktail dress short enough to display his endless legs, big sunglasses, drop earrings—was hot, confusing, and transgressive in a way I wasn't even ready for. He'd waved me through indifferently at Boybar when he worked their door. He vaguely recalled having seen me around: "I was probably on dope, but I remember your eyes." I felt a step more connected to those stolen nights: *I really was there, there's a witness, however unreliable.*

After one boozy Tuesday night with the decorator, I'd ditched my uptown clothes and stumbled down to Avenue C. Dean was holding court out by a nightclub entrance. Once inside the dark, hazy space, I came across an irregular hole in a wall. I was that deep drunk I'd get over hours by the decorator's side and the club's vibe was already otherworldly, but stepping over a pile of bricks through the hole to find a raw space with a swaying chandelier felt like entering another dimension. Only later did I learn that I was at the World for Dean's notorious 'Rock n'Roll Fag Bar' party, and they had in fact broken through the party wall into the adjoining abandoned building, outlaw style.

I later attended a screening of the film *Mondo New York* in which he appeared with his first band, the Weenies. I found the film's wide-eyed, sensationalist framing of New York's underground scene tiresome freak-gawking, but Dean's incendiary performance of the song "Fuck You" woke me right up. His appearance in the film had led to a deal with Island Records, immediately followed by a run-in with the music industry's homophobia that he was still railing against years later when I met him. It was the open wound that drove his work and I got behind his righteous crusade. The success he craved would be a victory for all of us.

I was newly sober when we met; Dean wanted to get sober, so I tried to support him. Ultimately AA was the one club he could not get into. Despite the program's warnings about avoiding people that might lead to relapse, I allied myself with him. My sobriety was one boundary Dean fully respected. We really bonded out in Cherry Grove, Fire Island, during a summer that Mario Diaz, the owner of the Cock, had rented a house and threw raucous parties for his circle. Dean and I shared a love for naked bodysurfing. I'd cheer him on as he caught waves; he would stiffen his long body into a surfboard and rocket into shore, scraping his bald head on the sand.

I followed Dean to his next party, at a former massage parlor on the Lower East Side called Happy Endings; it was equal parts dancing and sleazy antics. One night I had a spontaneous three-way with a couple in one of the bathrooms; I locked the door to keep anyone else out. When we emerged from the bathroom, Dean told me that the NYPD had just raided the place: "They came in, turned on all the lights, and made everyone just stand there while they searched for illegal activity…" I looked around to find the party getting back to full swing. "They just left," he said. "Well, they didn't find us," I replied, and we laughed over the NYPD's incompetence. We both despised Mayor Giuliani for his moralistic crusade against nightlife. He'd send the cops to crack down on venues without cabaret licenses where any dancing took place and Dean's venues were prime targets.

I would later work door for Dean at the Hole, a dive bar on Second Avenue; as his "drop," he entrusted me with thousands in cash. For the first time I felt truly a part of the scene, not just a bystander. The Hole was a narrow space and his parties would get so packed that the naked, viagra-popping go-go dancers could hardly swing around without hitting someone in the eye. Guests who'd make their way to the basement would find an active dark room reeking of empty beer kegs, sweat, ass, and cum. "I can't believe I'm getting away with this," he once said to me on an especially raunchy night there. I earned my cut as I watched him admiringly, raking in cash while pushing boundaries; but what really awed me about him was that his public spectacle of a life was wholly in service to his art.

I went with him to CBGB for a meeting with Hilly Krystal, the owner, to pitch his idea to host a night of queer music. In all my years hanging out in the East Village, I'd been too intimidated by its fag-bashing punk vibe to venture inside. In daylight, the run-down interior seemed held together by band stickers. Hilly, who knew and had supported Dean, gave him the go-ahead with a simple, "I trust you." I got the sense that he was open to breaking this new ground while being protective of what he'd built over the years. We returned to photograph near-naked twinks hanging on each other in the club's notoriously grubby bathroom to promote the showcase, which Dean named HomoCorps. As I was designing the print ad and flyers, I couldn't really grasp the name's meaning. He explained: "Because the music industry is homophobic *and* run by closet cases—just like the military." Headliner Rufus Wainwright packed the place; his celebrity following garnered a lot of press. Dean appeared fronting his second band, the Velvet Mafia. HomoCorps gave me—along with a packed-in queer crowd—a claim on the club's rowdy scene.

One of the changes in the aftermath of 9/11 was positive: Dean's activities were less scrutinized. Newly elected Mayor Bloomberg and the NYPD had other priorities. This was a relief to both of us, especially since I was now earning money from them, too. Dean next partnered with gay comic Jonny McGovern for a party called Triple XXX, for which I also designed the event's ads and flyers, including one I especially loved of a stripper standing on the bar with his white briefs around his ankles and dollar bills stuffed into his scuffed high-tops. The copy proclaimed that the party had "brought the Giuliani era to a screeching halt."

His next party, Magnum (named for the extra large condom) changed all that. He co-produced it with Johnny at the Park, an upscale venue in Chelsea; gossip columnist Michael Musto called it a "a raunchy gay sleaze fest." I got wild at the opening night party, or better said, a horny and very flexible twink got wild on me, twirling on my dick right on the dance floor, lifting his leg into a full rotation with his foot pointed in a move I later learned was called an *arabesque penché*. As we closed the party out, it pained me to see that the venue's pricey new high-concept interior had been trashed. Magnum was shut down soon after it started; the venue was summonsed for "lewd and licentious behavior," among other offenses. Dean blasted out a goading email: "If the police want to waste their time and money chasing naked, well-hung men around a nightclub, we are prepared to take a stand…" I cheered him on for tweaking the NYPD while quietly fearing for his safety.

Sure enough, Magnum put police scrutiny back on Dean; this go-round was worryingly more efficient than Giuliani's inept grandstanding. His options in nightlife having narrowed, Dean shifted gears and started escorting. "I used to throw parties," he said of the late-life career change, "now I *am* the party." Using the worker name 'Big Red,' he experienced an immediate surge of popularity. He was the new cock on the block, and his cock was even bigger than mine. He was raking in cash and used it to support his music like he had with his earnings as a party promoter. Though the paths that had led us each to late-in-life hustling were distinct, our bond deepened having been through these upendings. I'd lost my means of support to the real estate boom while he'd lost his to moralistic crusades—two sides of the same blade.

On our frequent late-night phone calls, I would read him my diary entries, and his thunderous laughter would reverberate over the line. He found my workmanlike approach and hapless episodes of on-the-job learning hilarious, and begged me to read some stories at the queer literature series he was headlining. It was called 'Reading for Filth,' and he would be presenting various texts himself: diary entries, music industry exposés, rants mocking establishment puritanism. Like he did with this parties, he mixed high and low: literary types such as Edmund White and poet Eileen Myles with emerging queer writers and downtown performers. I cherished Dean as my reader and was tempted to participate, but worried about blowing up my spot or breaking client confidentiality.

Dean and I had very different approaches to hustling. I was the emotionally detached careerist fulfilling a specific fantasy, the "Italian Stallion dream cum true" per my review, a "Guido stud for hire," as writer David Henry Sterry once christened me. Dean came with a backstory: "Sometimes I get to the door and the john takes one look and says, 'Oh my god, you're Dean Johnson!' and slams the door on me. But then others say, 'Oh my god, you're Dean Johnson!' and turn out to be huge fans…." With his performance background he gravitated towards role-play scenarios. When a client would ask him to enlist other escorts he would take it as a cue to produce and direct an elaborate piece of theater. He would sometimes bring me in on these scenes. I usually found it easier to go into a call with another escort, but with Dean, I'd get notes on my performances.

He gave me the rundown of the roster of clients he'd amassed, among them submissives, size queens, devoted cocksuckers, foot fetishists, tight-assed 'sons' looking to be violated by 'dad,' str8 hotties who "just wanna see it," and married men who "never do this." I continued to work my Guido stud lane while his emblematic whiteness—he was six-and-a-half feet tall, his cock a totem of mythic supremacy, his pale skin translucent in places—attracted those who fetishized his race. He appealed to Black guys with a taste for white meat and those into racial humiliation. Asian guys looking for some 'white on rice' hit him up, too. Dean had history with such role-play; for months, he'd regaled me with tales of his hookups with actor BD Wong and the protracted Viet Cong prisoner-of-war camp scenarios they played out in Dean's cell-like Cobble Hill studio. I hung on every gossipy morsel. As I watched him unleash his lunatic imagination and barbed wire wit on the profession to which I'd been studiously applying myself, he blew open my sense of what was possible in sex work.

In our underground grind, I tended to follow the unspoken rules of conduct: keep clear boundaries with clients, keep your emotions in check, keep a low profile. Dean delighted in trampling all of these rules. He happily treaded into taboo territory with clients—rape, incest, adultery—many of whom were working through some conflicted feelings. I wasn't surprised that his larger-than-life physical attributes inspired awe, admiration, and worship, but some of his clients crossed over into obsession—and Dean appeared to encourage them. Like many good hookers, Dean was part psychotherapist, his methods distinctly on the drama therapy-reenactment tip, but when he launched into his latest stories I often had a hard time telling who was the one being therapized.

He brought me in on a number of calls. Of course I was glad to have another income stream, but was also drawn in by the lunacy. For one, he recruited Dick—a lanky, dark-skinned actor/escort—and me to play college buddies who were to pass around the trick like a drunken sophomore slut. This trite porn fantasy improbably took place at the trick's hotel room at the Plaza. Listening to Dean rattle on in his deepest voice about seducing his bros at frat parties and locker room towel-snapping antics, I cracked up and broke the spell. To recover, I started taunting the trick, but then Dean pulled me aside: "We're supposed to ignore him completely...treat him like a piece of furniture."

"Sorry, I must have missed that."

Down in the lobby, I got one of his admonishments. My level of commitment to role-play scenarios couldn't match his overgrown theater kid energy.

For another, wearing sunglasses and ball caps, Dean and I were thieves breaking into a trick's room at the Hotel Pennsylvania, only to discover him hiding in the bathroom, where we were to brutalize him with "no limits." The poor guy chickened out while we were beating him. He had no idea what he was doing telling Dean Johnson "no limits" and I apparently had some anger to work through. Maybe I was acting out still-unresolved hostility towards the decorator; I didn't get any performance notes on this call. "It's one of those when the fantasy in his head didn't translate," I said to Dean in the cab downtown. He nodded as he counted out my take.

Another showed me some limits of my own:

"I've got a call tonight, a Black media executive in Murray Hill. Really cool guy, and his apartment is to die for. Do you want in?"

"Sure, what's the deal?"

"He's into race play. I'm his stern Masser, you'll be my cousin from a neighboring plantation, $250. ..." I was wary but needed that call to hit my sales goal.

"A stretch, but okay. Do we have to do Southern accents?"

"It helps..."

The media executive greeted us at the door in a coarse cotton shirt and breeches; we headed back "behind the barn" (his rear patio) where I'd see how "Masser Dean" punished with a switch and then rewarded with sexual attention his prized slave. In truth, Dean hadn't fully prepared me. The trick wanted us to use slurs—*that* slur along with some antiquated ones—to be delivered in our terrible southern accents.

I checked out when Dean launched into the prescribed racial abuse; he caught my eye and gestured impatiently for me to join in.

A half-forgotten recollection was storming through my head: I was thirteen, playing outside with the kid who lived next door and my little brother. The next-door kid saw a Black employee of the nearby country club walking to work and yelled *that* slur at him, laughing. My little brother copied him. I was horrified and ratted them both out. Maybe I'd half figured out why my "swarthy" Sicilian grandfather had been shunned by neighbors and even family, or maybe I'd already sensed that I too, would be an outsider and target of another slur. All these years later I still hadn't processed. I fixated on one image as Dean yelled *that* slur: the country club employee taunted by kids, fast-walking to the gate.

I couldn't bring myself to say *that* slur, but managed to cough up a line or two of dialog about "this here d———." Once the verbal abuse was more or less over, the scene shifted into routine sexual domination—the trick servicing us both on his knees—and I snapped back to the present. After the call, I got furious notes from Dean on my lack of commitment to the role. Even the trick had given me a withering look as we said our goodbyes. Race play may have been helping him to dismantle the power of those slurs, or maybe it just made submission that much hotter for him, but I was just not up for this job. While Dean and I had some overlapping skill sets there was some territory he could venture into that I could not. It pricked at my sense of worth to know that I wasn't "up for anything, short of blood," as I'd often asserted. Much as I told myself it was just a script, the trick *wanted* it, racial slurs even in a consensual context had made me as queasy as blood.

I was hearing more and more stories from Dean suggesting that on his sex work journey, my rule number one—*Don't get emotionally involved, it's a business transaction*—was roadkill. He'd fallen in love with one cocksucker and wound up scaring the poor guy off with his ardor. He disappeared for a while, and upon his return, chronicled a co-dependent, romantic-obsessive love triangle with a Scarsdale dentist and his wife. Beneath my fascination I worried about where such entanglements might lead him. He would announce that he was no longer going to charge this or that trick, but now they were "boyfriends," for me an unthinkable development. It reminded me of the unilateral decision he'd made about us the night we met. On a break at the Hole, I grew impatient as he rattled on about his latest "boyfriend" and summoned county music lyrics to snap at him: "You're looking for love in all the wrong places."

He sipped on his soda and replied, "Sweetie, there's no wrong place. I'm a romantic! Stranger things have happened on this planet."

Though working porn stars like Arpad were routinely flown all over the country for overnights and weekends, I didn't get many requests for long-distance travel calls. Any temptation to do porn and step up into higher earnings was offset by my desire to keep a low profile. I was happy burrowing into the greater metropolitan area, by far the largest marketplace in the country anyway. Most out-of-towners who really wanted to hire me would sooner come to the city for the weekend than fly me out to them. It was Dean who set me up with my one long-distance travel call, to San Antonio, Texas. We were to attend a party thrown by Tom, a fifty-something queen, and Anthony, his younger Texican lover. "I am the *scandal* of my socially prominent family...." Dean had reported Tom saying to him, in drawl. I was enticed by the picture Tom had painted of the party: a catered and staffed gathering of about a hundred men—San Antonio's gay A-list—on Tom's estate. The crowd would be peppered with escorts flown in for the occasion. The escorts would romp in the pool, mingle, and have a little fun with the guests.

Dean, who suffered from travel anxiety, proposed bringing along two of his hung buddies; he recruited me and Dick.

"It's eight hundred for the overnight..." he explained.

"That's a little light..." said Dick warily.

"Plus all meals and transportation. And the hotel," added Dean.

"Could be more, but okay fine..." I said. Dick shrugged.

"Oh GOOD. I hate flying alone. I get a little extra for booking you two."

Representing quite the variety pack of New York talent, Dick and I were there as Dean's emotional support animals as much as the gig. For the first leg to Dallas, we were assigned the very last (non-reclining) row in the back of the plane. As the smallest of the group (at six-foot-two), I was designated the middle seat; even the jaded flight attendant gave me a look of pity. We endured the flight but not without attracting attention from other passengers. Dean and Dick were both being fairly outrageous and not using their inside voices. Dean: "Oh, that young twink I raped in the basement of the Hole last night was *so* cute." Dick: "You'll see, wait 'til we get there. All the damn crackers in Texas are racist as hell!" Their voices carried at least ten rows forward; the passengers who overheard them likely did not understand Dean's role-play use of 'rape,' or appreciate Dick's painting with a broad brush, however accurate he may have been. I was squeezed in and scandalized for the length of the flight.

A white lady seated in front of us had her handbag accidentally dragged off when it got snagged on the service cart. Dick noticed and returned it to her; she eyed him suspiciously and went through it to make sure nothing was missing. "You see? This racist bitch thinks I stole her stuff, and I was being nice," he snapped, loud enough for her and others to hear. I'd seen the suspicion on her face Dick had seen, but this escalating conflict threatened to make my middle-seat entrapment a full nightmare. To my relief, the flight attendant rushed in to defuse the situation, thanking Dick profusely for his help. Despite the scene, Dean managed to charm everyone they had offended as we disembarked.

On the connecting flight, we were once again seated way in the back. Dean and Dick began to snipe at each other, two cranky, snarling alphas. I sought to keep our dysfunctional posse together and smiling. Upon landing, we were met by Tom and Anthony at baggage claim. An escort from Dallas in a tight black lycra t-shirt joined us, as did a cute bearish guy from Houston. I made small talk with the Houston guy and was initially seduced by his twang, but soon realized he was deeply insecure; I avoided him for the rest of the trip. This was the escort crew, with the exception of one local guy we'd meet at the party. I was alarmed; I'd met our hosts, two other escorts, and a couple of their friends, and hadn't connected with any of them. What did this gig hold in store?

We were driven to a Hampton Inn not far from the estate, and Anthony handed each of us an envelope with some cash and a note:

Good Afternoon Dominick, Thank you for cumming (sic) to our party and being the "crème de la crème." Just a few details. Enclosed is $20 for food if you want to eat something before you arrive. There will be food there for you also… The hotel has a wonderful breakfast in the morning…

The note, with its horny spelling variants and lewdness, went on to outline our schedule and transportation logistics. We were soon picked up in a black car and driven to a sprawling, elaborately decorated suburban tract house—hardly the 'estate' Tom had described. As I drifted through its many rooms—each painted a different jewel tone, each crammed with pretentious art and tchotchkes, each decorated within an inch of their lives, the decor a revolting blend of Southern Plantation style and Eighties postmodern prissiness—I was made queasy by the level of delusion.

The large backyard adjoined the neighbors' but a high fence surrounded it for privacy. I beelined for the caterer's set-up at the far end of the yard. The party was Incan-themed, inspired by the hosts' recently travel to Peru. I'd have been happy scarfing ceviche cups and *papa a la Huancaína* all night. Dick and Dean, on the other hand, popped Viagras, smoked a bowl on the patio, got naked, and jumped in the pool.

The party guests, mostly white gay boomers, telegraphed their happiness at seeing us there with leering stares and coquettish flutters. I got the impression that this was a major event in their social lives. They had on their party clothes and their party manners were in full effect. Tom's family background and the concept of a social order, with traditional strains of decorum and gentility, seemed to be held in high regard by these queens, though I did catch some of them talking trash about their hosts. To me, unfamiliar with Texan social codes, the whole scene felt like an unintentional parody.

While the horny guests wanted to get it on with us, they just couldn't act out sexually in front of their friends beyond a little groping; the end result being that they all wanted what they called "private shows." Dean and Dick were having none of it. After creating a scandal in the pool, they started dogging the one sexy guy at the party, the local hooker, a compact Middle Eastern guy with a shaved head and an intense stare who stayed busy socializing.

Dean and Dick had read the situation and took full advantage of the guests' timidity. They hung out outside all night, swimming, splashing around in the Jacuzzi, parading around their Viagra-enhanced boners. Only the boldest/drunkest of the guests would grope them. Dean let one guy go down on him in the Jacuzzi; he was happy as long as he had an audience. Dick seemed determined to keep them all at a distance and I couldn't blame him. It fell on me to be the workhorse of the New York trio.

With this crowd of Southern queens, I was Guido incarnate. I laid on the accent, and had packed a Speedo and an Italian lucky horn pendant on a gold chain. I started bringing my more relentless admirers—at least the ones I could stand—into one of the bedrooms for private shows. The first went down on me for a while until I couldn't take any more of his toothy machinations. I tried my best to make each one feel like the most attractive guy at the party. I must have laid it on a little thick, because each in turn entered into a dramatic mini-relationship with me. They'd professed their deep passion for me once we got into the bedroom. Later, they'd see me on the patio and watch as I took one of their friends in. They'd be furious and act all spurned. I had to laugh at the absurdity of it: *I'm the stud in a hothouse full of soap opera divas.*

By the time the party wound down, I'd done about half a dozen private shows and fucked Anthony in the media room. Anthony was a power bottom, and all the while I was fucking him, he moaned like a cow, out of his head with pleasure; then he'd snap out of it, shoot me a hard stare and intone: "Don't tell Tom!" Then he'd take another hit of poppers and be off again. Once I'd serviced my host, I figured that my work was done.

Dean and Dick brought the local escort back to one of their rooms. They invited me, but hot as I was for him, I needed some time away from my oversize, bickering, mismatched set of Black-and-white alpha companions. A few minutes later, I was in the lobby decompressing when I saw the local escort hobbling towards his car. "I'm going home. My ass is too sore to party," he said apologetically. Dean cashed me out and I went to bed. Our trip back, after a not-so-fabulous hotel breakfast spread, was uneventful. Dean and I compared notes and laughed a lot, causing more scandal among the passengers; his laughter was always thunderous, even on a crowded plane. Dick sat apart from us and listened to his iPod.

I got a conflicted vibe from Tom's guests: they were out, at least at this party, but still constrained by Texan social codes. So hungry for some out-of-town dick they were willing to humiliate themselves in front of their friends. The trip, if not a culmination of my career, was a kind of tragicomic milestone. It was the furthest I'd ever traveled for a call. It was the most theatrical of my performances; I'd never laid on the Guido shtick so thickly. Dean might have given me high marks had he been paying attention. It was ridiculous fun. At the same time, it was something of a spiritual dead end, lacking the higher purpose I sought to serve on calls. The window it had provided me onto the gay subculture of San Antonio was pretty depressing. I've since been back and developed a deeper appreciation for the city, but from my admittedly brief exposure in '06, I got the impression of a pretentious, insular scene.

The trip to San Antonio had given me pause, causing me to wonder where I was going with sex work and where it would ultimately take me. I wouldn't have to ruminate much longer on the topic, however. Soon after that absurd Southwest adventure, after years of struggling to find a fit in the business world and many false starts, I was called in to interview for a job in commercial real estate. I interviewed well, providing a reasonable enough explanation for the years-long gap in my resumé, and was offered a management position. I jumped at the chance even though it would technically mean a pay cut; I longed for the security, the health insurance, the 401K.

It was time. After three busy years as an escort, I was ready to hang up my jockstraps. I'd started out later than most and was aware that sex workers—like athletes or dancers—often have an expiration date. Though I'd met a few who'd continued working into their fifties, I was staring down at a trend-line towards diminishing returns. I recalled being deep in the trenches, running from back-to-back calls one Sunday night, struggling to achieve my sales goal after a slow week. It was an exhausting yet electrifying night: I'd somehow managed to arrange and show up for five separate calls, and like Neo in *The Matrix*, a super-charged zen warrior, I'd calmly dispatched all obstacles. Normally a one-shot wonder, I'd shot three times and was physically spent. Counting that night's take, I thought: *This can't last. Soon I'll be an aged-out hooker chasing down those last dollars. I'll get all whacked out. I've seen it happen to some of the older bulls.* This fear of staying past my expiration date had fueled my interest in landing a "legit" job.

Once the employment contract was signed I announced my retirement from sex work. One at a time, I informed my regulars, telling them I'd no longer be available. Their responses surprised and touched me. To a person, they were very happy for me, even proud. They congratulated me, wishing me success. Now that I was facing this transition, I realized that I'd formed attachments to several of them: HornyUWS, my first and steadiest, who could be clingy but I still enjoyed seeing; Headmaster, who'd lined up escort ass for me for years; the Undertaker; the Grammy winner. I'd always seen myself as a cold-hearted operator, wearing a mask that rarely slipped off, but the regulars knew me better. A few asked if they could continue seeing me "as my schedule allowed." I answered that I was going to have to focus on my new job for the time being, but left the door open with a select few; maybe I wasn't entirely ready to give up sex work. I pictured it becoming a sideline that would ease the transition.

I told some of my escort colleagues that I was retiring and suggested that they call certain of my regulars. A few went on to form steady trade with them. It was gratifying to play matchmaker in this way, to tie up loose ends. Some of my regulars had formed attachments to several escorts over the course of time, alternating from one to the next based on mood and availability. For them, I was part of a stable they'd hire in rotation, mitigating the loss of one.

I contacted the Webmaster at Hooboys, the male escort review site. I'd accumulated a few reviews from various tricks, all very flattering and positive. The guy who'd called me "an Italian Stallion dream cum true," a Broadway and cabaret performer, had actually tried to finagle a discount or even a free session in exchange for writing me more favorable reviews, but I'd done just fine with the few consistent reviews I'd garnered organically. The web site provided escorts with the option of listing themselves as 'retired'. My review page would still stand as some kind of online memorial, but there would now be an 8-bit emoji of a setting sun wearing shades at the top. It's still accessible via the Wayback Machine. I deleted my suggestive AOL profile, but maintained the account, if for no other reason than to keep a record of my correspondence. I continued to receive email inquiries for months, even years.

There would be obvious changes to my schedule and attire, but the adjustment I worried about most was being around civilians. As an escort, I'd withdrawn into myself. I'd maintained a couple of close friends, like Dean, and I had my queer sober tribe, but hardly engaged in the straight world beyond. I'd been mostly in lone wolf mode. Escorting required me to relate to only one other person at a time (occasionally two, for a couple or a double-up) and even then I was in transaction mode. In my new position I'd be dealing with a hierarchy: bosses, underlings, colleagues, clients, vendors, a whole constellation of professional relationships. I worried that after three years, my socialization had become so queer and so binary that I wouldn't succeed in the workforce.

From a glass-walled office, I was now managing the downtown satellite operation of a company headquartered in midtown. After years underground, I was sincerely enthusiastic about having coworkers and answering to clients. It was a domain of my own supervising a staff of two. I was asked to take an entrepreneurial approach to running the operation, as if it were my own business, so my experiences both at the loft and in sex work transferred well. I worked for two caring, thoughtful women who I adored, and once I'd demonstrated to them that I was capable, I had minimal oversight.

I adjusted to life among the day-walkers. It was the first time that I'd had such a structured schedule, but after years of unpredictable hours, I was all too ready to fall in to nine to five. The struggle to wake up early, after years of keeping nocturnal hours, was minimized by the fact that my new job was a 10-minute walk from home: I could sleep in, skip through Tompkins Square, and be at my desk on time. It was a rare blessing among working New Yorkers not having to crowd into a rush-hour subway car.

I had the right wardrobe for a corporate job from my time with the decorator. Thanks to him, I was well-versed in the status codes of men's business attire. Out of the closet came the custom fitted suits, the good shoes, the dress shirts with French cuffs, and whatever silk ties had survived that messy break-up. Out of the jewelry box came the sparkling cufflinks and that one fancy semi-occult watch. Looking the part gave me enough self-confidence to show up and figure out the rest. I'd occasionally be negotiating with real estate brokers, a very status-conscious clique. I could face them down in attire that would hold up to their scrutiny.

The changes to my routine took some getting used to but the sales component had a familiar feel. My experience in the sex trade had enhanced my business acumen. For me, sex work had been the labor-for-capital exchange at its most primal: my work for the value of your longings. I hadn't gone to business school but had field experience as a warm-calling seller. My new position required me to make the initial contact with the prospect, assess their needs, negotiate, massage the deal, and then deliver on the commitments I'd made. It took a similar combination of persuasion, communication, tact, and follow-through as escorting. I *really* wanted to explain this through-line between sex work and real estate to my new co-workers.

The fact that I'd organized sex work like a small business certainly helped. So many of the tasks that were required of me were familiar ground: I'd set weekly sales goals and tracked expenses, and used Excel to count up sales and to measure patterns and trends. All of this served me well in my new office. When I was asked to develop a targeted marketing strategy, I found that I was more attuned to the changing dynamics of web-based marketing than anyone else at the company. When complicated spreadsheets were thrown at me—revenue forecasts and operating budgets—they were familiar enough.

That I'd been so focused on working a specific geographic territory also turned out to be good preparation for my new position. Three years of taking calls throughout the greater metropolis had imprinted a complex map of geography and building stock, the map pins my tricks in their varied dwellings. Whether it was a ratty studio at the Chelsea Hotel, a suburban home in Babylon, a co-op in Hackensack, or a luxury suite at the Plaza, I'd been very attuned to real estate. I've gotten to know this vast metropolis building-by-building, neighborhood-by-neighborhood. I can still walk along many streets, point to buildings, and describe their interiors as I'd encountered them. Now that I was working in the field, this knowledge base was an asset.

Once I was fully settled in, I reached out to one regular with whom I'd left the door open, mostly because he lived around the corner from my new office. *Hello lunch break*. Desmond was a Jamaican-born business consultant who'd made millions selling his shares of some overvalued IPO stock right before the Dot-com crash. He'd text me: 'R U available?' I'd hustle over, and he'd go straight to work giving me a quick, slobbering blowjob. I'd bust in his face and he'd scrounge up my rate in crumpled twenties lying around his disheveled apartment. He'd go back to his laptop, I'd check my suit for stains, and return to the office with Starbucks for my team. Damn I shined like a superhero running between blow-and-go's and the management gig; as much as the extra cash helped me adjust to being on payroll, I thrilled in being the suit with a secret life.

One afternoon at work, after not having seen him for some time, Desmond reached out to me. The last time I'd gone over to his place, instead of the usual rushed scene, we'd talked. His voice was deep; his speech had a flat American affect he'd likely picked up in college, but his Jamaican lilt would sometimes break through. He told me more about his wild Dot-com ride: "I did it all from here, some research, some risk, some good timing…" he said, indicating his home trading desk setup. He seemed to relish in the cover working online gave him: no one in that world had a clue about his Blackness or his queerness. I told him about my photo studio and event business.

This time, instead of the usual 'R U Available?' his text read, 'I'm turning 40 this year, would you be interested in planning my party?' I booked a photo studio for the occasion, brought in a caterer, and hired my friend Viva Ruiz as the deejay. Viva, a big part of my East Village AA family, modeled a vibrant, creative, and expansive recovery. She's gone on to many inspiring projects in film, music, and activism. My trick-turned-client was thrilled with the results, and I began to ask myself if I could transition others. He would be the only one in the end, but it was validating that he saw me as capable in other ways. One day at the office as I scrolled through Desmond's old text messages on my BlackBerry, John's final relationship review came back to me: *You're too emotionally unavailable.* Desmond always meant his standard 'R U Available?' as he did, but I took it as a prompt to assess my emotional state. *Am I available? A little more every day.*

•

Now that I was semi-retired, Dean finally persuaded me to join an upcoming installment of Reading for Filth: "Just change the names to protect the guilty. We'll bill you as 'Dominick.'" The venue was Rapture, a bookstore/coffee bar on Second Avenue started by Joe Birdsong and Brian Butterick, who as Hattie Hathaway was a Wigstock legend—and as I would soon learn, a street hustler on Polk Street in San Francisco in his teens. I took the stage with a story I'd drawn from my diary; though I dreaded coming out as a sex worker to a roomful of friends and strangers, it needed telling. I hedged with a disclaimer: "If there's anyone here from my company or any of its affiliates, or any law enforcement, what I am about to read is a work of imaginative fiction. For everyone else, it's as true as it gets." It was a half-serious laugh line: I was really worried about blowing my cover. That same day, I'd rocked a suit and tie and gotten a paycheck from one of the largest real estate concerns in the city, and here I was pouring out a raunchy confession of outlaw sex.

I thought the quiet crowd could sense my unsteadiness. They laughed at a line I thought they'd find funny, breaking the tension, and went on to laugh in places I hadn't anticipated. I ended the reading with: "They say you can lose yourself in the hustle, but I know where I'm coming from," a bite on Blondie's "Call Me": *Come up off your color chart/I know where you're coming from.* The crowd broke out in applause. I got mostly encouragement afterwards, although there were a few creepy remarks from guys with trick energy. As usual, Dean gave me performance notes: "That was great, but you need to modulate and to play to the back of the room." He also wanted me to come back for the next reading.

The urgency to tell my story was stronger than my fear. I thought if people knew what my days had been like it would dislodge stereotypes around sex work. My experience hadn't been the descent into darkness common in pop culture depictions. I hadn't counted the effect of telling the story on me; carrying secrets around wears the body down, as I'd seen all too clearly with the decorator. Not only had Dean given me a platform, he was emboldening me to use my full voice and fill the space with it. As I became immersed in the business world, and my sense of worth in it had grown, I'd started to think that maybe sex work had been a mistake, another lost era after my dozen years with the decorator. Despite prior ruminations about sex work being affirming, the pervasive negative messages about it had started to wear me down. Even at my friendly and low-key office, people threw around disparaging jokes about hookers, not knowing there was one in the room pretending to find them funny. After my Filth debut, I consciously took back my run as a hustler, owned it, valued it; but I was *still* unsettled about my past as a kept boy.

    I worked up another story for my next reading, outlining the years I'd spent with the decorator. Dean found my naïveté as a kept boy/college student as hilarious as when I'd told him stories of my beginnings in sex work. He cracked up when I mentioned running into the bathroom at Bloomingdale's to change out of my suit to go back downtown, then said, "Sweetie, you're still splitting yourself in half." As I read through my script, he started telling me about this "pain gimp" who had contacted him: "He's got fibromyalgia and he's a BDSM bottom… he hires Doms to beat and whip him…he gets off on having control over pain when for most of his life, pain controls him." Dean found his profile so compelling, I think because he'd chosen his own pain over that which he couldn't control for years. As he'd inventoried in a Myspace post:

> I've never had any security, I don't own any property, not even a car, and I'm hard-core unemployable, I've suffered through years of heroin addiction, overdoses and withdrawals, hospitals, rehabs and asylums, career disasters and public humiliations, two decades of being HIV positive, homelessness, spinal surgery, the deaths of so many people I've loved—and I'm fine.

    Despite his travel anxiety, Dean took Amtrak to Washington, DC for an overnight call with his new fascination, who the *New York Times* later identified as Steve Saleh, "a former Commerce Department employee who is hobbled by chronic pain…" He came back from a long and intense domination session telling me about how they'd bonded over the course of their night together. I'd warned him before about getting emotionally attached to tricks to no avail. He and Saleh scheduled a repeat call a few weeks out.

A few days later, Dean got a startling email from Saleh: 'Jeremy is dead please call.' Jeremy Conklin was a young man who had moved to Washington from Massachusetts, and was staying in Saleh's apartment, which by all accounts was stocked with large quantities of pain medications, primarily Oxycontin in various dosages from 10 mg all the way up to 60 mg. His death was an apparent overdose. Soon after receiving the email, Dean told me he was going back down to Washington: "It's not a call. I'm going down for moral support. I'll just take a Klonopin for the train ride."

Early the next morning, his band mate Amanda, who sang back-up vocals on many of the Velvet Mafia's tracks, got a call from Dean's phone. The voice on the line belonged to a stranger. It was Saleh, telling her that Dean had taken a sleeping pill and wasn't waking up. She told him to call 911 and he hung up; then began a scramble to locate Dean. His bandmates tried to figure out where he was and who was the stranger on the phone. A few days later—after Dean had uncharacteristically missed a band rehearsal—the DC coroner's office announced that a previously unidentified body at the morgue was Dean's. It was the second apparent overdose in less than a week in Saleh's apartment. There was speculation that he was luring men with the promise of pharmaceuticals; he himself remarked that he was being painted in the media as some kind of "gimp black widow." Dean could be a garbage pail when it came to drugs, but I couldn't help but blame Saleh for a certain recklessness. The toxicology reports for both Jeremy and Dean showed Oxycontin. I found myself scolding this Saleh character: *Control your controlled substances, pain gimp!*

Dean's friends and collaborators rallied to mourn his death and celebrate his life. The next installment of Reading for Filth became an impromptu memorial service attended by hundreds. It was covered by the *Times* in an article called "Disquieting Death Stills the Night Life." I read a tribute to Dean entitled "The Real Big Johnson," a riff on the Velvet Mafia song "The Big Johnson." As I closed my eyes and breathed deep in the back alley of Rapture to steady my nerves, I heard Dean telling me to modulate and play to the back of the room. It was hard to play to the back of the room because the crowd was out the front door and onto the street by the time I got to the podium. I recounted how Dean had survived the scourges of AIDS, heroin, and Mayor Giuliani and laughed his thunderous laughter at all of the fuckery. I talked about his sex work as an act of survival and defiance; when the haters shut down his party, as he often said, he *became* the party. Dean had written a slogan for rentboy.com when the escort site enlisted him as their spokesmodel: "Money can't buy you love, but the rest is negotiable." I teased out the corollary, one I'd seen in action from Dean: "Make your love non-negotiable." Lady Bunny toddled over to me after I was done and said, "That was great, but you need to project more." It was Dean speaking to me again through his old friend from the Pyramid Club.

Mourning the loss of my best friend and confidante while being quoted in the *Times* had a reckoning effect. For all his faults, Dean had left a mark. Charting my non-linear path through city life since slipping into nightclubs with Joy's art-school clique at seventeen, it was hard to see what mark I'd left other than ruts. I seemed to have put all my faith in running between oppositions. In high school, I was high-achieving teacher's pet, but after the last bell, I'd run off to the city looking for trouble. I'd spent years shuttling back and forth between Upper East Side society and the downtown scene, at a time when uptown and downtown were two distinct cultural entities, with divergent customs, mores, dress codes. I'd been a studious college kid with a sugar daddy and now I was a hustler gone corporate, a real estate manager with a raunchy backstory. I'd often congratulated myself for these oscillations between good and bad, legit and underground, uptown and downtown, but they seemed to have gotten me everywhere and nowhere at once. Dean had committed to his role in the underground. From the perch of my legit gig, my stint as a hustler was a ritual dance to prepare me for the harsh shine of the working world. Even after retiring, I was still invested in Dominick's ability to ground me in the raw truth beneath the suit. Dean alone saw how I tended to trap myself in iterations of the same loop: "You're still splitting yourself in half…"

I'd slogged through the solitary routines of online-mediated sex work but they never brought me to the depths of isolation that losing my friend did. His loss hung on me like wet clothes, and I felt more estranged from the social world without my truest ally than when I didn't have one. Mutual friends like Viva and I drew together over our loss. Still, his absence was a throbbing abscess, its contours vague, sometime nudging me into depression, sometimes enveloping me in existential loneliness.

After retiring from hustling, after letting go of those lunch break calls, after those cathartic confessional nights at Reading for Filth, my sex life was finally restored to me. I didn't have to take work home any more. I lived with the constant low-grade fear that I'd be outed and fired from my new job. I hadn't used my name, but there were photos from past events online. It never came to pass; I somehow dodged reputational scrutiny. I was *available*. I could date if I wanted—though I don't know how to and didn't think I wanted to. I could fuck who I wanted, when I wanted, where I wanted. I was liberated from puritan judgments about my sexuality and my instinct to share it far and wide. After years of meeting the needs of others I was ready to bring out my own. It had been long enough that I didn't even know where to start—except to honor the Big Johnson by keeping my halves together, committing to the role, playing to the back of the room, fucking freely, and putting a deep growl into it.

9. ANDRÉS

"*Soy más subversivo que usted.*"

–Pedro Lemebel, "Manifiesto: Hablo por mi diferencia"

In November of 2019—just before the pandemic hit—I traveled to Santiago, Chile to attend a wedding and to visit Andrés, who was alive and thriving, a miracle considering his AIDS diagnosis thirty-three years earlier: "rapid deterioration within a few months…" The urge to re-connect with him in this new century, in a distant city, burned hot in me. We'd seen each other a few years back on his quick visit to New York, but he'd been preoccupied with his new boyfriend. This time it would be just us, and though resolution over our past seemed unlikely, I sensed that we had still more road to travel. Even before his diagnosis, Andrés was always pitched towards the next. For me, our youths bouncing between that aerie-like railroad flat, the Central Park Ramble, and the decorator's East Side residences glimmered on the horizon, a far-off urban dream of our conjoined recollection.

Santiago's late spring felt like summer. After a few days on my own, Andrés—ever the vagabond traveler—returned from Buenos Aires and greeted me at his art-filled apartment in the Bellas Artes section of the historic city center: "Yasss—" He seemed to have dropped the "child" upon seeing how I'd aged in the intervening years. He himself had long ago lost his hair and shaved his head. His facial wasting—an effect of long-term HIV—had been treated with injections of fillers, his forehead smoothed with botox. He was tan and fit from regular gym visits and cycling, his usual means of transit. He battled the signs of aging he never expected to face with liberal applications of lotion. The net effect of his self-care, including the cosmetic procedures, was a brown, athletic mannequin. It struck me as defiance rather than vanity from a man living a second life, a continent away from the epicenter of the disease that had vowed to kill him.

Seeing his reconstructed face again, my first impression came back to me, or at least another reconstruction. Like me, he'd been a suburban boy eager to get to New York City, having graduated from high school at seventeen. By the time we met he was this stylish polyglot who'd lived so much more life than me. Before starting at our alma mater, he'd met Joseph, a Columbia grad student from a wealthy Baltimore family, and moved in with him. He'd been spoiled: "Child, I was such a brat with him. I would take his Datsun 280XC on nightly rides to the Christopher Street Piers and whittle the hours away with the children. I racked up quite a few parking tickets…" Joseph was running a fever when he'd dropped Andrés off at my doorstep; he would die of complications from AIDS at twenty-eight. It was the only time I'd met Joseph, and we barely exchanged words, but his hollowed expression has stayed with me: *Did he know about his condition then? Did he blame Andrés?* His angry ghost haunted every reunion.

While I got lost in these shadows, the details of Andrés' new life burst forth in bright flashes: "You remember my last boyfriend, who you met in New York, who does drag? *Child!* He confessed to me that he started taking hormones and is transitioning. That's why he was so moody with me…*She*…She goes by Julieta now…We had to break up…" He opened the blinds and his apartment glowed with reflected light. "Those Argentine boys, yassss…I stayed in the Palermo section, you have to go, it's happening…I almost missed my LATAM flight to Ezeiza, and you know mama does *not* miss planes. There was an action in the Metro."

At the time of my visit, Santiago was in the midst of one of the largest populist uprisings in the world. I told Andrés about the day my husband and I arrived for the wedding: "The couple chartered a light blue bus to take us to the venue in the Maipo Valley. So we're getting to know the other guests, passing around sodas, and we see a surge of protesters on Providencia running towards us. And in the distance trucks with water cannons mounted on top, shooting…"

"Plaza Italia," said Andrés.

"Right, one of the bridesmaids told us that the monument was the flashpoint."

"Yasss, that's Baquedano on his horse…the protesters throw red paint on it and fly the indigenous flag."

"We were sitting ducks on that bus, all of us well-dressed wedding guests. It was like scraping up against history in the making…The trucks got closer and a woman up front, in all her finery, yelled at us to close the windows, to keep the water out. Then the bus backed away and headed to the venue."

As Andrés and I took our respective current selves in, he outlined the effects of the protests on his daily routines: "I can still bike to Vitacura for work, but getting home is the hard part. There's *always* a protest… I'm *very* sensitive to the *bombas lacrimógenas*…the tear gas canisters the *pacos* shoot off constantly.…*pacos*, that's what we call the military police…even a little smoke in my eyes and I have to get off the bike." He re-arranged a meticulously curated group of artifacts atop a dresser, only to put them back to their original placement. "You know those canisters are made in the USA, like you? Yasss, child, the imperialists are *still* trying it…You know the Lider—the supermarket downstairs? It closed for a week when the protests moved over here…They boarded it up but the looters got in anyway…It's been hard to get money, some days the ATM's are empty, other days the banks are boarded up…"

We'd reunited several times over the years, and his welcoming embrace was always quick, as if to signal that we needn't dwell on our fraught past. Usually he'd launch right into telling me about the packed itinerary he'd planned for us, and I would bristle at his meticulous, demanding Virgo energy. On this visit, the protests were thwarting his organizational mind. We'd be adrift amidst the smoke and the fires, and I actually looked forward to my time with him without his hard edges. It put us on a little more even footing, neither of us sure what might happen.

After the wedding, my husband had flown home, and I'd rented a short-term apartment near Andrés', anticipating his return. I was fairly proficient in Spanish, having learned from Andrés, then Machito, and lately with my Peruvian-born husband and his family. Over the years, I've used it more than the French I'd studied or the Italian I'd picked up on the Sorrentine Peninsula. My apartment was steps from Cerro Santa Lucia—Huelén to the Mapuche—the hill in the middle of the old center which was strategically captured by the Spanish invaders. I'd hiked to the lookout at the top of the hill, past fortifications and cannons which had asserted dominance over the great valley of the Santiago Basin, a vantage point used to plan the colonial city. The plaza we'd seen from the bus—which the protesters have since renamed Plaza Dignidad, from which the Chilean government recently removed the equestrian statue (in the name of protecting the national patrimony)—was walking distance away. To my north was Parque Forestal, the long, narrow park along the Mapocho River, and to my east was Lastarria, a cultural hub; both were also rallying points. As it turned out, the apartment was surrounded by daily protests; its walls muffled the sounds, but I still could tell they were coming in from all directions. *How will Andrés and I get anywhere with every road barricaded?* It was a question of logistics as much as one that hung figuratively over our long, complicated relationship.

Prior to his return, I'd taken long walks through the contested city. I'd wandered alone in New York as a teen, and it was still my default mode. One afternoon in San Isidro I watched as middle school kids in uniforms walked off their playground, covered their faces, and joined the protests. I couldn't help but think of US school kids their age, or even me at their age: *Would we show such unity? Would we channel our energies into mass actions alongside adults?* What had sparked the protests was a proposed increase in the Santiago Metro fare of thirty pesos; School kids were among the first to defy the increase with mass fare evasions. Andrés called it *"la gota que colmó el vaso,"* the drop that made the glass overflow. "It wasn't just that one fare hike; everything's been going up lately," he explained. "Rent, water, food, electricity, banking, phone bills…"

I'd wandered alone through a city covered in graffiti and paste-ups, creating an endless text, a city-as-text. Getting repeatedly lost with my attention on the words, I picked up some slang and looked up some poems. I read through overlapping messages decrying an unjust economic system (*no es depresión, es capitalismo*), denouncing the president, an elderly billionaire (*¡Piñera renuncia!*), decrying state violence (*¡estado asesino!*), demanding a new constitutional assembly to replace the constitution authored under the murderous dictatorship of General Pinochet, upholding the rights of indigenous peoples, denouncing the culture of machismo (*¡paco homofobico!*), asserting the dignity of the struggle.

Though I was a rare *norteamericano* on my own, I never feared the protesters; I was aligned with their causes. Nor had I resented the resulting inconveniences—the closed banks, having to go around an action—I was a visitor without obligations or schedule. Despite my somewhat untouchable status, what I most feared was getting caught up violence from the *pacos*. I'd been regularly pressed into action by protesters: "*¡Vamonos al toque, weon!*" (Let's go now, dude!") Nearly all of bystanders or shopkeepers I talked to backed the movement's broad demands for economic justice, human rights, and a reckoning on state violence, even through their weariness. When I told a pharmacist I was visiting from the United States, she gestured to the commotion on the street and asked, "But why now?" I had no real answer. I could have cut my trip short right after the wedding just to avoid the tear gas. Despite the obvious dangers I couldn't bring myself to leave. I wanted the rare gift of being alone with the city for a few days. If I worried about anything it was that something might prevent Andrés' return.

Our first evening together, we sat down for a coffee; Andrés flung open the windows as a syncopated rhythm rang out. "That's the *cacerolazo*. It started in the Seventies when Chileans would bang on empty *cacerolas* to protest food shortages," he explained, handing me a pot and a wooden spoon. At the same time every evening, people in their apartments would hang out of their windows and bang out the rhythm: *ting, ting, ting-ting-ting!* They'd be joined by marchers in the streets banging on whatever they could find, the cyclist's bells, and the driver's horns. I heard and felt the *cacerolazo* as the heartbeat of the movement as if through its chest.

On my last visit to Santiago, our days had been filled what could have been languid meanderings through the city's evocative nineteenth-century urban fabric—except that Andrés would program them to the quarter hour, insisting that we keep on his schedule, making them an obstacle course. We'd drop in on friends—*Run!*—shop in the central market—*Run!*—lunch at a favorite *cafetería*—*Run!*—then detour to visit a lovely garden. This time, we donned protective gear and rode bikes, bearing witness to protests while avoiding the tear gas. The bitter smoke could overwhelm us in seconds if we were to ride into a drift; I dropped my usual resistance to Andrés' controlling ways and let him guide us through the perils. Oddly enough, we moved at a more relaxed pace than his usual frantic itineraries. All around us, Santiaguinos had routinized protest, rallying where summoned via closed social media channels, showing up daily after school and work. Others sought to hold on to the solace of the everyday, despite sporadic closures of Metro stations, banks, and stores, and even disruptions to the main electronic payment system.

"You see that white liquid they are shaking on him?" Andrés asked as we rounded a corner, pointing to a protester with bloodshot eyes, coughing and crying. "It's an antidote made with baking soda. We get exposed to the toxins in those bombs every day, and no one really knows the long-term effects." Ever the scavenger, Andrés had picked up a spent tear gas canister on the Puente Purisima; their markings indicated manufacture by a company with the vaguest of names, Combined Systems, out of Pennsylvania. That these "less-lethal" weapons were US-made had sometimes put a chill on my reception, echoing decades of violent US meddling in Chilean politics. For me, it stirred up a specific moral outrage: *A whole US factory is free to make and export these, but how I supported myself for years is illegal?*

I'd overheard heated claims that the military police were intentionally aiming for the eyes of front-line protesters with rubber bullets, another "less-lethal" import. I did not want to believe them, thinking maybe the protesters were exaggerating for sympathy; then one afternoon outside of the Centro Gabriela Mistral, Andrés pointed out a baby-faced protester flanked by two friends, his right eye wrapped in black cloth. On the wall behind him were paste-ups with photos of protesters with various eye injuries, unwrapped. *They really are shooting at their eyes.* Having been through surgeries for retinal detachments, my right eye twinged with sympathetic pain, my horror degrees more visceral.

On nights at home, we'd scan twitter to find videos of the protests we'd attended; many captured the arrests of innocent young protesters just to clear the streets, subjecting them to rough treatment and the repercussions of criminal records. We'd go out when we could, too;

Santiaguinos would nightly overcome their sense of dread and various logistical challenges to convene, to commiserate, to share food and drink. A small act of normalcy in the midst of all of this, like slipping past burning barricades to buy ice cream at a *botillería*, as we did one hot night, could feel like a major triumph.

After posting on Instagram from Lastarria, I was contacted by a sweet Venezuelan couple who'd I'd met through Machito when they were visiting New York: "We are here too!" It turned out they were living not far from where I was staying. After being ambushed in their home during the depths of Venezuela's recent crisis, they'd fled and resettled in Chile as refugees. They'd become part of the immense Bolivarian diaspora: millions of Venezuelans who have fled their country since its economic collapse. They'd each gotten jobs in Santiago and were finding their way until the protests started. We met up for drinks in Barrio Paris-Londres. Having lived through the failed mass protest movement in Caracas—against corruption, hyperinflation, and austerity measures—and then their assault and sudden dislocation, they were triggered by the unrest in Santiago. They believed that the protests had likely been instigated by Cuban operatives intent on destabilizing South American democracies. I didn't argue, but couldn't square the organic, grass-roots movement I'd witnessed with the idea that it had been seeded by Castro's chaos agents. I was just glad to reunite with them and relieved that they were safe, if troubled that their trauma had made them susceptible to this narrative.

Having drinks on a street-side patio in a rare moment of calm, Andrés told us about his own relocation to Santiago in the grip of optimism following the return of democracy: "I wanted to come sooner, but had to wait until I could get my meds here…" He'd immersed himself in Chilean life and culture; though his Spanish was fluent, and his study of *chilenismos*—idiomatic phrasing specific to Chilean Spanish—had been meticulous, his speech still belied Anglophone patterns. "The neighbors call me *el Gringo*." It would turn out that he was uniquely suited to providing English lessons to employees of the burgeoning high-tech industry, in the shiny, modern Santiago of glass towers east of the historic center: "I give young Chilean engineers and managers one-on-one conversation lessons. Yasss, child, some of my pupils are fine. They call me Doctor. Their first lesson is learning to pronounce 'English.' The upper classes don't use the *sh* sound, so they all say 'In-glitch.'" He's since been contracted to translate Spanish texts into English; he calls me sometimes to check his translations. I'd been in awe of Andrés' capacity to adapt and thrive for years, but never so much as in this moment, as he indexed his second life in another hemisphere.

He'd found his way into a circle of queer artists and thinkers, among them the sculptor Hugo Marin, whom we'd visited on my last trip. Andrés raved to me about Pedro Lemebel, a performance artist and writer in this circle: "Child, a queen from the gutter of Santiago who's become a national folk hero." He bought me a copy of Lemebel's collection *Adios Mariquita Linda*, the title taken from a Mexican ballad about unrequited love. It was a stretch for my Spanish reading level, especially with all the *chilenismos* and queer slang, but he helped me when I got stuck. I'd make lists of words I couldn't grasp from the context, and he would explain them to me when he got home from tutoring the tech bros. "'Goodbye, pretty ladybug,' that's the literal translation of the title, but it misses the twist: *mariquita* is a slur for effeminate, like fairy or sissy," he explained. The man who'd turned me out and then pimped me out was now my tutor, and all these years later, I let down my resistance and became receptive to his instruction.

I immersed myself in Lemebel's work and story as his city raged and burned, reading by nightlight until my eyes strained. I couldn't think of anyone in the English-language canon quite like him: queer, outsider, working class, yet highly celebrated. Lemebel himself once characterized his voice as *"mariconaje guerrero"* (warrior faggotry). The hustler in me immediately allied with this outlaw stance. Growing up, his marginalization as an effeminate, uneducated poor person with indigenous roots from the slums of Santiago was total. He'd gotten an education and embarked on a teaching career, but was fired because of his obvious homosexuality. He once delivered a biting critique of the state to an assembled group of officials in full drag. He'd shown a level of bravery in the face of a disenfranchising and violent regime I couldn't even come close to mustering with my soft oppressor.

Andrés gifted me a copy of his Lemebel's one novel, *Tengo miedo torero,* in translation. Set in Santiago circa 1986—the same year Andrés had gotten his terminal diagnosis—it's a love story between a balding gay man known as the Queen of the Corner and a handsome student revolutionary who is meticulously planning to ambush the dictator Pinochet. The Queen's form of resistance pinged with me: squatting in a condemned house, she lives out her *mariquita* fantasies while the city outside her fringed curtains is engulfed in conflict. Her musings are interspersed with satirical sections depicting a henpecked dictator, his wife, and her adored gay hairdresser. The two stories—of the protagonist and her beloved guerrilla, and of the dictator and his fashion-obsessed wife—take place in parallel, converging towards the day of the ambush. Plotlines converged and timelines collapsed as I tore through the novel one insomniac night. Outside the window were echoes of the unrest depicted in the novel: tear gas bombs, targeted harassment and arrests, police violence, surveillance tactics. I'd seen in the streets how queer resistance—the biting humor, the necessity of imagining a possible future, one less brutal, more beautiful—suffused the moment. Even the slogan of the current resistance movement, *¡Chile Despertó!* ("Chile has woken up!") suggested to me one of Lemebel's poetic images, that of tragic diva stoically enduring indignities until one fateful, dramatic turn.

I continued to obsess over Lemebel when Andrés and I weren't out on the streets, and my old friend guided me. I searched for an English translation of the poem Lemebel had famously recited in drag: *Manifiesto: Hablo por mi diferencia*. Finding it stiff and formal, I undertook a close reading of the original, while Andrés filled me in on the historical references, double entendres, and *chilenismos*. The way Lemebel invokes past abuses to color the depth of his suffering under authoritarian rule really stuck with me. One heralded father of the Chilean state, General Ibáñez, who ruled during formative periods in the 20th century, is exposed as a murderous homophobe. Homosexuals, rounded up and imprisoned by Ibáñez, were executed by way of *fondeamiento*, the practice of throwing detainees off of ships at sea with weights bound to their legs; off the coast of Chile is an especially deep trench. *"Manifiesto"* is a lament for those forgotten victims: "Shed us a black tear/For the fairies consumed by crabs." I shuddered imagining the last moments of their lives. Ibáñez also created the very police force that was committing human rights abuses during my visit.

We'd seen the conflict over the equestrian statue to Baquedano, another father of the modern state whose legacy has been reassessed. Indigenous groups gathered in Plaza Dignidad decried his "Pacification of Araucanía" as a brutal massacre, the man an emblem of murderous colonialism. Protesters were thrilled when the monument was removed. It struck me as among the most absurd images to come out of Santiago: the scene of dozens of military police guarding an empty pedestal. The clash between the leftists who demand the removal of such monuments and the traditionalists who insist that they were part of the national patrimony reminded me of the clash over monuments to dubious historical figures such as Confederate generals and Columbus back home. The hyping of Columbus in the early 20th-century had been a strategy to counter nativist anti-Italian sentiment, although his elevation hardly resonated with my family. His monuments did not uplift or instill ethnic pride in us; his day was just another shopping day.

Among the miles of graffiti I saw in Santiago were many paste-ups devoted to Lemebel, and a line from *Manifesto* repeatedly scrawled on city walls as an encouragement: "*Soy más subversivo que usted*" (I am more subversive than you). Andrés pointed out another Lemebelian graffito on a monumental bust in front of the Catholic University: *Ya no tengo miedo torero*. This turned the title of his novel into an assertion of courage: 'I'm not scared any more, bullfighter.' In a city on edge, burning, crying, transforming, to see tributes to a queer outcast had its own tear gas bomb effect on me. Lemebel had choice words for the gay rights movement in the United States: he called it a "cold pink spring" for "white, rich, and elegant gays ...who only look at each other" and are "misogynist, fascistic, allied with the male that sustains the power." Coming from that cold pink spring, seeing a queer person so embraced and upheld on the walls of the city made me feel like I belonged, however accidental my presence.

I sensed that Andrés had latched on to my interest in Lemebel in order to keep my attention away from our past, but we did have some moments of reckoning. We laughed over our drunken performances under the decorator's bed canopy, over abandoning him to the Luna Park in Italy, over his appearance on a hired boat in our secret cove. He revealed another detail about that Concorde flight which had driven him mad with envy: "Child, I even called the Port Authority Police and reported that you were being taken against your will on British Airways flight 4 out of JFK." Apparently nothing had come of it, but I had to laugh at how he'd tried get the decorator arrested: "If anyone, *you* were my trafficker," I said, tweaking him.

The first section of *Adios Mariquita Linda* consists of sketches of Lemebel's love affairs with street trade, mostly *sureños*, young men from the south of Chile noted for their earthiness and swagger. I devoured his comic, transgressive descriptions of these young men, which unleash a desire that is both lecherous and nurturing. In the same streets Lemebel trod, Andrés and I played a licentious game of scanning the evening protest to find its sexiest activists. We were at once infatuated with their earnestness and fearful for their safety. Once I found my favorite—pensive, lean, black-clad, a shock of hair standing up under the goggles perched on his forehead—I wanted to huff on his grimy neck. Between the highly emotional stakes of the protests and our days being infused with regular discussions of Lemebel's body of work, we'd manifested a Lemebelian chorus of complex desire, queens on the corner looking for our handsome student revolutionaries, to nurture them, to serve their cause, to ravish their taut bodies.

Late at night, I'd open Grindr and find young Santiaguinos hungry for sex. *Ping! Ping!* On my way to the apartment of Daniel, a queer activist and cat dad, I was almost swept up in a march trying to get across La Alameda, a wide main avenue. The leader of the march fairly insisted that I join in, but when I told him, *"Es que voy a cojer…"* ("It's just that I'm going to fuck"), he shrugged and let me go. I was relieved, but he'd come close to recruiting me.

I nearly got into trouble with Daniel's nosy, half-drunk neighbors, who were staked out in front of the apartment building and wary of strangers. After vouching for me, Daniel confirmed my suspicion that sex had become a vital coping mechanism to relieve the tension in a city under siege. He was fiercely proud of how the warrior faggotry of Lemebel suffused the movement, and just as amazed as I was at how his country had embraced him: "Can you imagine? Pedro is taught in high schools now." Bonded over Lemebel, our sex was vigorous, life-affirming, loud: we really gave his neighbors something to gossip about. They saluted me on my way out.

My last night in Santiago, I had another GPS-enabled hook-up. Miguel was a writer, proficient in English, and a bit morose; I gave him a copy of my chapbook and mentioned my interest in Lemebel. "Oh, for sure, he is the mother of this movement," he said. He became animated as he explained to me how the protests, having sprung from that small increase in the Metro fare, had grown intersectional, to include demands from the indigenous, feminist, queer, and environmental organizers I'd seen on the streets. "It is absolutely Lemebelian!" he proclaimed before we started making out. I was both turned on by his conviction and relieved that this spark of queer power had changed his mood. From what I could see he was right: the movement at large was demanding no less than the deconstruction of the patriarchal pact of oppressor church and colonizer state that had brought the Chilean people to this despair.

Back in the States, shuddering with relief, I was a glass overflowing with optimism—until concluding that our fractured populace would never coalesce like the Chileans. If I couldn't imagine how *¡Chile Despertó!* might inform our captive politics, at least I could model my own liberation on their example. I would wake up as a wronged diva under siege. I would paper my city center with demands. I would converge with the like-minded on wide avenues. I would force the removal of the monuments *I myself had built* to my dead oppressor. He would no longer be the weight bound to my legs, plunging me to the depths. His fictions would dissolve like old paste-ups. I would uphold my queer outlaw body in the wider struggle.

Since my visit, Andrés has extensively tattooed his aging body; like his city, his forearm is a word cloud of the origins and main grievances of the *Chile Despertó* movement. His life story—born in Santiago, moved to the United States as a child with his family to escape the dictatorship, fought for his life during the AIDS epidemic, returned after Pinochet's arrest to live a second life immersed in Chilean identity—resonates with Lemebel's advocacy for an anti-colonial queerness—*"una identidad chiloca"*—to counter the hegemony of imported gay globalism, that cold pink spring.

He and I have shared a bond across time and continents which is sometimes held together by a mere string: an exchange of text messages, a FaceTime signal bouncing from Hells Kitchen to Bellas Artes. He will always be the person who turned me out and pimped me out—the vampire who turned me—and I will always be the person who took his sugar and his seat on the Concorde. Whenever I talk about my time as an escort, whether in conversation or at a public appearance, he'll ask, "Child, where's my cut?" My complicated love for him has morphed over years of shifting dynamics, sex, trade, medical drama, parties, loss, vagabonding, and creative resilience. I cried a lot in Santiago, shudderings of empathy and remembrance, tears of my own manufacture commingling with those of the Chileans.

10. COLOR CHART

Color me your color, baby

Color me your car

At sixteen, I was riding in the back of my mom's car, a Top 40 station playing on the radio, when it hit me, edgy and fast: crashing guitar licks over a driving beat. It raised my heart rate and lifted my sweaty butt off the seat, like when the car would gain lift going over a bridge. The singer's high-register seduction had struck me with a direct signal. My mouth hanging open, I looked to my little brother, then fifteen, for some kind of affirmation; he reached between the front seats to change the station. "Leave it!" I screamed, karate chopping his arm, and the signal continued: *This car? This '78 Mercury Marquis in the metallic blue factory finish?* My adolescent body—stretched by a recent grown spurt, sprouting with hairs, battered by hormonal turmoil—quaked with possibility. The DJ announced: "that was Blondie with their hit single, 'Call Me.'"

The next time I heard the track was in the discount department store on the gritty side of my Long Island suburb. In wide aisles under the fluorescent fixtures, from the beacon of the record department, Debbie Harry cooed in my ear. Flipping through the racks of albums, I was too cowed to ask for help. I'd seen enough DISCO SUCKS T-shirts under the leather jackets of the self-appointed enforcers of social order to know what would happen to me if word got out. If you liked New Wave, as my circle did, you were fags, but if you liked disco? You were a *faggot*. I left the store without it.

I eventually found the single at the Sam Goody's in Roosevelt Field, a vast shopping complex built on a former airfield. The record label was Chrysalis, which struck me as something precious and rare, insect and mineral. The subtitle printed below the spindle hole read, '(Theme from the Paramount Picture AMERICAN GIGOLO).' While the movie opened wide to middling box office, the song topped the charts and split open a debate about musical genres: *Was it rock? Was it disco?* How that debate which seems so trite now had roiled me. I plucked that contraband forty-five out of the shopping mall record store and played it on the stereo in the family room but only when I was alone with the blinds drawn. I tried figuring out how to move to it, falling into something between a pogo and a pony.

In my melodramatic and oversensitive way, I made a big deal out of something I'd been denied just for being a year too young. The suggestive references to that unseen R-rated movie left deep impressions. The word *gigolo* hadn't been in any of my spelling bees, but the inferences were enough to fuel my adolescent fantasies of seductive power and ease at negotiating the social world, two attributes I distinctly lacked at sixteen. My home town, a redlined suburb once Meroke territory, was a mixed Italian and Jewish enclave, mostly transplants from Brooklyn. They'd settled in tract houses built on marshland, protected against postwar social upheavals and racial strife. The flatness I felt growing up there was not just in the social construct, it was in the very geography: Long Island is a glacial moraine, meaning long ago, a huge glacier dragged its ass over a once-contoured landmass, leaving a big rut. I longed to pull myself out of that rut, but as adolescence raged on, I felt it only deepening.

I hadn't always felt such Pleistocene despair. As the first male child of the second US-born generation of my Italian family, I'd once enjoyed favored status. I was the first grandson twice over. My family had held on to traditional values through the sexual revolution: picture Seventies hairstyles and outfits with Fifties moral codes. I was treated like a prince, lavished with indulgences like extra cookies from my Grandma. I alone had a seat at the dining room table for Sunday dinners, while my little brother and the cousins were banished to a folding thing in the alcove.

By sixteen I was lost in the wider world, barely able to form friendships. The erotic demands of Debbie Harry—her sultry cooing in Romance languages, her whispered promises—stalked my adolescence.

Her voice tuned out my disordered emotions, though the vocals posed unanswered questions: *Is this woman's voice the inner voice of the gigolo? Who's calling whom and where do I fit in? Could this sultry lady voice be an expression of my inner thoughts? Or am I the gigolo, whatever that might be? Card cheat, salesman, Italian vagabond?*

There were boys in my class who to my mind had gigolo attributes: feathered hair they would effortlessly toss, seductive smiles with an accompanying glint, an ease in their maleness. I did not yet know if I wanted them or their attributes. Boys couldn't sing along to Debbie Harry—that was suspicious—so I kept the song in my mouth and kept up my guard. Still, those crashing guitar licks pulsed at my temples as I stared down at my changing body in the shower, as I dodged the social enforcers, as I ached for and feared those gigolo boys, as I drifted through suburban nights. I kept my longing directed at the gleaming edges of the Twin Towers, navigational markers I'd identified on the far horizon.

"Call Me" echoed back at me the night I "turned my first trick," as Andrés had so bluntly put it on the midnight cross-town bus, returning from the decorator's townhouse with crisp hundreds tucked into our jacket pockets. He'd sung out those polyglot demands in a high camp pitch as he sashayed up and down the aisle of the bus, to the wearied amusement of the late-shift workers. I was a little too drunk and a little too naïve to make sense of it all, but I knew he'd pulled me out of the contained student life I'd been living and opened up a city with endless possibilities—a *queer* city, a city fueled on desire— just a bus ride away. My buried teenage fantasy had been re-ignited, those crashing guitar licks fired up.

Andrés had manipulated me into the decorator's bed with a slow roll-out of the truth behind our dinner dates, but I'd been pliant. That Theme from the Paramount Picture had prefigured the scenario, transmitting its hints through my black curls and into my soft head. Having not seen the movie, I had to supply my own pictures. After we'd thrown ourselves on the decorator's designer sheets like we were jumping into a pool, Andrés turned to me, took my head in his hands, and kissed me. I could tell he was taking advantage of the situation to do what he wanted; he'd always been good at working the system. The performative context gave me permission to kiss him back. We made out under the chintz-lined canopy and the decorator's leering gaze, our first intimate moment tied up in voyeurism and transaction, but later at home, we erased his gaze and looked upon the stars visible in the night sky through the windows of our tenement flat.

My infatuation with Andrés never had a womb in which to gestate or be delivered from. It was hobbled from the beginning by the decorator's intrusion, and soon after by an even more ominous intrusion: Andrés' AIDS diagnosis. Despite the flippant way I've often encapsulated his role in my development—*he turned me out and then pimped me out*—he was undoubtedly my first gay lover. My love for him was in turns reckless and thwarted, but that love wrested me out of my sexual confusion. I didn't exactly know how to love him, but wasn't given the chance to fail at it. I wouldn't get that chance until Machito.

•

I finally watched Paul Schrader's stylish, uneven *American Gigolo*, years after my kept boy experience, well beyond the decorator's extinguished gaze and my stint as a by-the-hour escort. The film had served as a cultural reference point for male sex workers for decades—just not for me, even while I was one. I watched it on a streaming service from the co-op I'd purchased with the money in the matured annuity my lesbian financial planner had wisely recommended. I was relieved that the MPA ratings system had prevented me from seeing it at sixteen; I shuddered imagining what likely would have been poor choices trying to emulate its style.

Watching through to the final scene, of an imprisoned gigolo saved by his lovestruck client, it hit me that the film was telling a gay story with straight characters and a happily-ever-after ending for mainstream audiences. I cracked up at the scene when Julian, the gigolo character, meets up with his gay pimp and alludes to dalliances with men, while insisting that he doesn't do "fag jobs" any more. *What hustler in the history of the world had "moved up" from gay to straight?* It painted an absurd picture of me and my fellow hustlers in some minor-league bullpen just waiting to get called up into the heterosexual majors. I'd marketed myself as bi and had gotten few requests from women. The one call I did with a woman and those few male/female couples were some variety in my routine. They'd proven, at least to me, that I was up for just about anything. I doubted Schrader was going for a camp effect, but that's what the scene gave me.

Perhaps the one sequence that struck me as authentic was the famous one depicting Julian getting ready, the considered wardrobe choices. I'd summoned that same narcissistic self-regard to show up for calls, except instead of racks of Armani, I was picking through worn-in jockstraps, tight jeans, and fitted tees. Schrader asks the audience to believe that the character's unlikely trajectory from pimped, endangered gay hustler to well-paid gigolo is the root of his vulnerability. *American Gigolo* scanned like a mockery of my own trajectory from kept boy to rented stud. I had a secret sexual past and it had made me vulnerable, but hustling was the very thing that allowed me to work through it.

As this muddled tale of conflicted sexual actors and kink violence unfolds, a drug-addicted gay hustler is revealed as the murderer. Julian's male pimp, Leon, who represents a threat to his heterosexual fiction, is dispatched by being thrown off a balcony. I'd called Andrés my pimp for his agency in my sex work history, but he's proven to be more than a disposable character, one whose sole purpose is to push the protagonist into action. He'd pushed me into action, ridden along for a while, and moved on to a whole new picture. He's also served as my witness, memory-keeper, and fact-checker; so much of this story would be vague impressions without him.

After semi-retiring from escorting, and while I was still writing under my worker name, I blogged for rentboy.com. Sex workers and some clients would write in with questions, and I'd offer advice based on my experiences. Writing those dozens of blog entries was fulfilling and had given me the first opportunity to process what I'd recorded in my diaries. My blogging led to appearances on Dan Savage's podcast and in his advice column in the Stranger. Savage called me in to address a question he was regularly asked: a straight guy was looking to "break into the gigolo industry." I replied: "There is no gigolo industry…the vast majority of clients for sex work are men…pursue a profession with the potential to bring you into contact with a wealthy female clientele—business consultant, art handler—and be exceptionally good and loving to all the women in your life." After this was published, I got emails for years from straight young men with limited reading comprehension asking me how to become a gigolo. I still get them. At least these emails remind me of the reach and fantasizing allure of cultural products like *American Gigolo*.

On the other side of sex work, the film I couldn't see at sixteen struck me as having straight-washed a queer narrative while villainizing its vestigial gay characters—and its only Black character. How might that plotline have damaged a suggestible queer boy like me? Unlike the way the theme song had attached to my story, the film, despite its lush imagery and certain authentic flashes, did not track. It might have pinged for me as a meditation on isolation if not for the thinness of the melodrama. From the perch of my apartment paid for with sex work, *American Gigolo* became for me an object lesson on how *not* to depict sex workers or steal queer narratives. Instead, the way it's embedded in the culture, with its stereotypes and distortions, was one of the things that drove me to tell my story.

I didn't see myself in the film, but I "saw" myself in its theme song. "Call Me"—and all that it conjured for me—accompanied me as I navigated longing, from my confused adolescence to my colonized twenties to my redemptive stint as an escort. I'd taken the lyrics, its beat, repetition, sultry coaxing, and charged inferences as a sort of instruction manual in the absence of any other. It slipped between genres the way I wished to slip between uptown and downtown, between kept boy and guido stud, and other oppositions. Even as the decorator lay dying and I lashed out against my kept boy status, I'd framed my emotions through it: *I've been rolled in designer sheets and I've had enough.*

•

Dean Johnson was a regular guest at my house in the Grove, which I'd paid for with my sex work savings. I couldn't dream of a more apt use for that stash. The Grove had been attracting queer New Yorkers since the late 30's, among them performers, artists, and writers from the theatre scene. They were literally outlaws in their day: drag was illegal, gay men couldn't dance together, and congregating risked raids, arrest, and exposure on charges of perversion. The Grove had been their sanctuary and I've become part of that current of queer sanctuary-keepers. The house is the same age as me. It was built by John Eberhardt, a set designer who'd also built the legendary Belvedere hotel, a Venetian-inspired confection on the bay. His cottages had mid-century layouts and applied decorative themes: French Classic, Roman Villa. They were beach shacks in drag. Our place, the Hansel side of a two-unit house called Hansel and Gretel, was working Bavarian Alpine lodge drag.

Eberhardt, who'd adopted his partner Craig in the days before gay marriage, had sold it to Tony and me himself. We fixed it up and filled it with art—our respective art school work, a moody seascape from Andrés, paintings, photos of friends and ex-lovers. I hung "Academic Study of a Youth"—the painting that used to stare down at me from over the decorator's mantle—in the living room; it is slowly deteriorating from the marine air. This Wildean artifact on display is my kept boy identity disintegrating for all to see. After Eberhardt's death, Craig took me aside and confided: "John and his buddies robbed a bank and hid the money out here. That's how he financed all of his building." I hadn't known this when I'd joked about my own financing of the property, but this revelation tied me a little more tightly to the Grove's queer outlaw spirit.

Keeping the place operational and hosting Dean and our tribe has fueled that spirit. We learned from our neighbor Danny Fields, who was the Ramones' manager, that Patti Smith's keyboardist Richard Sohl once stayed in the house, and sadly died there. Burlesque artist Linda "Dirty" Martini performed a memorable sword act on our deck and later cooked us spaghetti and meatballs. Early in her career, Lady Gaga was put up at Hansel by Dean's promoter partner Daniel Nardicio, when he'd booked her for a gig at the Ice Palace. Between the time she'd been booked and her scheduled appearance, her stardom had skyrocketed, but she honored the gig. Wanda Sykes stayed in the house on the visit to the island she met her wife. Over the years, our recurring guests have included queer performers, artists, writers, and sex workers. Through all the shimmering seasons, my happiest memories of the Grove are of naked bodysurfing with Dean in rough waters that would scare off most others, catching waves and rocketing into the shore. Now I take to the waves solo.

After Dean's death and impromptu memorial service, I appeared at subsequent Reading for Filth installments. I jumped into telling more stories, including the one about my misspent youth as the drunken decorator's romantic obsession: "This was the Eighties, a decade I think we all misspent." I shared with the audience the stories of two memorable tricks—the Upstate Undertaker and the shy, delicate young guy I called "Cherry"—and two horror stories: the coked-out fisting bottom who maced me, and the yuppie on crack with a big bank balance. In another installment, I gave a brief history of how the Internet took trade off the streets and evinced the reading, writing, and composition skills of hookers everywhere. I'd first read these stories to Dean, and this was how I sought to deliver them to a roomful of people, like a late-night phone call to my confidante but delivered in full voice: *Modulate, and play to the back of the room.*

From Reading for Filth I moved into other writing communities. The Red Umbrella Project, or RedUP, was a peer-led advocacy organization with the mission of "amplifying the voices of sex workers" founded by Audacia Ray. RedUP ran writing workshops and reading events, and published an annual journal. For me, RedUP's effect of fostering community among sex workers broke through my social isolation, but sadly it didn't hold through the organization's fractious dissolution once Ray stepped back. RedUP ultimately fell victim to founder's syndrome.

Through RedUP, I was contacted by writer David Henry Sterry and contributed a version of one of my Reading for Filth scripts to an anthology of sex worker writings he was editing for Soft Skull Press. It was credited under my worker name; I wasn't ready to disclose widely my sex work past. The same year, I published a personal essay in Salon under my given name. I'd interviewed my mom and other family members about my grandmother's brief friendship with Marilyn Monroe; their warm remembrances informed the essay. It was my first time being paid for writing and one piece I could share with my family without hesitation. While acknowledging the progress I'd made with RedUP as a participant, facilitator, performer, and ultimately board member, I credit Dean with first putting me on this track.

I've felt his loss with every step forward. We vibed on a rare frequency, as brothers, co-workers, co-conspirators. With Dean, I didn't remain passive follower to an instigator, as I had with Andrés and Joy before him; when he goaded me, it was to step into my own power instead of burnishing his. Other than my mom, no one else believed in me as a writer, and no one actively supported me the way he did. He'd found my diary entries hilarious in their earnestness, but also knew from his own experiences that writing alone had kept me sane through the isolating routines of sex work. Like me, he'd known the pangs of disembodiment that hit those of us who rent out our meat-suits, even for an hour at a time. With my diary-keeping, I wasn't just honing a craft, I was writing to survive.

Dean had his struggles with addiction, and sometimes I felt that he was using me as his sober crutch. Ultimately, I lost him to pharmaceuticals, not the street drugs of my downfall. I'd copped a measured resentment about over-prescribed pharmaceuticals for the role they'd played in the decorator's death, but with Dean, I was in full-blown rage over Big Pharma's corrupt practices. I hadn't grieved the decorator's death so much as I grieved his later life diminished by drugs and alcohol. Death struck down Dean at a moment of vulnerability and grace: out of his comfort zone having traveled alone to a strange city, showing up for a friend in distress, whatever judgements I'd made about his boundaries.

The decorator was largely forgotten after his death; I am the only one who cares to remember him, it seems. In the years since Dean's death, his life and work have been memorialized with events, most recently in 2019 with "Night of the Living Dean," featuring live performances of his music, readings, and other inspired acts. From my reading:

> There was a spiritual component to Dean's lifelong work, all of it, the parties, the music, the drag, the performance, the hustle. In 2007, the Times quoted me saying, "Dean was a New York landmark, like a tall tower or a tourist attraction." Today I'm gonna tell you something else about Dean that you weren't ready for back then: Dean was a Pagan God. His irreverence was absolutely necessary and his fury was holy: "Fuck thermonuclear war, fuck Mary Tyler Moore." Big Red was the God in charge of dislodging the Judeo-Christian hold on the sacred, with its tedious cycles of guilt, castigation, and redemption. We are sacred. This gathering is sacred. Music, dance, celebration: sacred. Sex is sacred, drugs are a sacrament, prostitutes and artists are sacred, our naked bodies are sacred, queer people are sacred.

Like Andrés before and after, Dean Johnson was my polestar. My sex work diary, which he had championed, was the first honest writing I'd done and is the root of my entire writing career. The singular project of all of the work I've produced since has been to liberate my queer body. I've absorbed the philosophy Dean lived by, which valued free expression, sexual freedom, and bodily autonomy above all else, even extending to public nudity and public sex. I carried forth the lessons of the life he'd lived and his last years beside me: Laugh through your pain. When the haters shut down your party, be the party. Make your love non-negotiable.

What made me a good hustler for all the ways I never measured up to Dean's manic vision? In some ways I was built for it, like athletes or dancers are built for their pursuits. Alongside my body, I brought curiosity, empathy, and love to every call. I was able to rehabilitate my work ethic, which the decorator had fully corrupted, between the day-drinking and his constant mooning. I'd made some progress on that front at the loft, but the loft remained an albatross of my grandiosity. In contrast with my prior gigs, and for all the ego-stroking, the sex work I practiced was humble, and humbling. I protected myself with a writing practice that has culminated all these years later in these very words. In my best assessment, the plum which drove me to succeed in sex work was not the cash, the education, or the exercise of my heart muscles. The work gave me back my agency, something I'd been too willing to give up, to Joy, my prom date-turned-Scientologist, to Andrés, who dazzled me blind to the grubby reality of the rich old man at his side, and to the decorator, whose corrosive deceptions did him in and nearly took me down, too.

•

When I launched into the research and interviews for the Marilyn Monroe essay, I unearthed some difficult truths alongside glamorous sparks—especially about the impacts of colorism. The decorator had fetishized my Italian heritage and I'd leaned into ethnic caricature while working as an escort. What I learned about my Italian-American identity was more complicated than either lens allowed. In his day, my brown-skinned Sicilian grandfather on my mother's side, Antonio Rizzo, was commonly referred to as "swarthy." He'd faced degrees of colorism as an immigrant to the United States and among fellow Italians. My fair-skinned Amalfitana grandmother's family had slurred him as *quello Africano* ("that African") when they were first introduced.

When the Rizzos moved to California, they settled in Sunnyside, a working-class neighborhood with a large Sicilian population, among them the extended family of one Giuseppe DiMaggio, a fisherman who had brought his trade to the waters of the San Francisco Bay. One of Giuseppe's sons was Joe, the swarthy baseball hero. It was when Marilyn Monroe was dating Joe that my grandmother met her, through her ties to the DiMaggio family. The adulation of Joe as an athlete by a broad swath of Americans represented a shift away from the othering of Sicilian Americans. Joe's much-touted "class" undermined prevailing narratives about Sicilian immigrants. As I learned about DiMaggio's arc of acceptance, this note rang familiar. I remembered family friends talking about my grandfather's "class." It was one of those back-handed compliments inferring stereotypical expectations of Sicilians. In published historical accounts, Sicilian immigrants had been called "filthy," "sneaking and cowardly," and "lawless."

 Returning to the New York area, Grandpa Rizzo had sought to buy a house in a redlined Long Island suburb with a large Italian-American presence. The developer sold to him only reluctantly. He showed him a house on an irregular plot along a creek, requiring a lot of bulkhead work, which others had passed on. He would tell the story about the developer with a note of triumph; that irregular plot would become his sanctuary where he tended an extensive kitchen garden, whose spit of beach connected him to his beloved sea. For years he was estranged from my father's parents, who lived three doors down, for reasons that were never fully spelled out to me; it was easy enough to draw inferences. "Southern Italian" was once a separate racial category, those so classified subject to employment restrictions, derision, and occasional violence. Even when I was growing up, we did not identify as "white"—we identified as Italians, a category apart. Grandpa Rizzo would eventually find acceptance as an immigrant success story but not before running a gauntlet of colorist suspicion.

 Through my history of being romantically fetishized for my Italian looks and later trading on ethnic caricatures in sex work, I sensed there was something more complicated at the core of my identity. How the raucous tenor of our family dinners seemed to stand up against assimilationist pressures. Against this history it pains me to see fully assimilated Italian-Americans burn our history of immigration and turn perpetrators of xenophobia. Too many to name assume the role of enforcers of the boundaries of whiteness or otherwise prop up the white supremacist project. My feeling of betrayal is so pronounced I wonder if I'm channeling the operatic family melodrama I'd grown up with. Living for so long under these two stereotypes—exiled prince and guido stud—has prompted me to stir at these deeper currents of my identity and the Italian-American condition.

•

My one time double-up partner, Arpad Miklos—born Peter Kozma—grew up in Hungary. He had a degree in chemistry, and worked as a chemist in Budapest until he was recruited by British porn producer Kristen Bjorn. He moved to the United States and embarked on a prolific porn career as a muscled top stud. I met him just when he'd branched out into escorting. A porn legend, an overnight with him was in the thousands, a rate I would never command. In our conversations, I got the impression that much of his earnings were wired back to his family in Hungary.

We'd see each other occasionally in the intervening years since our double-up, often at Hustlaball, the annual party thrown by rentboy. com for escorts and porn actors. Because I was writing "Ask Dominick," the advice column for the company's blog, I'd get invited. When *Butt* magazine and American Apparel marketed a pink beach towel with Arpad's smiling likeness on it, using a photo shot by Marcelo Krasilcic (who I knew from my days at the Loft) I bought a stack. The proceeds went to the Ali Forney Center, a New York City shelter for LGBT youth. I'd gifted them to friends, a couple who'd hosted me at their rental house on Martha's Vineyard. That project, along with a tender music video he appeared in for the band Perfume Genius for their ballad "Hood," signaled to me that Arpad was interested in moving away from porn and into more creative projects. I was glad to see him taking this direction, aware of the difficulties porn actors faced transitioning into other areas. He seemed to be forging his own path.

In February 2013, Arpad—Peter—took his own life. He used his knowledge of chemistry to commit a clean, solitary suicide. "There will be judgment and the haters can speculate," he wrote in a note left behind, refusing to explain his motive. His death shocked me as it did many who'd looked upon him as a happy and successful sexual warrior. He'd always been super health conscious and didn't use recreational drugs as far as I knew. I'd seen him at the prior year's party and said a brief hello; he seemed withdrawn. His closest friend, who I knew from RedUP workshops, also noted that he'd been down lately. There was a fair amount of gross speculation about the impact of porn and sex work on his outlook, but few pointed to the estrangement from his family and his life in Hungary I'd sensed in our conversations. He'd been away for decades, unable to return, his status an unsolvable limbo, another real consequence of the broken US immigration system. If he could have gone back even if his papers were sorted, how would he have been received, the chemist-turned-pornstar? I'd felt the isolating routines and diminishing returns of sex work, but not such estrangement. I'd tracked how demoralizing Machito's distance from family and country had been for him, aware that I had a role in it. My brother Arpad found his agency, too.

•

In the summer of 2019, while in Washington DC for a writing conference, I put aside a day to visit the National Museum of African American History and Culture. The then-recently completed building, a collaboration between British-Ghanaian architect David Adjaye and the late Philadelphia-based architect Philip Freelon, drew inspiration from Yoruba terra-cotta figures and ironwork from the slave ports of New Orleans and Charleston. The building cut a singular figure next to the neoclassical masses of the Smithsonian, while nodding silently to the Washington Monument, its obelisk form, the geometry of its pyramidion. As I entered the museum's wide "porch" entrance from the Mall, I noted the building's simple box form, its skin of bronzed lattice panels, its tiers of angled layers forming a crown.

I found the interior welcoming and well-organized; culture, activism, and education are on the upper floors—held up in the light—while history is laid out in a timeline coiling through the basement, a passage through darkness. I decided to work my way down from the top, starting with the arts exhibits, thinking their content would be more relatable, less challenging. In the music section, I stopped to listen to an audio recording of Big Mama Thornton singing "Hound Dog" and read a text that indexed how she "dressed in work shirts and slacks…eschew(ing) the norms of gender and race."

I next came upon something unexpected: a small display dedicated to the late Frankie Knuckles, who died in 2014 while the museum was under construction. His name (a street/stage name: he was born Francis Warren Nichols) appeared in large letters on the vitrine. Inside, there was a text outlining the late deejay and producer's impact on the music industry, a photo of Knuckles at the turntable, and a series of mixtapes. As my astonishment over what I was looking at cleared, I was overcome with emotion and started sobbing.

I'd danced to Frankie Knuckles sets at his residencies in New York, mainly at Sound Factory, a converted warehouse with a custom-engineered sound system, in the early 90's. The all-night club brought together the gay tribes of New York City: house queens, vogue queens, banjees, Chelsea boys, Brooklyn guidos, and undercover yuppies. One Saturday I'd checked out of my arrangement with the decorator I went with a crew of friends from Cooper Union's Art school. Deep into a night-long set, Knuckles broke the Whistle Song, which would become his top-charting hit. Blissed on ecstasy, after hours of elation and exhaustion from dancing to one of his sound journeys, the track broke through to me. The soft meanderings of the flute intro provided relief, even solace, from the insistent bass beats; then came this chorus of whistles. It it's not a commonly heard sound—whistling is generally individualistic—but on this auroral track, I heard a whole squadron of syncopated whistlers, a sonic dream of unity among differences built into the mix. The simple whistling melody conjured a restless, melancholy figure, blowing into the emptiness, braving solitude, finding their tribe in a space and time beyond language.

Years later, Frankie Knuckles was back in New York and hit me up after this gig—that is, he hit "Dominick" up. He would become one of my regulars. He was the "Grammy winner" I'd described in my diary my first week on the job, the one famous person I'd immediately recognized. I'd played it cool because he didn't seem to want to deal with a fan, but on subsequent calls, I let him know about my Sound Factory nights. He once told me, "I make love, that's what I do…" He was referring to our intimate moments, which were indeed tender and loving, but it seems to apply to his every act: the arc of his deejay sets, his music career, his gentle demeanor, all a form of love-making.

I shuddered through the rest of the music exhibit, reckoning that my tears were over Knuckle's posthumous inclusion at the museum. Scanning the museum text, it drily described house music as "initially produced within the subcultures of Black, Latino, and in the lesbian, gay, bisexual, and transgender (LGBT) urban communities…" but stopped short of recognizing Knuckles as a gay man. As I moved on, I questioned my emotional response to his sparse little vitrine. The ways I've experienced grief aren't always linear. I surely loved Frankie as a man and admired him as an artist, but hadn't given him much thought in the intervening years. The news of his death had hit me at a time when I was basking in recognition for having published that personal essay in Salon. It was the first time I'd been paid for writing, the first time I'd published under my government name, the first published writing I could show my mom.

When I was escorting, I'd tried to find something to love about every man I spent an hour with; with Knuckles alone, I felt *his* love—free of objectification or fetishization—piercing me. He was the one needle in that whole haystack. Through my unbottled grief for his loss coursed feelings of pride at the sight of a fellow gay New Yorker being recognized by this national institution. I tried holding in my tears; they somehow felt inappropriate up in the light. Another museum-goer stopped in her tracks upon noticing my sobbing and simply said, "It's going to be okay."

•

It was later that same year that I travelled to Santiago, unwittingly arriving in the midst of one of the largest populist uprisings in the world. As Andrés and I navigated the city of his birth and re-birth, then under siege, we'd look upon each other with mutual wonder for what we had witnessed of each others' lives since that novela-dramatic meeting on my doorstep. From his native city (which is an equatorial inversion to New York) he'd watched me throw off the mantle of kept boy he'd placed my shoulders like a cute new outfit for a night at the club. From my co-op at the nexus of the public transit systems I once relied upon to work my territory, I've watched as Andrés slowly reconciled his two homelands, Chile and the United States, in an era of increased dissolution and fracturing.

Being on the ground as the Chilean people struggled to effectively decolonize their country—under the guidance of a queer mother of the movement—brought me to another emotional reckoning. I'd choked up on the streets of Santiago more than the smoke of tear gas bombs could explain. I'd felt their movement in my skin. That I saw my internal struggle aligned with a global movement was simultaneously affirming and alienating. I was either running behind or dwelling in delusion. *Had the decorator felt my indifference seeping through my skin as he'd worn me down?* Like colonizers, the decorator had inhabited and advanced a fiction: a myth of status and civilizing taste. He was coercive if not violent. There had been a brief uprising, but it was squashed. For years, he dispossessed me of my natural resources and poisoned my soil.

In the contested streets of Santiago, I saw how my afterlife of a life has pulled me out of this fiction. I've looked beyond the palaces and the ruins. I've set the streets of my fictional principality on fire. My emotional and sexual colonizer was a sad, lonely, sensitive queer man sharing his vision while passing down his trauma; that relay hopefully ends with me. This pull, and the pull of other bodies in my orbit—Machito's shipwrecked existence, the loss of my late-to-the-game hustler brother Dean Johnson while he was on a travel call, the suicide of a man I'd looked upon as a paragon, the recognition of my love-maker Frankie Knuckles—had inched me towards understandings that clicked into place in the acrid haze of Santiago's streets. I even owe a reckoning to Dominick, my dad in his right name. It wasn't just a worker name, a name I'd borrowed to shield my identity; it was a *fathering* identity that protected and raised me.

I've shed the body that was kept. I was unable to tend to its lushness and gave it over to false promises. Once I got it back I still didn't know how to live in it so I went on a mission to destroy it. The moment that body showed a hint of failing it became unbearable. That body has since been replaced cell by cell and disappeared from the mirror. It turned out that buying into the self-image of an exiled prince was not elevating; it only confined me within the boundaries of that fictional principality, one I'd let be taken over by an overseas invader. I found my true state of boundlessness through sex work.

I still live in the body of a sex worker. Sometimes I'd like to have it spelled out—Can I get a SEX WORKER box under orientation on forms? I still pick up on trick energy from civilians. Civilians often disparage people who have engaged in sex work with a glib, "Once a hooker, always a hooker." Well, sure: what I learned about longing has stayed with me, and I've carried it forward into my afterlife. I was able to navigate my own disclosure over many years, while many sex workers understandably choose silence as they move on to other lives. Some are outed with dire consequences. I couldn't simply put away what this body carries in storage, in a safe, in a lockbox.

From the day we met, I was upfront with my husband about my past as a kept boy and an escort; he paused to consider and found acceptance. I appreciated the clear terms of escorting and brought that expectation to marriage, too. My sly husband, Millennial to my Gen-X, leans into the kept boy narrative, and maybe he's got a point. While we each have our own lives and careers, our relationship is imprinted with the dynamic. This would be the third iteration and he gets to write it with me, not have it written upon his brown body. We enjoy ongoing banter about the transactional dimensions of our bond: I give him a stable home, he gives me company benefits, and we huddle in our burrow. As I once advised a lovestruck trick: *Every relationship is a little transactional.* I've found my way to a bond in which my full past can be acknowledged and built upon. I love how he thinks of my sex worker history as a resource: if ever a question comes up among his friend group about a kink, a fetish, or sexual health, I'm their go-to.

Time under the decorator beat at me in menacing solarity, his gaze sun-like in its relentlessness. The clouds of dope and weed only provided transient cover. My un-kept life after his death—scraping past my Jesus year, my spellbound underground as a sex worker, the zeros clicking and the world carrying on, towers falling, my reality stamped but not upended by AIDS, the recent pandemic—has felt lunar in rhythm. Some regions remain in shadow, some orbits tidally locked, the trajectory pulled at by other bodies in orbit: Machito's nearly crushed compactness, Dean's long pale plank, a lived manifesto, Arpad's, idealized to a million gazes, intolerable to the one from within, Lemebel's uplifted, scarred, and painted, Andrés' inked, resilient, and restored, and my own in a free state.

Fin

DEDICATION

To Marie Corvino née Rizzo, who'd read my postcards from Europe and say, "You should be a writer." (Also not sure you'll want to read this.) To the real Andrés, lover, pimp, instigator, chaos demon, polyglot, dandy, memory-keeper, explorer, artist, witness, survivor, gringo, *chiloca*; and to his tattooed body.

To Audacia Ray, for her mentorship through RedUP's writing workshops; to Brontez Purnell (lit daddy), who selected a trio of my short stories for publication; to Bruce Benderson (mom), for his enduring friendship and sharp mentorship; to Saeed Jones, for lessons in chaos at the Lambda Literary Retreat; to Tim Murphy, with whom I workshopped the later chapters; and to Kitty Austin, my reader with the goods.

To Viva Ruiz and all who work and fight to destigmatize and decriminalize sex work, for our bodily autonomy, and sexual liberation.

To the lost: Joseph, Alvaro, Bradley, Stuart Greet, Frankie Knuckles, Dean Johnson, Peter Kozma (Arpad Miklos), and Domenick Barry Corvino.

And the found: Jean-Pierre Lopez, my companion in this afterlife.

ABOUT THE AUTHOR

A 2021 Lambda Literary Emerging Fellow, Dale Corvino found his voice at the underground literary salon "Dean Johnson's Reading for Filth." In 2018, he won the Gertrude Press Fiction contest, judged by Whiting Award recipient Brontez Purnell. Recent nonfiction includes a profile of Chilean writer Pedro Lemebel for the *Gay & Lesbian Review*, an essay on queer longing in the digital era for Matt Keegan's 1996, and a chapter in the *Routledge Handbook of Male Sex Work, Culture, and Society*. BONDS & BOUNDARIES, his debut short story collection, was released in 2023 from Rebel Satori Press.

DALE CORVINO

www.ingramcontent.com/pod-product-compliance
Lightning Source LLC
Chambersburg PA
CBHW021811150625
28210CB00003B/17